THE
community
foundation
FOR NORTHERN VIRGINIA

Sponsored by The Community
Foundation for Northern Virginia

CEONet

Denver Retreat
June 11, 2023

CEO
Excellence

*The Six Mindsets That
Distinguish the Best Leaders
from the Rest*

Carolyn Dewar,
Scott Keller,
and Vikram Malhotra

SCRIBNER

New York   London   Toronto   Sydney   New Delhi

Scribner
An Imprint of Simon & Schuster, Inc.
1230 Avenue of the Americas
New York, NY 10020

First Scribner hardcover edition March 2022

For information about special discounts for bulk purchases,
please contact Simon & Schuster Special Sales at 1-866-506-1949
or business@simonandschuster.com.

The Simon & Schuster Speakers Bureau can bring authors to your live event.
For more information, or to book an event, contact the Simon & Schuster Speakers
Bureau at 1-866-248-3049 or visit our website at www.simonspeakers.com.

Manufactured in the United States of America

3   5   7   9   10   8   6   4

Library of Congress Cataloging-in-Publication Data has been applied for.

ISBN 978-1-9821-7967-0
ISBN 978-1-9821-7969-4 (ebook)

To
Thomas, Gray, and Evening Czegledy
Fiona, Lachlan, Jackson, and Camden Keller
Mary, Malu, Devan, and Nik Malhotra

And to our
Partners and Colleagues at McKinsey & Company
for giving us the opportunity to continue the search for excellence

Contents

STAKEHOLDER CONNECTION MINDSET:
START WITH "WHY?"

PERSONAL EFFECTIVENESS MINDSET:
DO WHAT ONLY YOU CAN DO

CEO
Excellence

Introduction

Excellence is never an accident.
—Aristotle

At the annual Leadership Forum hosted by McKinsey & Company in the picturesque waterfront town of St. Michaels, Maryland, thirty soon-to-be CEOs were gathered in the conference room. On this rainy fall evening, the retreat's first day, everyone snapped to attention as the moderator, Vik (one of your coauthors), posed an intriguing question: "What does a CEO really *do*?"

Without pause, the first guest speaker, a chief executive of one of the world's largest technology companies, responded, "I can say with confidence that the role of the CEO boils down to . . ." He then expanded on each of three items with conviction and clarity. At the end of the night, everyone left feeling a mysterious veil had been lifted.

That is, until the following morning's speaker, the leader of a multinational financial services company, answered Vik's same question. The guest articulated what she viewed as the three primary roles for a CEO, punctuating each with potent, reinforcing examples. They were an altogether *different* set than offered by the first night's speaker. That evening, the third and final CEO speaker, leader of one of the world's most prestigious academic medical centers, presented—you guessed it—yet another categorically different list of the three "most important" aspects of the CEO role.

The next morning Scott and Carolyn (your two other coauthors) brought the retreat to a close, doing their best to crisply summarize the key takeaways. On the subsequent hour and a half drive to the nearest major airport, the three of us discussed how starkly different each guest speaker's list had been. We guessed that if we'd had a fourth speaker, we'd have yet another take on the CEO role. We all

1

agreed that each piece of advice raised by our speakers was important and helpful, but in aggregate, the information felt disjointed.

It was unsettling. As CEO counselors, we know that how a person performs in the CEO role *matters*. CEOs who rank in the top 20 percent of financial performance generate, on average, 2.8 times more total return to shareholders (TRS) during each year of their tenure than do average performers. More concretely, if you invest $1,000 in a Standard and Poor's (S&P) 500 index fund and over ten years your investment grows at historical averages, your investment will make you just under $1,600. If you invest in the companies led by the top quintile highest performing CEOs, you'll gain more than $10,000. That's a big difference.[1]

What's more, the extent to which a CEO is a significant predictor of a company's performance has more than doubled since the mid-twentieth century.[2] This "CEO effect" will undoubtedly become even more important in an increasingly volatile, uncertain, complex, and ambiguous world, one in which stakeholder capitalism is on the rise—calling leaders to move far beyond Milton Friedman's notion that companies exist solely to create profits for shareholders. In fact, the actions of today's companies will likely have more impact on societal issues such as the environment, health care, wealth inequality, and human rights than those of governments and charitable organizations.

By the time we got to the airport the three of us decided to work together to definitively answer the question: "What does a CEO really *do*?" That knowledge in itself would be extremely valuable. But we wanted to go beyond that, to find out how the best CEOs work differently from the rest and why. This would mean getting deep inside the minds of those who truly excel in the role.

Such an effort, we felt, would be welcomed by CEOs and their many stakeholders—boards, investors, employees, regulators, customers, suppliers, and communities. After all, in the past two decades, 30 percent of Fortune 500 CEOs have lasted less than three years, with two out of five new CEOs failing in their first eighteen months on the job.[3] These leaders could certainly have benefited from a primer on what the role entails and that includes lessons gleaned from the best.

By all counts the role is also getting harder. Today's CEOs have to navigate far more than the traditional running of the business. They must deal with the exponentially accelerating pace of digital transformation and the workforce retraining and cybersecurity challenges that come with it. Leaders need to pay more attention to their employees' health and well-being, racial diversity, and feelings of inclusion. Concerns around sustainability, the public desire for more purpose-driven organizations, and calls for CEOs to be spokespeople on broad societal issues are all on the rise. Leaders must not only hear those calls but be prepared for a level of public scrutiny and activism that is driven by social media and can spark outrage (rightly or wrongly) within a matter of hours.

As a result, the probability that a CEO will crash and burn is now higher than ever. From 2000 through 2019, the average CEO tenure in the United States decreased from ten years to less than seven.[4] In the same time frame, turnover rates globally have increased from roughly 13 percent to almost 18 percent.[5] It goes to show that even when there's a stable economy buoying bottom lines, the challenges to contend with at the top can be overwhelming. Add to this the reality that, as General Motors' chief executive Mary Barra told us, "Becoming a CEO is unexpectedly lonely. I've always had a regular dialogue with whoever my leader was, and all of a sudden, you don't have a leader to go to."

Of course, most of the problems faced by large, public company CEOs aren't substantively different from those faced by other leaders—whether they're running a small business or a nonprofit. Insights from the best CEOs running large companies, we felt, would be helpful for just about anyone. Bolstering that belief was the popularity of an article that Scott and Carolyn published on McKinsey's website in the fall of 2019, "The Mindsets and Practices of Excellent CEOs," which quickly became one of the most read articles of the year and has remained in the top ten ever since.

Who *Are* the Best CEOs of the Twenty-First Century?

What exactly does it mean to be a top-performing CEO? After all, aren't a company's results heavily influenced by factors outside of a CEO's control? Yes, they are. In fact, more than half of the factors that determine a company's financial success—such as previous research and development (R&D) investments, inherited debt levels, geographic GDP growth, and industry trends—are largely out of a sitting CEO's control. But that still means roughly 45 percent of what can drive results falls into the hands of one person: the CEO.[6] We wanted to identify those CEOs who moved the needle most in those areas that can be influenced by the top leader.

Overview of methodology used to identify high-performing CEOs

2400+   CEOs of 1,000 **largest public companies** over the past 15 years[1]

998   ...with at least 6 **years in role**

523   ...and delivering **"excess TRS"** in the top two quintiles[2]

146   ...also recognized in "best CEO" **industry lists**[3]

Evaluated for diversity of industry, geography, gender, race, ownership structure[4]

+ 54   Best CEOs in underrepresented areas who meet our tenure and performance and/or reputation bar

200   *of the best CEOs of the 21st century*

1. Top 1,000 companies in the global *Forbes* 2000 list as of March 2020 that ranks largest companies in the world based on a composite of revenue, profits, assets, and market capitalization

2. Total return to shareholders over tenure in excess of the return their industry peers delivered, adjusted for geographical variations in growth

3. *Fortune's* Most Powerful Women in Business, *Barron's* Top 30 CEOs, *Harvard Business Review's* Top 100 CEOs, *CEOWORLD's* Most Influential CEOs, and *Forbes's* America's 100 Most Innovative Leaders

4. Ownership structure examples: public, private, family-owned, not-for-profit

As the above chart shows, we started with a list of all CEOs who've led the one thousand largest public companies at some point during the last fifteen years. There were more than two thousand of these. We then filtered this list based on tenure, removing any CEOs who spent less than six years in the role. That way we could ensure that those we targeted had a consistent track record of success. That brought our list to just under one thousand CEOs. Next, we filtered the list for those aspects of performance that the CEO can influence, adjusting for as many external factors as possible. We looked beyond absolute returns and chose those who, in their tenure, delivered results in the top two quintiles of "excess TRS" (the total return to shareholders in excess of the return their industry peers delivered, adjusted for geographical variations in growth). That narrowed the list to 523.

From there we wanted to take into account factors such as the individual's ethical conduct, employee sentiment, a company's environmental and societal impact, the strength of its succession planning, and in the cases of those who'd retired, whether the business continued to outperform financially in the years after the CEO stepped down. These measures are already rigorously incorporated into many existing "best CEO" lists such as the *Harvard Business Review*'s Top 100 CEOs, *Barron's* Top 30 CEOs, *CEOWORLD*'s Most Influential CEOs, *Forbes*'s America's 100 Most Innovative Leaders, and *Fortune*'s Most Powerful Women in Business. We used an appearance on one or more of these lists as a further screen, which left us with 146 CEOs.

There was one problem with this group, however: It was skewed heavily toward the white male profile that has prevailed in the business world for far too long. Only 8 percent were women and 18 percent were people of color. Further, the list was US-centric and underrepresented CEOs from certain sectors such as health care and energy, which doesn't reflect the topography of today's global business landscape. We therefore opened the aperture to look for additional excellent CEOs in our underrepresented segments, while maintaining a high bar for performance and reputation. We included, for example, CEOs from outside of the largest one thousand companies (though still large in terms of generating billions of dollars in revenue or having many thousands of employees) who led remarkable transformations while delivering top-two quintile "excess TRS."

With this new screen, we were able to add almost 40 percent more women—CEOs such as Nancy McKinstry of Wolters Kluwer, who transformed the Dutch publishing house from a digital laggard to a leading provider of expert solutions and software with revenues of over $5 billion and almost twenty thousand employees worldwide. She was the top-rated female CEO in *Harvard Business Review*'s Top 100 CEOs list of 2019. Similarly, the number of people of color on our list rose by roughly 30 percent. In that group is Malaysian-born Lip-Bu Tan of Cadence Design Systems, a vendor to semiconductor and system companies. He took over the company in a period of turmoil and by the end of 2020 had increased its revenue to almost $2.7 billion and multiplied its stock market capitalization by more than thirty-eight times to almost $40 billion through a singular focus on the customer and a shrewd market expansion strategy.

As we further balanced our mix across sectors and geographies, we also wanted to make sure that we included a sample of privately held firms and not-for-profits that passed our performance and reputation bar. This led to the inclusion of CEOs such as Alain Bejjani of Majid Al Futtaim, who is shaping the influential, privately held Middle Eastern retail conglomerate as a global pioneer in customer experience. Majid Al Futtaim's revenues have grown from $6.8 billion to almost $10 billion during his leadership, and the company employs over forty thousand people across sixteen countries. Toby Cosgrove of the not-for-profit Cleveland Clinic also made the list. He transformed the regional health network with $3.7 billion in revenues in 2004 into a preeminent multinational health system with $8.5 billion in revenues by the time he stepped down in 2017.

In the end we added fifty-four CEOs to our list to make it a round two hundred with a diversity of industries, geographies, genders, races, and ownership structures represented. Having done so, we now had our list of those we felt could most credibly be considered the best in the world in the twenty-first century to date. Stunningly, we estimate that the economic value created by this group of two hundred leaders in excess of their peers is approximately $5 *trillion*. That's equivalent to the annual gross domestic product of the world's third largest economy, Japan.

Our final research step was a pragmatic one: Statistics told us that a sample size of at least sixty-five CEOs would yield a 95 percent confidence level in our conclusions, and so we spent a year interviewing that many leaders in depth. (See appendix 2 for snapshot bios of all of the CEOs we interviewed.)

Who then are our elite CEOs? When you think of the best, you immediately picture such iconic and outspoken founder-CEOs as Jeff Bezos, Warren Buffett, Mark Zuckerberg, and Elon Musk.

Yes—much has been written about them, and they indeed made our list of two hundred. However, in our review we purposefully minimized the number of founder-CEOs, given that their large ownership stakes often allow them much more freedom to act.

Microsoft CEO Satya Nadella was a non-founder who made our cut. He was the architect of a remarkable cultural transformation at the software giant, making bold moves to grow the company and leading with empathy—a trait he learned from his experience raising a son with cerebral palsy. Another CEO on our list was Shiseido's Masahiko Uotani. As the first outside CEO in the 149-year history of this Japanese beauty giant, Uotani transformed the company by empowering his people and unleashing innovation. His approach was shaped by lessons he'd learned while running Coca-Cola in Japan for nearly twenty years under five different CEOs. During his tenure the region became the soda maker's most profitable.

Marillyn Hewson's humble leadership style was shaped partly as the result of her father's unexpected death when she was nine years old, leaving her mother to raise five children. As Hewson worked her way through school, she never imagined she'd someday become the CEO of Lockheed Martin and in that role cement its position as the world's largest and most influential defense contractor through a customer-first strategy. Gail Kelly doubled the cash earnings of Australia's oldest bank, Westpac, during her tenure and became Morningstar's 2014 "CEO of the Year" by applying a no-nonsense leadership style that was forged early in her careers as a schoolteacher in Zimbabwe and bank teller in South Africa.

Each CEO has their unique background and journey that made them the leader and person they are today. Despite their differences, they all have in common that they've excelled *in the CEO role*. Through our conversations and research, we uncovered both how and why.

What Separates the Best CEOs from the Rest?

We spent hours with each of the CEOs we interviewed and often extended our conversations over multiple sessions. The goal of our discussions wasn't only to gather information but also to prompt deep reflection on why these leaders have done what they've done. To reach this level of insight, we used an interview technique that originated in clinical psychology known as laddering. It involves using various methods of inquiry, such as storytelling, asking provocative questions, posing hypotheticals, role-playing, and circling back to previous statements to uncover multiple levels of why someone holds a particular opinion and takes a specific action.

The first thing that became abundantly clear during this process is that there are far more than *three* things that every CEO does, despite what our guest speakers had implied at our Leadership Forum at St. Michaels. From our interviews *six* key responsibilities emerged: setting the direction, aligning the organization, mobilizing through leaders, engaging the board, connecting with stakeholders, and managing personal effectiveness. And each of these responsibilities had a number of sub-elements. For example, setting the direction has sub-elements related to choosing the vision, deciding on the strategy, and allocating resources. Aligning the organization has facets related to culture, organization design, and talent management. And so on. As we kept interviewing CEOs, they time and again validated our conclusion that the six responsibilities and their sub-elements were all important to being successful in the role.

The six responsibilities of the CEO

Vision	**Set the Direction**	**Engage the Board**	Relationships
Strategy			Capabilities
Resource Allocation			Meetings
Culture	**Align the Organization**	**CEO Excellence**	**Connect with Stakeholders**	Social Purpose
Organization Design			Interaction
Talent			Moments of Truth
Composition	**Mobilize through Leaders**	**Manage Personal Effectiveness**	Time and Energy
Teamwork			Leadership Model
Operating Rhythm			Perspective

These six responsibilities aren't unique to the best CEOs—they just describe fully what the job is. When we initially shared this taxonomy with many of the CEOs we interviewed, we received two responses. The first was resoundingly affirming. As Mastercard's former CEO and current executive chairman Ajay Banga told us, "This is an outstanding way to frame it. It's how CEOs should be thinking about their role." The second was also positive but tempered by the feeling that, "this is a *lot*, can it be simplified further?" However, when we then spent time with these leaders discussing what they felt could be taken off the list, in all cases we ended up coming back to the idea that each of the six responsibilities and their sub-elements is vital.

What *is* unique to the best is the mindset with which they approach each of the six responsibilities, and the actions they take on each sub-element. These are what enable great CEOs to, in the words of Eaton's former CEO Sandy Cutler, "play big ball, not small ball. By that I mean spending time on things that no one else can in ways that magnify your effectiveness without getting mired in things that don't make a difference."

As part of our research, we also looked to see whether the amount of time that the best CEOs spent on each of the six responsibilities shifted during their tenure. Was there a pattern or life cycle? Did they spend more time on, say, setting the company's direction and redesigning the organization early in their jobs compared to later? We even went so far as to have our CEOs complete an exercise where they allocated one hundred "importance" points across each of the six responsibilities during their first eighteen months, last eighteen months, and in between.

After looking hard at the data, we concluded that there is no clear pattern. How the CEOs prioritize each of the six responsibilities depends on a complex interplay between the specific business situation and the CEO's unique capabilities and preferences. The key takeaway was that despite their different approaches, every CEO at every stage of their tenure meaningfully tended to all six responsibilities. The best CEOs kept all six plates spinning at all times, even if the external and internal environment meant that some needed to be spun faster or slower than others.

Lastly, we examined the financial performance of the company during an excellent CEO's tenure to see if there were predictable ebbs and flows over time. While doing so, we were aware of the research done by executive search firms that suggests there is a pattern: CEOs start strong in year one, have a "sophomore slump" in year two, then recover and do well in years three to five, get complacent in years six to ten (if they stay that long), and return to glory in the golden years of eleven to fifteen.[7] While this may be true looking across a sample of all CEOs, we found the best CEOs exhibit no such pattern. They instead create significant value on a sustained basis year after year during their tenures. They do so by periodically redefining what it means to win and refreshing their strategies with new, bold actions.

With all this in mind, we've organized this book into six sections, each dedicated to the mindsets that separate the best from the rest in each of the six responsibilities of the CEO role. In each section you'll find three chapters that explore in depth how the mindset translates into best practices. In each chapter you'll not only understand what the best practice looks like, but how the best CEOs make it happen. At the end of the book, we'll step back and discuss how chief executives prioritize their six responsibilities and how they successfully transition into and out of the role. We will also explore how the CEO job might change in the future.

Why CEO Excellence Is Elusive

As our research concluded and our findings crystalized, three things in particular struck us more deeply than we'd imagined: how unique the role really is, the number of contradictions a CEO faces, and the sheer amount of work involved in doing the job well.

On the first point, virtually every CEO told us that they thought they were well equipped for the job because of their experience in having led large business units or functions, only to find that to simply not be the case. It wasn't that managing a profit and loss statement, setting a strategy, or leading a team was radically different than what they'd done before. What took them aback was how the top job is the only role in an organization that is literally peerless. A CEO is accountable for everything. In the words of Dick

Boer, former CEO of Ahold Delhaize, parent company of Stop & Shop and other food retailers, "When you run a business unit or a region, at the end of the day you have peers and you're on a team. As the company CEO, it's solitary. You can't say, 'Look, I can't do it because . . .' No. It's you. You can't blame anyone anymore, for anything. It's you to blame."

Beyond the solitary nature of the role, the second major challenge was best expressed by Jacques Aschenbroich, the CEO of Paris-based global automotive supplier Valeo, who articulated it for us: "The CEO role is the intersection of all contradictions." Interview after interview brought to light the kinds of contradictions Aschenbroich was referring to. Delivering short-term results versus investing in long-term performance. Taking time to gather facts and do analyses versus moving fast to capture opportunities. Respecting the past and creating continuity vs. disrupting the future. Maximizing value for shareholders versus delivering impact for other stakeholders. Having confidence to make tough calls versus having humility to ask for and receive feedback. You might say that F. Scott Fitzgerald's observation that "the test of a first-rate intelligence is the ability to hold two opposed ideas in the mind at the same time, and still retain the ability to function" applies fully to the role of the CEO. As we'll see in the chapters to come, the best CEOs masterfully reconcile these apparent contradictions to create positive and mutually reinforcing outcomes.

Doing so isn't easy, however, which leads us to the third challenge—the vast amount of work involved, as witnessed by the sheer weight of the six responsibilities that falls on a CEO's shoulders. From the outside, the role can seem like it's little more than setting the overall direction and giving speeches. The reality, we found, is far different. As the leader of the global sportswear company Adidas, Kasper Rørsted, explains, "A big part of your job is dealing with all the unsolved problems." It's no wonder that Stanford University Professor of economics Nicholas Bloom, who has spent much of his career researching CEO effectiveness, says, "It's frankly a horrible job. I wouldn't want it. Being the CEO of a big company is a hundred-hour-a-week job. It consumes your life. It consumes your weekend. It's super-stressful. Sure, there're enormous perks, but it's also all-encompassing."[8]

Our deepened understanding of these three challenges gave us even more resolve to provide definitive answers to the questions we were asking: "What do the leaders of the world's most successful and most influential companies and organizations really *do*?" and, more important, "why do they do it that way?"

What Sets This Book Apart?

When we started on our journey, we wondered if our questions had already been answered. We first checked whether our CEOs already had access to the type of book we wanted to create. Their answers validated our quest. As Greg Case, the CEO of the global professional services firm Aon, said to us: "Systematic pattern recognition on what people who have succeeded in the role have done across multiple years, industries, and geographies, all backed by analytics? At some level it's hard to believe that hasn't been done before, but if it has, I'm not aware of it. This could be really powerful."

We were aware that such work still might exist somewhere in academia. We reviewed all of the studies we could find where the scientific method had been applied to understanding the CEO's role. The earliest was from the late 1960s when Canadian academic Henry Mintzberg shadowed a number of CEOs full-time for a week. He reported back that a CEO plays ten roles: figurehead, leader, liaison, monitor, disseminator, spokesperson, entrepreneur, disturbance handler, resource allocator, and negotiator.[9] While groundbreaking, Mintzberg's findings were descriptive versus prescriptive, and didn't attempt to distinguish the best from the rest. The same was true for the other studies we could find, all the way up to some of the most recent work by Harvard professors Nitin Nohria and Michael Porter, whose excellent study of how CEOs spend their time didn't speak meaningfully to the *effectiveness* of how that time is spent or what the best CEOs do differently.

Otherwise, the vast majority of the research looked at the traits of successful CEOs. Though each of these studies had a unique spin—whether it came from Harvard, Wharton, the World Economic Forum, Forbes Coaches Counsel, or an executive search firm such as Russell Reynolds, Spencer Stuart, or ghSMART—the findings generally pointed to CEO success being driven by traits such as relationship building, resilience, risk-taking, decisiveness, and strategic thinking. For those aspiring to the role, these findings might help lead to a job in the corner office. Such traits, however, don't help someone understand what they actually need to *do* to succeed in the role once they have the job.

One notable aspect of these studies is that they all debunk the myth that successful CEOs have a seemingly Hollywood-scripted level of charisma to motivate and inspire. Our experience resonated with these findings. Sure, the more charismatic leaders tend to grab the public spotlight, but certainly the group of excellent CEOs we interviewed were far more inclined to ask good questions than dictate preordained answers and to let their actions speak louder than any rousing speeches.

As we worked through the research, an observation offered by Steve Tappin, the author of *The Secrets of CEOs*, put an exclamation point on why we should continue down our path. Having studied the lives of hundreds of chief executives, he told CNN that "probably two-thirds of CEOs are struggling. I don't feel there's really a place where they can learn to be CEOs, so most of them are making it up."[10]

The absence of the kind of playbook we envisioned did make us wonder if trying to write one would be a fool's errand. Perhaps each CEO's personality and situation are so different that there actually isn't anything generalizable beyond how time is spent and what traits are exhibited. Stanford's Nicholas Bloom seems to support this notion. He argues, "You look at the data, and there're ten different recipes for success. Maybe they each work for a particular case study, but I still struggle to find anything that's a secret recipe beyond saying: sure, there are some people who are better than others but it's damn hard to tell what it is that sets them apart."[11]

Our intuition and experience told us otherwise, and as senior partners at McKinsey, we felt well equipped to look for answers. After all, we spend the vast majority of our professional lives counseling CEOs and, as a firm, we have unrivaled access to more CEOs than perhaps any other institution. Our colleagues reside in sixty-seven countries and serve a breadth of clients constituting over 80 percent of the Fortune 500 and Global 1000. Further, every year more than $700 million of our firm's resources are invested in doing research and analysis, the vast majority of which is on CEO-relevant topics.

Ultimately, the six crucial mindsets that our research unearthed are what we believe differentiate the best leaders of the twenty-first century from the rest. These mindsets enable them to navigate the dominant features of their environment—new competition, disruptive change, digitization, pressing social and environmental issues, or economic meltdowns—with wild success, while others wallow in mediocrity. The simple fact is that the top of the pack *think* differently, which causes them to take profoundly different actions day in and day out.

Keep in mind that we're not suggesting that the best CEOs excel in *every* aspect of the role—in fact, we've yet to meet one who does. Rather, the best CEOs are excellent in a few areas, and do a solid if not exemplary job in the others. In our final chapter, we'll discuss how CEOs know to pick their spots, but note that it's this realization of only being able to do a few things extremely well that explains why the CEOs back at the St. Michaels Leadership Forum each focused on a different short list of priority areas—those that made sense for them to excel at given their situation. Having said that, our research indicates that the more areas a CEO excels in, the better their results are likely to be, making this book, potentially, a powerful field guide for any leader of an organization—be it public, private, or not-for-profit.

We're also confident that many of the mindsets and practices that underpin success can be used by any young, *future* leader looking to be their best. With this work, our greatest hope is that all of our readers will be inspired and informed in ways that enable them to build a leadership legacy they're proud of and for which the world will be grateful.

DIRECTION-SETTING MINDSET

Be Bold

Boldness has genius, power, and magic in it.
—Goethe

In today's complex world, many CEOs try to minimize uncertainty and guard against making mistakes. It sounds sensible. After all, the old adage that "discretion is the better part of valor" would seem to make sense for a job that has such a huge impact on a company's stakeholders. Ultimately, however, such a cautious mindset has proven to deliver results that follow the dreaded "hockey stick" effect, consisting of a dip in next year's budget followed by the promise of success, which never occurs.

The best CEOs recognize this dynamic and, in turn, approach setting the direction of their company with a different mindset. They embrace uncertainty with a view that fortune favors the bold. They're less a "taker" of their fate and more a "shaper"—constantly looking for and acting on opportunities that bend the curve of history. CEOs who embrace this mindset are well aware that only 10 percent of companies create 90 percent of the total economic profit (profit after subtracting the cost of capital) and that the top quintile performers deliver thirty times more economic profit than the companies in the next three quintiles combined. And here's the kicker: The odds of moving from being an average performer to a top-quintile performer over a ten-year period are only one in twelve.[12]

Knowing just how low the odds of success are, the best CEOs apply boldness to each of the three dimensions of direction setting—vision, strategy, and resource allocation, as we'll discuss in the chapters that follow.

CHAPTER 1

Vision Practice
Reframe the Game

Your playing small does not serve the world.
—Marianne Williamson

In a pivotal scene in the biographical movie *Invictus,* Nelson Mandela asks Francois Pienaar, the captain of the South African National Rugby team, "How do you inspire your team to do their best?" Pienaar unflinchingly responds, "By example. I've always thought to lead by example." Mandela reflects, "That is exactly right. But how to get them to be better than they think they can be? That is very difficult, I find. How do we inspire ourselves to greatness?"

The answer to Mandela's question becomes clear during the rest of the film. Though not expected to perform well, the Springboks won the 1995 World Cup—driven less by a desire to be rugby world champions than the opportunity to unite a nation fractured by the legacy of apartheid. Mandela and Pienaar effectively reframed the very nature of what winning meant, and by so doing dramatically increased the team's work ethic and motivation.

As we spoke to the most successful CEOs, we were struck by how they similarly reframed what winning meant for their companies. They didn't just raise aspiration levels; they changed the definition of success. Mastercard's former CEO Ajay Banga, for example, shares his game-changing vision and how it came about: "I was walking through the office and saw this slogan written in a staircase: 'Mastercard, the heart of commerce.' It made me think, 'But commerce is mostly in cash, right?' I realized that in the company nobody talked about cash. If anything, they talked about Visa and Amex and China UnionPay and local schemes.

"That led me," he continues, "to figure out the percentage of transactions in the world that were happening with cash. That number exceeded eighty-five percent just for consumer transactions. From then on I talked about our vision as being to 'kill cash.' Instead of fighting for a piece of the fifteen percent of transactions that were electronic, we fought for a piece of the eighty-five that weren't (yet). We then converted the vision of killing cash into strategies for growing the core, diversifying our client base, and building new businesses."

To take another example, imagine if Netflix cofounder and CEO Reed Hastings had promoted among his employees a vision "to be the number one DVD company in America." Back at the turn of the century no one would have batted an eyelid at such a vision, which ostensibly was Netflix's core business. Had that been his goal, it's doubtful we'd have interviewed Hastings for this book, and probably his company would have gone the way of then-dominant video rental company Blockbuster. From the outset, however, Hastings had his eyes set on a bigger, bolder playing field than DVDs. In a 2002 interview with Wired.com, he was asked what his vision for the company was. "The dream twenty years from now," he said, "is to have a global entertainment distribution company that provides a unique channel for film producers and studios."[13] He added in speaking to us, "That's why we called the company Netflix and not DVD BY MAIL."

Hastings's response may seem logical today, given what Netflix has become. With his more expansive vision, however, the big strategic moves that followed made sense in ways they would never have otherwise: moving into video streaming, betting on the cloud, creating Netflix Originals, driving exponential globalization, and so on.

The table below shows how some of the CEOs we interviewed boldly reframed their game:

Table 1: What does winning look like for our company?			
CEO	Company	"Win the game" vision	"Reframe the game" vision
Doug Baker	Ecolab	Lead the industry in industrial cleaning and food safety	Lead the world in protecting people and resources
Ajay Banga	Mastercard	Win in payments	Kill cash
Mary Barra	General Motors	Win in the global auto industry	Win by transforming transportation
Sandy Cutler	Eaton	Top-quartile-performing vehicle component manufacturer	Leading energy management company making power safe, reliable, and efficient
Piyush Gupta	DBS Group	Win in financial services by using technology	Be the technology company that makes banking joyful
Herbert Hainer	Adidas	Outgrow our competition	Help athletes perform better than their competition
Mike Mahoney	Boston Scientific	Leader in manufacturing implantable medical devices for heart disease	Global leader in innovative, fast-growing medtech solutions
Ivan Menezes	Diageo	The leading beverages company in the world	The world's best-performing, most trusted and respected consumer products company
Shantanu Narayen	Adobe	Providing the best creative professional desktop tools for websites	Powering the world's best digital creativity, document, and customer experiences
Masahiko Uotani	Shiseido	Create a Japanese beauty products icon	Create iconic global beauty brands with Japanese heritage

The "reframe the game" visions in the table above may look obvious after the fact, but getting to the right one is harder than one might think. As Hastings, a self-professed student of how corporations rise and fall, describes: "You definitely want to define what your space of interest is, what you'll go after and defend. But firms can get that definition wrong all the time." In the rest of this chapter we will explore how the best CEOs get it right—creating a game-changing vision for their organizations. They do so by . . .

. . . finding and amplifying intersections
. . . making it about more than money
. . . not being afraid to look back to look forward
. . . involving a broad group of leaders in the process

Find and Amplify Intersections

The best CEOs build their vision by looking for where various aspects of their business and the market intersect. Hubert Joly, the former CEO of electronics retailer Best Buy, explains that setting the right course is, "at the intersection of four circles: what the world needs, what you are good at, what you are passionate about, and how you can make money."

When Joly took over the company in the summer of 2012, Best Buy was on the brink, losing $1.7 billion that year. Amazon and various technology companies were vertically integrating, service quality in stores had plummeted, trust in leadership was low, and the share price was dropping rapidly. Joly knew the company was in need of an immediate turnaround, but as he did his diligence in his initial days on the job, he knew he'd eventually need a vision that would reframe what winning looked like to inspire his troops.

Joly was confident that his industry would keep growing because consumers would look to electronics to help fulfill their needs for entertainment and beyond. His insight was that Best Buy could play an important part in this world by helping customers navigate it. Choosing the right electronics is hard. Seeing the differences in picture quality between TVs or hearing the differences in speakers or headphones can't be done online. And being able to talk with someone who's knowledgeable can be extremely valuable, especially on large purchases. Once products are in homes, setting them up is often confusing. Who better than Best Buy to help?

Looking at the intersection of the first three circles of market need, company capability, and passion, Joly saw a potential vision that would reframe the game. "Best Buy is here to enrich lives through technology," he says. "We're not in the business of selling TVs or computers. And we're not fundamentally a retailer. We're in the business of enriching lives by addressing key human needs, whether it's entertainment, health, productivity, or communication."

One question remained, however: Could money be made doing so? Joly understood that many customers were going to Best Buy stores to learn about products and then purchasing them cheaper online. Employees were demoralized. Investors balked at the idea of price matching, seeing a cost structure that could never compete with online. Joly disagreed. He felt if customers were provided with superior value from the experience, they'd leave with more products.

He also saw that consumer electronics companies looking to vertically integrate needed a physical presence. Best Buy could provide this by offering these companies stores-within-a-store—a portion of the floor space allocated to the merchandise of just one vendor, often with dedicated sales support. As he describes, "We could provide a real service to Apple, LG, Microsoft, Samsung, Sony, and later to Amazon, Facebook, and Google. They needed to find a bricks-and-mortar presence, and we could give that to them overnight versus their building thousands of stores at great cost and risk. That way we were like the coliseum where the gladiators fight, we could collect tickets from everybody—from customers and from vendors. It was a win-win-win."

Given Best Buy's dire straits, few CEOs would have taken such an expansive view of the playing field. Joly's bold, reframed vision meant Best Buy's turnaround involved unorthodox approaches such as partnering with versus squeezing vendors and lowering versus raising prices. And it was indeed visionary: By the time Joly stepped down in June 2019, Best Buy's shares had soared 330 percent from $20 to about $68 while the S&P 500 rose only 111 percent. Finding the right intersection indeed pays off.

Other CEOs we spoke to looked for intersections similar to Joly's. Lars Rebien Sørensen, the former CEO of the Danish pharmaceutical company Novo Nordisk, saw the unmet medical needs in society related to diabetes. He also knew what his company was good at: biologics (drugs that are produced from living organisms or contain components of living organisms). "It was the only thing we understood well, and biologics were difficult to copy," shares Sørensen. Sharpening the vision further, Sørensen was passionate about taking a patient orientation, instead of catering to physicians as was the industry norm. "We have to do what's right for the patient and convince the doctor to be our partner," he says. To build passion in the workforce, all employees were asked to meet with patients and understand what their lives were like and how Novo Nordisk's products were transformative. "It helped our people see that they were contributing to something much bigger than the job they thought they had." Finding and amplifying the intersections worked: Under Sørensen's tenure, Novo Nordisk revenue grew fivefold and net profit elevenfold, and today the company controls nearly half the insulin market globally.

When Lip-Bu Tan at Cadence Design Systems asked a successful investor for advice on how to become the best stock in their portfolio, the answer was instructive. "First of all, you have to be mission critical to your customers, not just a 'nice to have,'" Tan shares. "Second, you've got to be a category leader—number one or number two in your product lines. Third, your current total available market (TAM) is only worth $10 billion. How are you going to grow to be a $150 billion platform—how will you expand into new markets?" By looking for where those three pieces of advice intersected, Tan was able to reframe Cadence's game and expand beyond making software that designs computer chips to also providing system design and analysis software for such industries as hyperscale computing, aerospace, automotive, and mobile.

Make It about More than Money

When Paris Saint-Germain star Lionel Messi races down the pitch and scores, he gets an assist from his high-tech, laceless Adidas soccer boots. Sure, Messi has a sponsorship agreement with the company—the world's second largest athletic apparel-maker after Nike—but the man who has won more player-of-the-year Ballon d'Or awards for soccer than anyone certainly would only wear the best technology.

Messi's shoes, however, do more than help him score goals. They manifest the vision that former CEO Herbert Hainer set for the German company in 2001. When Hainer took over, the company was losing market share and stumbling on new footwear designs.[14] A less bold CEO would have put the financial clamps on the organization and tried to turn around the profit and loss (P&L) by pushing employees to sell more shoes, clothing, and accessories more efficiently.

Hainer was well aware that the financials were vital, but he didn't lead with them. Instead, he reframed the company's vision to be all about helping athletes fulfill their potential. As he describes, "The goal wasn't to be the biggest and the richest, it was to start creating products that help athletes perform better, so the runner can run faster, the tennis player and the soccer player can play better. If we did that and provided good service to our consumers, the financials would follow. All we had to do was help people achieve their personal best, and by doing so we'd also be making the world a better place. I wanted to give the company the belief that this is more than just a revenue game and we are more than just a revenue company."

Hainer's vision was backed by action. When investors would punish Adidas for having a lower profit margin than Nike, he'd respond calmly that Adidas's product development costs were higher because they were going to make the best performance product. "We will never disappoint an athlete with our product that they are wearing," he says. "If we help them make their dream come true—winning an Olympic gold medal, the French Open, etc., then we have achieved more than just revenue numbers." Yet, as planned, when it came to the numbers, Adidas scored big. By the time Hainer retired fifteen years later, he'd revived the Adidas brand and had seen the company's market capitalization rise from $3.4 billion to over $30 billion.

Looking back at the boldly framed visions in table 1, it's striking that none of these successful companies focused on achieving financial outcomes—profits were an outcome of achieving their vision. Oliver Bäte, CEO of the world's largest insurance company, Allianz, explains why: "Nobody gets galvanized by, 'I need to double net profit.' Sorry, even my top team doesn't. So the question is, what can you rally people behind? It's really different to tell people, 'We want to be the loyalty leader in everything we do,' than, 'We want to double return to shareholders.'"

When Aliko Dangote, the founder and CEO of Nigeria's Dangote Group, started his company in 1981, it was a small commodities trading firm. Yet, over the decades, his vision was always consistent—to scale up, industrialize, and be Africa's flagship company in key sectors. Today, the group is West Africa's largest conglomerate, with more than $4 billion in revenue and thirty thousand employees. Dangote describes how the clarity and power of vision continuously provide a crucible for change: "Africa is a richly endowed continent, and this for me is more than enough imperative for sustainable growth. Africa has six of the world's ten fastest growing economies, 60 percent of the world's uncultivated arable land, and by 2050, one person in five in the world will be African. Our workforce understands that we have a clear vision to develop the continent, meet core needs, and improve the livelihood of the populace."

Medical device company Medtronic's former CEO Bill George describes how this dynamic played out at his company: "Our most important metrics weren't revenues and profits but how many seconds it would take until someone else was helped by a Medtronic product. When I joined the company, it was one hundred seconds. When I left the company, it was seven." The focus on restoring people to full life and health and letting shareholder value creation be an outcome of that creates a powerful motivation far beyond making money. As George describes, "employees want to jump out of bed in the morning to invent something new, produce a high-quality product, or help doctors in an operating room. This holds true whether we're talking about South Korea, China, Poland, or Argentina. It motivates senior leaders, the woman on the production line, an engineer back at the lab, and the person who will drive through the night halfway across the state of Michigan to deliver a defibrillator so a doctor can start a procedure at seven o'clock the next morning. That's a true story."

Look Back to Look Forward

Reframing the game doesn't necessarily mean creating a vision that departs from a company's heritage. Our research found that the best CEOs often dig back into a company's history to find out what originally made it successful and then take that central idea and expand it in ways that open up new opportunities.

Intuit, the maker of QuickBooks and TurboTax, is a Fortune 500 company with eleven thousand employees. Scott Cook, who cofounded that Silicon Valley start-up in 1983, sought to create a customer-centric company that would always strive to fall in love with customers' problems, and never the company's solutions. The company's founding mission was to "end financial hassles," and the company continuously evolved its solutions to serve its customers.

When Brad Smith, a West Virginia native who'd worked his way through PepsiCo and the payroll company ADP before joining Intuit, took over the top spot in 2008, he faced some daunting challenges. The company had a proud twenty-five-year history of being a great desktop software company, but the world was shifting, and its products were becoming less relevant. Smith felt the essence of Cook's vision was still relevant, but how it was expressed and pursued needed to change. "We kept the spirit, but made the words from our original mission more contemporary," he says. "Our intent to power prosperity and champion the underdog has never changed. I simply needed to reaffirm it and ask what the most contemporary way is to do it. We refreshed our mission and once again evolved our solutions by leaning into the cloud, capitalizing on three macro trends—social, mobile, and global."

Reframing the founding mission into a compelling, contemporary vision for the company and mobilizing employees around it worked. Under Smith's eleven-year tenure, his vision of "powering prosperity to meet the needs of an increasingly connected world" helped Intuit double the number of its customers to 50 million and triple earnings while revenue doubled.[15] He grew the company's stock market value from $10 billion in 2008 to $60 billion as of 2019. Smith's advice to new CEOs is to have "a vision that is so clear a leader doesn't have to do anything but get out of the way. That's the most inspiring vision of all."[16]

Smith's experience was echoed by many CEOs to whom we spoke. As we already saw, Mastercard's Ajay Banga was inspired by an old corporate tagline. Gail Kelly at Westpac looked back to its service heritage as Australia's oldest bank. Microsoft CEO Satya Nadella looked to the origin story of the company that was about building technology so that others can build technology and felt, "Right there lies everything that needs to be known about Microsoft during my tenure."

Thus far we've discussed how the best CEOs create visions that boldly reframe the game. Indeed, every CEO we spoke to did so in one form or another, even those who took over already well-performing organizations. McKinsey & Company's former managing partner (our CEO equivalent) Dominic Barton summarized the prevailing sentiment: "As the leader, you have the power—and the responsibility—to raise the level of ambition in your organization." Raising the ambition level isn't just about the vision, however. It involves a highly inclusive process.

Involve a Broad Group of Leaders

The best CEOs create a game-changing vision for their company. When it comes to sharing it with the organization, however, they rarely dictate their views. Why?

Nobel Prize–winning Israeli psychologist Daniel Kahneman conducted an experiment that provides a memorable answer. Kahneman ran a lottery with a twist.[17] Half the participants were randomly assigned a numbered lottery ticket. The remaining half were given a blank ticket and a pen and asked to choose their own lottery number. Just before drawing the winning number, the researchers offered to buy back all the tickets. They wanted to find out how much they'd have to pay people who wrote down their own number compared with people who were handed a random number.

The rational expectation would be that there should be no difference in how much the researchers have to pay people. After all, a lottery is pure chance. Every number, whether chosen or assigned, should have the same value because it has the same probability of being the winner. The answer, however, is predictably irrational. Regardless of nationality, demographic group, or the size of the prize, people who write their own lottery ticket number always demand at least five times more for their ticket. This reveals an important truth about human nature. As Medtronic's Bill George puts it, "people support what they help create." In fact, they're some five times more supportive than those who aren't involved. The underlying psychology relates to our desire for control, which is a deep-rooted survival instinct.

This "lottery ticket effect" was tapped into by virtually every excellent CEO we spoke to. Maurice Lévy, the former CEO of the multinational advertising and public relations goliath Publicis, used the approach throughout his career. In 1987, the Moroccan-born executive took the reins of what was then considered a French "also ran" advertising company and successfully transformed it into one of the world's top three agencies. Lévy used mergers and acquisitions (M&A) to expand the group's reach to over a hundred countries. The rallying cry of the company was *"Viva la difference,"* which emphasized providing clients with services culturally attuned to local environments.

By 2015, his strategy of acquisition-led growth had largely played itself out. It was time to reframe the game. Lévy saw that Publicis was operating as a collection of individual entities—a separate agency for each solution and market. Further, he saw that consulting firms like Accenture were disrupting the industry, using data and technology to build brands. Even though he felt he had a clear view of what needed to be done, at age seventy-three he knew that, more than ever, the vision for Publicis needed to be owned by the next generation and beyond.

To capture the "lottery ticket effect," Lévy engaged his executive team and the next level of management—roughly three hundred leaders plus fifty recently promoted managers under the age of thirty—in a multi-month-long process. He invited guest speakers to help educate his leaders on global trends and disruptions. Among them were Eric Schmidt of Google, Mark Zuckerberg from Facebook, Salesforce.com founder Marc Benioff, and Harvard leadership professor Rosabeth Moss Kanter. Inspired by what they heard, the executives worked in subgroups where ideas for the future of Publicis were debated, combined, and prioritized. Ultimately, what emerged was a new vision of "the Power of One." This was a radically reframed vision, one that would serve customers through cross-functional teams in ways that broke down the firm's large number of traditional silos.

The ultimate benefit of "the Power of One," however, was that Lévy created a deep sense of ownership that led to a broad leadership coalition. The process, he says, "Gave us incredible energy and great solutions." When he stepped down two years later, the little French "also ran" company he'd taken over thirty years earlier had grown to an $18 billion market cap, and become a global powerhouse.

The vast majority of excellent CEOs we spoke to found ways to include their employees when setting their vision, with similarly impressive results. Majid Al Futtaim's Alain Bejjani says, "We aimed to have the most inclusive process possible. Doing so built a broad sense of ownership, and we also found that some of the most insightful answers came from people we wouldn't normally have approached for input, which in hindsight would have been a significant loss."

As Adidas's Herbert Hainer shares: "It took us five months, but people had the freedom to really speak out about what they think is right for the company. This unleashed enormous spirit, new ideas, and creativity. And within twelve months, our share price doubled—we had momentum like hell. This was, in my opinion, the magic moment." Best Buy's Hubert Joly reinforces that point, "Of course you have to create a plan, but you have to co-create it. It doesn't need to be perfect—the key is to create energy and manage energy."

Raising the spirits of your leaders doesn't happen overnight. Sometimes a CEO needs to drive toward the ultimate vision in a series of steps. Piyush Gupta experienced this as CEO of the DBS Group when he took over in late 2009. "Coming from being the worst bank in Singapore in terms of customer service quality, no one believed it was possible to even dream of being the best in Asia," he explains. "The confidence and capacity just weren't there. It was like taking a minor league team and saying not only that they can play in the major league, but they can win the championship." Gupta settled on an initial vision of being "the Asian bank of choice" as a compromise that his leaders could embrace.

By 2013, DBS was recognized in many regional rankings as Asia's best bank, and the stage was set to dream bigger. At an off-site that year, "250 of my leaders told me that they wanted to be the best bank in the world." He beams. "That was just a magical moment, knowing my leaders truly believed we could play at that level." In 2018, DBS was indeed recognized by *Global Finance* magazine as the best bank in the world, the first Asian bank to receive the accolade from the New York–based publication. *Euromoney* and *The Banker* magazines also bestowed the same honor on the company. Gupta didn't stop there. His team began to pursue an even more expansive vision to redefine financial services by adopting a tech company mentality toward the ultimate goal of "Making Banking Joyful."

It was somewhat disconcerting to find that the best CEOs used the terms vision, mission, and company purpose as largely interchangeable. Communications and HR professionals, academics, and we as consultants can argue all we want about the nuances of each term, but the fact remains that the best CEOs don't worry much about the distinctions—what matters for them is to have a clear and simply articulated North Star for the company that redefines success, influences decisions, and inspires people to act in desired ways.

To achieve such impact, the best CEOs apply a mindset of boldness, resulting in a vision that looks beyond winning the game to reframing it, just as Nelson Mandela and Francois Pienaar did in helping the South African rugby team. They weren't just playing for a championship; they were playing to unite a nation. To create similarly game-changing visions, the best CEOs find and amplify intersections, focus on more than money, aren't afraid to look back to look forward, and capture broad ownership via the "lottery ticket effect."

Once the vision is set, regardless of at what point in the journey, CEOs face another challenge: how to make that bold vision a reality. A Japanese proverb puts it starkly: "Vision without action is merely a dream." We now turn to what the best CEOs actually *do* to make dreams come true.

CHAPTER 2

Strategy Practice
Make Big Moves Early and Often

You can't cross a chasm in two small jumps.
—David Lloyd George

What was US president John F. Kennedy's vision for the United States? On May 25, 1961, before a joint session of Congress, he stated it clearly: "To win the battle that is now going on around the world between freedom and tyranny." What was his strategy? A series of big moves, one of which has become synonymous with the very idea of taking a giant leap forward: the moonshot. During his speech that day he not only asked for funding to put a man on the moon, but also for three related big moves: increasing unmanned space exploration, developing a nuclear rocket, and advancing satellite technology. These asks were in addition to a handful of other needle-moving actions being pursued by his administration such as setting up the Peace Corps, creating new civil rights legislation, and reinventing economic cooperation with Latin America.

Kennedy's story shows how a "be bold" mindset applies not just to vision but to the strategies employed in pursuit of it. A leader who sought to minimize uncertainty and guard against making mistakes would never have chosen as audacious a strategic move as a lunar landing; instead they would have simply increased funding for science and technology. Like Kennedy, the best CEOs boldly make big strategic moves early and often during their tenure.

Take Satya Nadella, for example, who took the reins of Microsoft in April of 2014. He became CEO when the technology company looked like it was on a fast track to irrelevance. The longtime motto of "putting a computer on every desk" had served Microsoft well in the past but was now antiquated. As we touched on in the previous chapter, Nadella drew on Microsoft's origin story to boldly reframe the company's vision going forward. He redefined the mission to be "empowering every person and every organization on the planet to achieve more."

Nadella then pursued a number of big, moonshot-style strategic initiatives to propel the company toward its vision. Over the next few years, the new CEO made more than $50 billion of acquisitions that helped strengthen Microsoft's productivity. He boosted services, including the purchase of platforms such as LinkedIn for business networking and GitHub for software developers. He doubled investments in the company's cloud services and artificial intelligence businesses. He also moved Microsoft away from a "software in a shrink-wrapped box" model to online subscription services. At the same time, he made the tough decision to sell Microsoft's mobile phone business, despite having spent billions trying to catch up with Apple and Google.

Nadella's bold moves—paired with some important changes he made to Microsoft's culture, which we'll discuss in future chapters—have paid big dividends. From the day Nadella took the CEO job through 2020, Microsoft's revenues have increased more than 60 percent. The stock price has grown almost sixfold during a period the S&P 500 has grown only twofold. As we write, Microsoft is the second most valuable public company on the planet.

We could fill pages with similar rundowns of the big strategic moves the best CEOs have made. More instructive are the results of an analysis of 3,925 of the largest global companies over a fifteen-year span. McKinsey ran the numbers to determine which big strategic moves yield the highest probability of a company's jumping from an average to a top profit generator. The research shows the following five strategic moves matter most, as long as they're pursued with a "man on the moon" kind of boldness:[18]

1. **Buy and Sell.** The best CEOs execute at least one deal per year on average, and over a ten-year period these deals cumulatively amount to more than 30 percent of a company's market cap (although typically no single deal amounts to more than 30 per-

cent of the company's value). This puts a premium on having a deep capability to identify, negotiate, and integrate acquisitions. The top CEOs are as bold about selling as they are about buying, which can also take the form of spinning off businesses. Aon is a poster child for making deals. In CEO Greg Case's words, "We're always shaping and improving our portfolio. Over the last fifteen years, we've done over 220 acquisitions and more than 150 divestitures, some big and others small."

2. **Invest.** If you want your company's investments to be big enough to move the needle, your capital expenditures to sales ratio needs to exceed 1.7 times the industry median for ten years. That's a big number, but when capital is spent wisely it can enable a company to expand faster than its industry. General Motors' Mary Barra exemplified this strategic move when she committed more than half of GM's product development capital ($27 billion through 2025) to pursue leadership in the global electric vehicle market.

3. **Improve Productivity.** The most successful companies reduce administrative, sales, and labor costs more deeply than others, and in so doing achieve 25 percent more productivity improvement than their industry's median over a ten-year period. This is exactly what Allianz's Oliver Bäte did to help him pursue his renewal agenda, "Simplicity Wins." In an industry that had seen flat expense ratios at 30 percent for decades, Bäte—soon after he became CEO—drove the company's expense ratio below 28 percent while increasing customer loyalty from 50 percent in 2015 to 70 percent in 2019, and increasing internal growth rates from negative rates in 2015 to 6 percent in 2019.

4. **Differentiate.** The best CEOs improve their business models and create pricing advantages in ways that are big enough to change a company's trajectory. As a result, their companies achieve an average gross margin that exceeds the industry's by 30 percent or more over a decade. Former LEGO CEO Jørgen Vig Knudstorp used this strategic move well in pursuing what he called, "a strategy of niche differentiation and excellence" that

aimed to refresh at least half the company's core products every year. He created, for example, digital platforms that strengthened communication among LEGO fans, developed products for girls, licensed collections (e.g., Star Wars), and launched the successful LEGO movie franchise.

5. **Allocate.** This move is deemed big when a company shifts more than 60 percent of its capital expenditures among business units over ten years. Doing so creates 50 percent more value than companies that reallocate more slowly. Resource reallocation involves more than just capital, however; it also means shifting operating expenditure, talent, and management attention to where it does the most good. As such, it's a vital enabler of the other four big moves and given its importance it will be covered in the next chapter, and then again when we talk about talent, and further still when we talk about leading the top team and creating the right operating rhythm.

CEOs who make too few moonshot-size moves—or make them too late in their tenure—fall behind the pack. An analysis of the data shows that of the companies in the middle quintiles of economic profit creation, roughly 40 percent didn't make any big moves at all over a ten-year period. Another 40 percent only made one. Meanwhile, the research also shows that making two of these big moves more than doubles the likelihood of rising from the middle of the pack to the top, and executing three or more makes such a rise six times more likely. Furthermore, CEOs who make these moves earlier in their tenure outperform those who move later, and those who do so multiple times in their tenure avoid an otherwise common decline in performance over time.

While the research is categorically clear on what separates the best from the rest, every CEO needs to determine which specific big strategic moves make sense for their company. Pursuing M&A is one thing, but how does one know what companies to buy and sell? Capital expenditure makes sense, but how does one know where is best to invest? Similar questions can be asked for each of the five moves, and getting the answers right is vital given the magnitude of such initiatives. As Steve Ballmer told Satya Nadella when he handed over the CEO reins at Microsoft, "Be bold and be right. If you're not bold, you're not going to do much of anything. If you're not right, you're not going to be here."

Being bold and right is far easier said than done, and in practice even the best CEOs don't get everything right all the time. Netflix's Reed Hastings shares how not every big move he made was the right one. In 2011, Netflix was on a roll. The company had a fast-growing online subscription business where customers got their favorite DVD rental movies mailed to their homes. However, CEO Hastings saw that the market was shifting, and that the future would be streaming video where customers could get their movies delivered over the internet. It was a classic innovator's dilemma—for Netflix to keep growing it would have to cannibalize its DVD mail business. Hastings's solution was to split his DVD-by-mail and unlimited-streaming package into two separate services—and charge a 60 percent price hike for customers who subscribed to both services. The customers balked at the higher fees and at having to subscribe to the new DVD-by-mail service, which was to be named Qwikster.

After millions of Netflix customers fled and the company's stock price dropped 75 percent, Hastings in an email to his subscribers wrote: "I messed up. I owe everyone an explanation. The key thing I got wrong was not fully explaining the pricing and membership plan changes announced a couple months ago." It turns out that an explanation wasn't enough. Customers *really* didn't want two separate services at a higher price. By the fall of that year, Hastings shut down Qwikster before it even opened and returned to a single subscription model named Netflix.

"In hindsight," explains Hastings, "we were too focused on not dying with the DVD. We looked at all these companies with collapsing business models like Kodak and Blockbuster. It was really a hard problem. We learned an important lesson. The fact that your company may not be strategically positioned for the next ten years—your customers don't care about that."

That said, in spite of not being perfect in execution, Hastings had moved quickly and still made the right call on the bigger decision to move from DVD to online. He identified an opportunity where many others saw a challenge. In the face of persistent skepticism and competition, he managed to grow Netflix through rapid technological expansion and addressed the evolving needs of an ever-growing customer base. While the DVD-by-mail service became a niche, Netflix has grown into an immense streaming business with two hundred million subscribers, $20 billion in revenue, and nearly nine thousand employees. From a start-up in 1997, the company is now worth more than $200 billion.

As Hastings experienced, making big moves in a fast-moving, uncertain environment with many variables that can't be controlled is risky. The easier path is to shrink back and stay safe, yet the best CEOs show courage to act in the face of uncertainty. Feike Sijbesma, former CEO of Dutch life sciences and materials sciences powerhouse Royal DSM, explains, "When we did daring things my board asked, 'Are you sure?' My answer was, 'Of course not, there's no way to be sure.' We created a culture to be open about having insecurities, but also to have the guts and determination to go after the opportunities."

The best CEOs aren't only willing to venture into uncharted waters—they're also willing to boldly stay the course on stormy seas. In his strategic push to make his UK spirits company more customer-centric, Diageo CEO Ivan Menezes diverted commercial and marketing efforts away from distributors and toward consumers. As sales declined in the short term, Menezes found himself under fire from investors and even faced some skepticism from inside the company. "The entire organization was watching to see if we'd blink," says Menezes. "But we stuck with it, explained why, gained credibility, and really set the foundation for growth." Since then, Diageo has gone from strength to strength, achieving top quartile shareholder returns in its peer group.

The many similar stories we hear from CEO after CEO remind us of the definition of courage offered by Piers Anthony, author of the Xanth fantasy series: "Being terrified but going ahead and doing what needs to be done—that's courage. The one who feels no fear is a fool, and the one who lets fear rule him is a coward."[19] Medtronic's George puts a fine point on the importance of this aspect of the role. "I've seen some otherwise very well-qualified CEOs who lacked courage," he observes, "and their companies managed for a while but atrophied over time."

As we explored where this courage comes from, we found the best CEOs . . .

   . . . are exceptional futurists
   . . . keep an eye on the downside
   . . . act like an owner
   . . . regularly apply "heart paddles"

Be an Exceptional Futurist

Virtually every CEO we spoke to emphasized the importance of having a clear point of view on where the world is going. They keep careful track of shifts in technology, changes in customer preferences, new competitors, and threats on the horizon. Doing so enables them to place bets before these trends become conventional wisdom and to maintain conviction when others inevitably criticize their choices to invest in markets that may not exist or technologies that are considered long shots.

Ed Breen ran multiple companies and built his career by capitalizing on future trends. Over the course of his twenty-three years in the CEO role, he earned a reputation as a master strategist, able to handle complicated conglomerates and activist investors. Before he became CEO of Tyco and then Dupont, in his early forties Breen was the CEO at General Instruments, a Pennsylvania manufacturer of set-top boxes connecting televisions to cable. It was the late 1990s, and the world was still largely analog at the time, but Breen foresaw a shift to digital. Digital set-top boxes didn't exist and would be expensive to develop. Breen had conviction, however, and put 80 percent of the company's R&D toward solving the problem. The investment paid off: GI was the first out of the gates with a digital box. Unfortunately, the technology was expensive to produce.

As Breen recalls, "I'd just been made CEO the year before and I'm sitting there amazed, thinking, 'No one else has figured out to build a digital set-top box yet, but we did it.' But now what? Like with any electronics product, we needed volume to get the cost of the components down. I went to Malone [John Malone, CEO of cable giant TCI] and said, 'Look, this technology works. TCI can lead the industry with it. Let's do a deal that makes this financially viable for both companies to install it in all your systems around the country. But you have to commit to getting 100 percent of your set-tops from GI.' And then I went to [the cable provider] Comcast the next day and offered them the same deal. And then over a week, I personally ran around to everybody and signed the top ten cable operators." Having made the big investment that allowed him to differentiate GI in the market, Breen then undertook a big efficiency move. "My focus the next year was, 'cost reduce, cost reduce, cost reduce these boxes.' And we got them down to literally half the cost we started at." GI went on to win big in the multi-billion-dollar cable set-top market and over the next couple of years Breen watched the value of his company skyrocket.

Another instance of Breen's anticipating future trends occurred later in his career while he was at DuPont. It was 2017, and he concluded that the agriculture industry was going to consolidate down to just a few players. Breen had studied the trends and economics of the industry, and realized that anyone who was fourth or fifth in this market would struggle. There were seven divisions in DuPont at the time, and agriculture was just two of the seven, but it accounted for more than 50 percent of the company's actual equity value. Breen worried that restructuring the agriculture business could negatively affect DuPont's stock in the short term. However, it became clear to him that merging with Dow Chemical and spinning off what is now Corteva Agriscience was the way to go. Many people were skeptical, telling him: "You'll never get the Dow merger. You'll never get it the way you want." Investors were equally doubtful, imploring Breen: "There's no way you're going to get Dow and DuPont to do something together. They're mortal enemies and it's not going to work." Breen reflects, "Probably ninety-nine percent of people wouldn't have pursued the deal. That was one of the biggest decisions I ever took in my career."

In spite of the opposition, Breen was convinced that the move made sense for both companies given the industry trends. "They're better on the crop protection side, we're better on the seed side. That makes a heck of a company. We'd be a strong number two player in the industry." In what some analysts have called the most complex corporate deal ever, Dow and DuPont merged into a single entity, were reconfigured, and then split into three separate companies: Dow (commodity chemicals), Dupont (specialty chemicals), and Corteva (agriculture seeds, traits, and chemicals), all of which were better equipped to compete in their respective fields. Looking back at his career, Breen reflects, "CEOs make important decisions every day, but some decisions are just so huge that nothing else even comes close. I've made approximately fifteen really major decisions in my career, and I'm in my twenty-third year as CEO. Those big ones better work." Breen's *have*, in large part because he was able to see around corners.

All of the excellent CEOs we spoke to had similarly lucid views as to what the future would bring. Italian utility Enel's CEO Francesco Starace had a deep belief that the renewable-energy space would become very big, competitive, and global. He also believed that "the future will bring along a compression of time, not an elongation of it." Combining these thoughts, he moved away from making large capital investments in thermal and nuclear power plants to a more granular approach of multiple investments aimed at renewables that have no more than three years of full development and construction time. By doing so, Enel has grown into the world's largest private renewable energy provider and the largest utility in Europe by market cap.

GM's Mary Barra is courageously making big moves based on the four trends she sees transforming mobility: electrification, autonomy, connectivity, and sharing. DSM's Feike Sijbesma foresaw the further concentration and commoditization of bulk chemicals and petrochemicals and at the same moment a growing opportunity in health, nutrition, and sustainable living. This prompted him to shift the company's business focus, while at the same time contributing to the planet and society as well as his shareholders. Microsoft's Satya Nadella has done the same based on the trends he saw relating to social, mobile, and cloud technologies. Today he's given credit for doing so, but as he describes, "Five years ago people were saying, 'Oh, this will never work.' So it's a lonely place. You've got to be the one to take some risk, and that emanates from your world view. As a CEO, you have to have an absolute first-class view of where the world is going."

Where do these CEOs get their crystal ball? The answer is more straightforward than many might think. "Early in my career, I wondered how to develop a vision and a strategy," DSM's Sijbesma shares. "Do you sit in your study and yell, 'Eureka! I have it'? I don't think that's how it works. I started reading more about all kinds of subjects, including unrelated subjects, to combine the unrelated things into something new—not only in technical innovation but also in business. I also started traveling a lot and building a network, connecting with a lot of people in business, science, and society." Inspiration for DSM's bold transformation came also from the input of this network. He gained conviction from visits with industry experts, including in the Middle East, that DSM would never be able to compete with the oil and chemical majors. At the same time, through his involvement with the United Nations (UN), among others, he realized opportunities were emerging in a whole new area of sustainable development and healthy food. "That's how we got the idea to move out of petrochemicals and use the proceeds to move to nutrition and health," he reveals. This eventually became a total transformation of DSM over the course of fifteen years.

For LEGO's Jørgen Vig Knudstorp, an unlikely group of customers was instrumental: the adult fan community. "They were viewed as a gray market and a little bit of a weird group," he shares. "They got together every year and so I joined them for one of their conferences. I camped there for six days and just had endless conversations with five to six hundred people." By doing so, Knudstorp gained their trust, and they helped him see what was possible. "They kept sending me emails and inputs and so on. They were much more advanced than the child user, but they were the lead user. If I could deliver something that satisfied them, I could deliver something that satisfied the average user as well. They were the credibility." LEGO's adult user community now totals more than one million people worldwide and accounts for 30 percent of LEGO's global business.

The best CEOs hardwire their view of the future into their company's strategic planning. As Sundar Pichai, CEO of Alphabet and its subsidiary Google, describes: "I think about our mission and the fundamental trends we're seeing, and based on that I write down the five to ten themes that we really want to execute on well." Pichai then works with his management team and nominees from different levels of the organization to sharpen his themes. With those ideas in mind, each part of the organization develops a set of objectives and key results (OKRs) that are ambitious and shared internally. Pichai then reinforces the themes in all review conversations: "If 'Asia Pacific–first' is one of our five themes, I could be in a YouTube review and probe the team: 'Can you tell me how you're solving for Asia Pacific first?' "

Keep an Eye on the Downside

To be clear, boldness doesn't mean recklessness. Excellent CEOs fully understand the risk/reward trade-offs of potential big moves. Explains Dupont's Ed Breen, "One thing I always study the most is the downside scenario. If I don't get this perfectly the way I think it's going to go, what is my downside scenario? And can I live with it? I always feel angst over that more than anything. I would never make a decision where I was risking too much. But if I can live with the downside scenario and I still end up being better off, that's a good risk/reward."

Ecolab's former CEO Doug Baker agrees that taking risks only makes sense when the trade-offs are understood. "Most of the time, you're making strategic decisions with imperfect information," says Baker, who became head of the water and hygiene services giant in 2004. "If you wait until you have everything you want to know, then you're likely to miss the opportunity. More often than not, you have to make calls with incomplete information. I often ask, 'Which mistake can you more afford to make?' " Baker, for example, is willing to build, say, a $75 million new plant in China to manufacture water treatment solutions, and risk that the market may disappear because, if it does, it won't kill the enterprise. When big moves are made through this filter, "The worst mistake I can make," says Baker, "is to throttle back—it's essential to keep growing, keep investing, keep moving, but to do so in a way that increases the company's odds of success."

That doesn't mean Baker only took moderate risks during his

time at the helm. At the World Economic Forum in Davos, Switzerland, in January 2011, he was having a coffee with the CEO of Nalco, a global water treatment company. Previously, Baker and his leadership team had identified water technology, Nalco's prime business, as a strategic priority. As Baker recalls from the Davos meeting, "The CEO was worried about his debt. He brought it up four times in our brief conversation. I thought, 'Maybe we should go look at this company.'"

After kicking the tires, Baker decided to pursue Nalco aggressively. One thing that reduced the risk of the deal for Baker was that he knew that his biggest competitor was being acquired, which would give Ecolab some room to move while the competitor was in disarray. He also knew he could spin off parts of Nalco to reduce the overall risk. In July of that year, Ecolab announced it was buying Nalco in a deal worth $8.1 billion, which at the time was equal to 75 percent of Ecolab's market cap.

This big move and more than a hundred other smaller acquisitions that Baker made gave Ecolab an expanded offering of products and services and geographic reach that allowed the company to provide one-stop shopping for its customers. These investments paid off. In his sixteen-year run as CEO, Baker increased Ecolab's market capitalization eight times over, while revenue increased from $4 billion to $15 billion. One of *Harvard Business Review*'s Top 100 CEOs for multiple years, Baker went out on top in his final year as well, cited by *Barron's* as one of its Top 25 CEOs for 2020 and recognized for his work during the global COVID-19 pandemic to protect employee pay, support customers and restaurant workers, and donate almost one million pounds of cleaning supplies to those in need.

Many CEOs beyond Breen and Baker spoke to us about how they practically managed the downside risks of big moves. "Most things that bring you down are the unintended consequences, that's the way we avoided disaster," shares the former CEO of automotive parts maker Delphi, Rod O'Neal. "One cause of our success was the things we didn't do. We didn't go big in India or South America or Russia. We avoided all the pitfalls of what a lot of companies were trying to do." O'Neal avoided the pitfalls through a process of methodically working through potential unintended consequences. "If you make a given decision, you can't just consider the first domino you trip, which is probably a good outcome," he shares. "What could be the second-, third-, fourth-, fifth-, sixth-, and seventh-order consequences? We would go down the decision tree and see what outcomes could occur as things played out. If we came across one that, no matter how remote it was, we couldn't survive it if it showed up, we made another decision. We didn't play the game of saying, 'Oh, man, that'll be a disaster if it shows up, but it probably won't, so let's try it anyway.'"

Over time, the best CEOs avoid the downside by forming some rules of thumb based on pattern recognition. At Danaher, Larry Culp, who was the company's CEO from 2001 through 2014 and who went on to become the chairman and CEO of GE, applied three hurdles for making an acquisition. "We've got to like the space and the company," he says. "We've got to be able to add value. And the math of the deal has to work. But we have to come at it in that sequence, because if you flip it the way most bankers want you to, you're going to get in trouble. We were quite candid with ourselves as to where we could add value and if we were the best owner."

Culp's conviction was forged from experience. "In the early days, we very much had a deal mindset," he recalls. "We weren't at all discriminating as to what we'd buy. The math was the first hurdle and everything else was secondary." When Culp became CEO of Danaher, his bias was for higher-gross-margin, less-capital-intensive instrumentation businesses, resulting in a portfolio that had strategic coherence as it grew. And grow it did, as over the course of Culp's tenure Danaher's total return to shareholders was 465 percent versus the S&P 500's 105 percent. During that stretch market value grew from $20 billion to $50 billion and revenue quintupled.

To help analyze risks, the best CEOs apply the right analytics. Adobe CEO Shantanu Narayen shares what happened behind the scenes during the company's big move to migrate all of its customers to the cloud. "We intuitively knew migrating our products to subscription was the right vision. To test this conviction, we literally covered the boardroom with pricing and unit models, predictions for how quickly perpetual licenses would fall off, and how quickly online subscriptions would ramp up. We spent hours knee-deep in modeling output." Doing so increased the entire team's commitment. "It really takes guts, but through this discussion we saw that we could manage through it and that Adobe, our customers, and our shareholders would benefit in the long run."

Act Like an Owner

When top CEOs are faced with making big, bold decisions, they say that the best way to arrive at the right answer is to think like an owner.

Reflecting on what had the biggest impact on his thought process as a first-time CEO at General Instruments, Ed Breen explains, "I had a couple of really tough decisions that were make-or-break for the company. I remember going to Ted Forstmann, our largest investor and board member, to discuss them, and he said to me, 'Ed, it's your company. You know, why don't you look in the mirror and make the decision?'" The advice had a profound impact on the new CEO and from then on he always made decisions as if he owned 100 percent of the company. "That way," Breen shares, "you don't have to worry about all the various constituencies, because you know you've made the right decision for the company. It's not that you ignore them—whether it's vendors, customers, employees, or investors—but, once you know you've arrived at the right decision, it's just a matter of how you handle it with the board, the management team, the employees, and so on."

Thinking like an owner helps resolve the tension between the short and long term. "As a CEO, you're responsible for the long-term fate of the company," says Valeo's Jacques Aschenbroich, who thinks like an owner. "If I want to improve the results tomorrow, it's very easy. I control R&D; I control capex. It will be fantastic, but we'll be dead in a few years' time. I don't think you are a true CEO if you don't think long-term. You alone represent the company and you have to act in the best interest of the company." Ronnie Leten, the former CEO of the industrial giant Atlas Copco, went so far as to tell his board and his team, "Let's act like a family business. I'm the head of the family. We create value over time for our children and grandchildren. If we do it this way, we'll continuously create economic value through economic cycles."

Early in his tenure at Itaú Unibanco, which became the largest financial conglomerate in the Southern Hemisphere and tenth largest bank in the world by market value, former CEO and now co-chairman Roberto Setúbal found that acting like an owner gave him the conviction to make a very bold move. "I was the CEO at the bank when inflation stopped overnight. For the first time that I'd worked there, the bank started losing money. I was panicking. But I knew my role as CEO was to make decisions like an owner, to do whatever it would take—no matter how controversial—to constantly increase the long-term value of the bank." At that time, banks didn't charge fees on accounts, but the reality was that if Itaú Unibanco didn't change, it wasn't going to make it. The bank made a big announcement on TV and in the newspapers about the new fees it would charge. Setúbal's competitors told him he was crazy and that his customers would close all their accounts. "They were wrong, though," says Setúbal. "Our clients accepted the fees because we chose to be very transparent about it. It turned out that people were tired of other banks trying to charge hidden fees."

Alphabet's Sundar Pichai drew inspiration from how founders Larry Page and Sergey Brin made bold strategic moves. "Often when a CEO tries to make a significant shift, the organization takes one step in that direction," he reflects. "Larry and Sergey were very good at taking what looked like irrational positions that led people to ask, 'Why are you doing that?' But by the magnitude of their aspiration, they did bend the organization. You're instantly working on something that most other people are not doing. You naturally attract the best people. Even if the teams achieved one-tenth what they set out to do, we still end up with big innovations."

Regularly Apply "Heart Paddles"

What Roberto Setúbal described above is but one of a number of big moves he made throughout his twenty-two-year tenure as CEO that helped differentiate his bank from the competition.

"You have to reinvent yourself. The world changes. You have to change," he advises.

In his first act, he turned Itaú from a regional to a nationwide bank by quickly acquiring and integrating four large and troubled state-owned banks. In his second act, he invested heavily to move the bank from being retail only to a leader in corporate and investment banking, while expanding into the affluent retail segment, and into three other Latin American countries. In his third act, he implemented an agile operating model, radically reduced overhead, increased efficiency, overhauled the company's performance culture, and negotiated and executed a merger with Unibanco. In his final act, he aggressively drove growth in Brazil, pushed further Latin American expansion, and prioritized investments to digitize the bank.

Applying "heart paddles" to create a series of performance-enhancing S-curves

Example: Roberto Setúbal at Itaú Unibanco

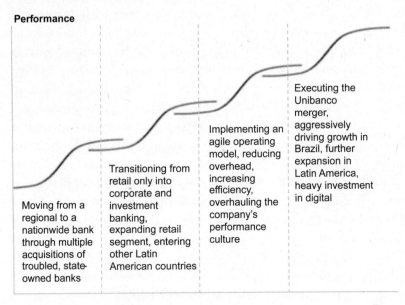

Setúbal's experience illustrates how many of the best CEOs think of making big moves: as a series of "S-curves" driving change over time. This means they ramp up into a period of intensive activity and radical improvement through a set of big moves, followed by a period of restoration while still improving incrementally, followed by another ramp-up in big-move intensity, and so on. Excellent CEOs are always looking to the next S-curve while ensuring the current one is delivered on. Microsoft's Satya Nadella describes the tension: "There are some things where you have to be long-term and patient. Some things where you have to be impatient. That's a fascinating thing—what is tempo? You've got to balance the future and the present. Only the CEO can do that."

Like Nadella, the best CEOs think hard about what tempo to set for the big changes they're making. Doing this isn't easy but it's necessary. Says McKinsey & Company's Dominic Barton, himself an expert in advising companies on transformational change: "No one likes change, so you need to create a rhythm of change. Think of it as applying 'heart paddles' to the organization. The average lifetime of an organization in 1935 was ninety years, in 2015 it was eighteen years. You have to ask the question: 'Why should we exist ten years from now?' It's an existential issue to change enough, regularly enough. If you're not doing this, you're not going to be around." While leading McKinsey, Barton effectively moved the firm from providing good advice to also becoming an implementation partner to its clients. Among many "heart paddles" applied, he retooled the firm's fee structure based on the impact of advice given to its clients, expanded services beyond consulting to include helping clients implement change, and invested heavily in building advanced data and analytics capabilities.

Best Buy's Hubert Joly describes why and how he applied heart paddles to his organization, moving from one S-curve to another. "We started with a turnaround, something we called 'Renew Blue.' There came a point where it became apparent we should declare the turnaround over. In the mind of some people that era was associated with a very conservative environment where we had to focus a lot on cost reduction and couldn't take as many risks or we'd lose credibility. It's a lot easier to manage Wall Street if you're hitting your targets."

At that point Joly felt Best Buy was ready to move into a growth phase, meaning it needed to take more risks to unleash its potential. The CEO moved into the next phase of his strategy: "Building the New Blue." During the turnaround, Joly had already made a series of bold moves such as offering price-match guarantees, exiting international markets, and reinventing vendor partnerships. Now with his eye on growth, he applied the heart paddles again by building a leading position in the smart home market, expanding into senior care through sensors and AI, and launching Total Tech Support, a program that provides customer support regardless of where the technology was purchased.

We're often called on to counsel CEOs who start strong by making a series of bold moves but a few years into their tenure experience waning motivation and increasingly static performance. These CEOs got the memo on "make big moves early" but not the one that added, "and often." Every big move should have a start and a finish, with the completion of each phase building confidence and creating capacity for further change. When the equivalent of a lunar landing is achieved, victory should be celebrated and lessons should be learned, but then it's time for the next bold move to take the company even further, faster. Doing so accounts for why, as we described in the introduction, the best CEOs achieve above-market performance on a sustained basis, avoiding the slumps that the less skilled experience as they go.

Johan Thijs, CEO of Belgian-based bank-insurance group KBC, exemplifies how the best leaders approach S-curves. In 2019, the financial services giant had consistently posted profits that were among the very strongest in the European market. The firm was always highly liquid and well capitalized. For three years running Thijs had appeared in the Top 10 of the *Harvard Business Review* Top 100 CEOs in the world list. If ever there was an "if it's not broke, don't fix it" scenario, Thijs was in it. So what did he do? What *all* great CEOs do, "We reassessed our strategy," he says. "We're continuing down our chosen route but are now shifting up a gear." The company celebrated and retired its previous S-curve, known internally as the "More of the same, but differently" strategy. Then it ramped up its next S-curve, dubbed "Differently: the Next Level." This new set of big moves emphasizes artificial intelligence, rapid decision-making, and product and process simplicity, all to become the most data-driven and solution-driven digital first bank-insurance company in the world.

Big moves bring with them big risk. The best CEOs know, in the spirit of hockey Hall of Famer Wayne Gretzky's observation, "You miss every shot that you don't take," that the bigger risk is to be timid in the face of uncertainty. Excellent CEOs get comfortable with acting boldly by having a clear point of view on the future, fully understanding the risk/reward trade-offs, acting like an owner, and applying "heart paddles" throughout their tenure.

While there's no guarantee of success, the fact remains that without making big moves early and often, there's little chance for a company to become a top performer. We mentioned earlier that one of the five big moves correlated with success—resource allocation—is essential in enabling other big strategic moves. Having covered the topics of vision and strategy, we now shift our focus fully to resource allocation—the final vital practice in setting a company on the right path.

CHAPTER 3

Resource Allocation Practice

Act Like an Outsider

Insanity is doing the same thing over and over again, but expecting different results.
— Rita Mae Brown (often attributed to Albert Einstein)

When Nazi Germany annexed Austria in 1938, discrimination against the Jews prompted mathematician Abraham Wald to immigrate to the United States. As the United States entered World War II, Wald was asked to apply his statistical skills to various wartime problems. One such problem was providing advice to minimize bomber losses due to enemy fire.

In studying numerous bombers that had made it back from combat, the experts found that some parts of the planes were hit more often than others. Military leaders wanted to have these parts reinforced to minimize damage. Wald wasn't a military leader, however. Applying an outsider's perspective to the problem led him to argue that the parts hit *least* often should be the ones that were protected. He surmised that if planes were hit in a critical area, it was unlikely they'd make it back to base. Those planes that were able to return probably hadn't been hit in a critical area. Thus, he reasoned, reinforcing parts of planes that had sustained many hits and lived to tell the tale would be unlikely to pay off.

Most CEOs believe, as with Wald, that if resources aren't deployed in the right areas, battles will be lost. In fact, 83 percent identify capital allocation as a key lever for growth—citing it as even more important than operational excellence or M&A.[20] They're right that it's important. As we discussed in the previous chapter, the top decile of high-performing CEOs is much more likely to shift around large amounts of capital, and they do it far more often than average performers. In spite of this awareness, a third of companies, our research shows, reallocate a mere 1 percent of their capital from year to year, whereas the highest performing companies average over 6 percent.

When allocation decisions don't line up with the company's vision and strategy, the latter become just hollow words in corporate presentations that quickly lose credibility and potency. Further, if a CEO cannot allocate capital more effectively than capital markets, the business will lose its legitimacy in the eyes of its shareholders and might even trigger an activist investor campaign to break up the company. Add to this the "tragedy of the commons" problem—the notion that individuals will neglect the good of the whole if they're focused on self-gain—and it's easy to see why the best CEOs are front and center in allocating resources.

So what gets in the way of lining up resources behind the vision and strategy? Internally, it has to do with the political challenges of taking away from A and giving to B. "Resource allocation is one of the most important things," says Adidas's Kasper Rørsted. "Most people don't want to give up resources, so very often the CEO has to intervene." External barriers can also get in the way. Although the stock market loves reallocation in the long term, it actually doesn't like it in the short term because it tends to depress profits for the first couple of years. For both internal and external reasons, then, it's easy to see why CEOs need to apply a mindset of "be bold" to resource allocation—or else it'll never happen the right way.

Coming in from the outside can make it easier to move resources around. Boston Scientific's CEO Mike Mahoney shares his experience: "Being an outsider helped me tremendously. Those that had been in the company for a long time were overly focused on the drug-eluding stents (DES) and cardiac rhythm management (CRM) markets. They're important businesses, but there are so many other opportunities in faster growing markets where we could leverage our innovation and lead in. We needed a new strategy and we needed to move quickly." Mahoney and his team systematically shifted R&D dollars—80 percent of which at the time were focused on the low-growth, core businesses—into faster-growing markets including endoscopy, neuromodulation, peripheral interventions, interventional oncology, and urology. The moves to reinvest in the medtech space proved to be the right ones as both revenue and EBITDA (earnings before interest, taxes, depreciation, and amortization) have increased by more than 50 percent and market capitalization has increased over seven times during Mahoney's eight-year tenure to date.

The best CEOs know that one doesn't have to actually be an outsider to be emboldened like one. In the early 1980s when Intel plummeted from $198 million one year to $2 million the next, creating a crisis, the president of the company at the time, Andy Grove, asked his CEO, Gordon Moore, "If we got kicked out and the board brought in a new CEO, what do you think they would do?" Moore answered without hesitation, "They would get us out of memory chips." Grove stared at him and said, "Why shouldn't you and I walk out the door, come back, and do it ourselves?"[21] The rest is history as Intel exited DRAM memory chips and staked its future on a new product: the microprocessor. In doing so, Intel helped usher in the computer age and had a run of success that lasted for decades.

The globally diversified conglomerate Danaher is a powerful example of a company that turned an outsider's view of resource allocation into a business model. Originally a real estate investment trust, Danaher evolved into a broad portfolio of science, technology, and manufacturing companies across life sciences, diagnostics, environmental and applied solutions, and dental. Under the leadership of Larry Culp, the company relentlessly applied the Danaher Business System (DBS) approach to resource allocation. DBS identifies the best investment opportunities, drives operational improvements to free up resources, and creates world-class capabilities in the businesses Danaher acquires. In applying DBS the Danaher management team spends over half of its time focused on resource reallocation, including M&A opportunities, organic investments, and divestments. During the fourteen years under Culp's leadership, the company made $22 billion worth of acquisitions and divested over a third of its businesses.

Thinking like an outsider when it comes to reallocation means a CEO isn't wed to tradition, encumbered by internal loyalties, or willing to bow to short-term pressures. Instead, they regularly ask themselves what a new CEO with no emotional ties or history would do if brought in to take over the company. Practically speaking, this translates to allocating resources by . . .

> . . . starting with a zero base
> . . . solving for the whole
> . . . managing by milestones (not annual budgets)
> . . . killing as much as they create

Start with a Zero Base

We talked in our chapter on vision about one of psychologist Daniel Kahneman's experiments with a lottery ticket and its related lesson for building a sense of ownership. Here we share another of Kahneman's experiments in which one grocery store puts Campbell's soup on sale for 79 cents with a sign above the display that says, "Limit 12 per customer." In another grocery store, the same sale is happening at the identical price, but with no purchase limit. On average, how many cans do you think are purchased per customer in the first store? The answer is seven. And in the other store? Just over three.[22]

What's going on here, and why is this relevant? The experiment shows the power of what is called an "anchoring heuristic." A heuristic is essentially a mental shortcut or rule of thumb the brain uses to simplify complex decisions—also known as a cognitive bias, something we'll discuss in further detail in our chapter on decision-making. An anchor is a piece of information someone relies on to make a decision. In the supermarket experiment, shoppers' brains anchored on the purchase limit of twelve and adjusted downward. Those who bought only three cans of soup didn't have the number twelve in mind, so they made what might be considered a more normal-size purchase, or one adjusting upward from zero.

Now let's apply this learning to the way most companies traditionally approach resource allocation: It starts with last year's budget or some other form of historical baseline (the "anchor"). This means that capital is likely to get distributed based on the way it always has been in the past. If Sally's division got a 2 percent bump this year, she'll probably get the same next year (or not far from it). But what if the "anchor" is replaced by zero? No investment is taken as a given—every investment is scrutinized, alternatives explored, and approval justified by how it helps deliver against the company's strategy and vision. This is what we mean by taking a "zero-based" approach to resource allocation. It's a more arduous approach, but the best CEOs believe it's well worth it.

When Mary Barra started out as CEO of GM in 2014, she put capital allocation at the top of her priority list. At the time, the automaker was operating in many markets around the globe but not always successfully. It was trying to be everywhere for everyone with everything. In essence, GM had spread its capital and other resources too thin, so it wasn't winning even in important markets.

Wanting to allocate capital appropriately, Barra started to take a hard look at the returns on the capital she was deploying. As she describes: "I'll never forget the meeting where a regional president in Asia wanted us to make a several-hundred-million-dollar investment in a country for a product, and the plan was 'We're going to do this, and we're going to lose money.' It wasn't 'We're going to make this money, but it's high-risk.' So I asked, 'Why would we do this? Why would we allocate capital, knowing we're not going to recover it?' "

The regional president argued: "We've been here forever. We can't leave the market. But if we don't invest in this product, we won't have anything to sell." As she heard this, Barra recalled something one of her board members once told her: "There's nothing strategic about losing money."

Barra recalls what happened next: "I looked at my CFO and said, 'We can't do this. There's no way we're going to deploy money without a plan to be profitable.' " It turned out that she and her chief financial officer (CFO) were perfectly in sync and put everyone on notice that if they didn't come up with a profitable plan, they weren't getting capital. "Either you fix the profitability of your region or your country, you fix the products and the segments we're competing in, or we're going to get out."

Over time, Barra finally decided to exit the market because GM didn't have the kind of products, brand, or strong dealer networks necessary to win in that market. "In that market," says Barra, "we tried really hard. GM had been there for twenty years, but we had to recognize that we hadn't entered the market appropriately with the right strategic plan."

During her tenure, Barra has continued to take a zero-based approach to capital allocation. In market after market she carefully analyzes where GM has the best chances of winning and generating an appropriate return. When doing her strategic reviews she engages in deep analysis and has tough conversations with her executives along the lines of: "Is there a different business model we can use? Can we source product from somewhere else? Or do we need to exit the market?" When she meets resistance from one of her executives, she asks: "Would you put your own dollar into it? If you wouldn't put your own money into something, why should we?"

Barra's approach of questioning everything and ensuring that every major investment reflects her company's vision, strategy, and financial goals was echoed by virtually every excellent CEO to whom we spoke. For example, Medtronic's Bill George talked about the importance of "the ability to see things through a fresh set of eyes" and LEGO's Jørgen Vig Knudstorp shared, "You're never going to have a chance unless you radically reallocate resources, so with that we started producing a product portfolio every year that was fifty to seventy percent new."

Solve for the Whole

Beyond taking a zero-based approach for each potential investment, the best CEOs use a mantra of "solving for the whole" that helps them cut through to the right answer quickly.

At Lockheed Martin, CEO Marillyn Hewson describes what this looks like in practice: "Before I became CEO, I'd been a leader of one of the business areas, so I knew how to get more than my fair share of dollars. When I got the top job, I told the leaders of these different business areas: 'We're going to look at your investment plan from top to bottom. We're going to put all the plans together, and we're going shave off the stuff at the bottom and we're going to double down on the things that we all collectively know we need to go after as a corporation. And it may mean somebody gives something up over here. Or it may mean that somebody takes the lead over there. But if we don't do that collectively as leaders of the corporation, as leaders of Lockheed Martin—not just leaders of Aeronautics, or Space, or Mission Systems—then we're not going to be as strong as we can be as One Lockheed Martin.'"

Dupont's Ed Breen illustrates the point by way of example: "The team will come in and say, 'We want to spend $500 million in capital.' Then the CFO needs to sit down with me and say, 'That might be a decent project over there in Business A. But you know what? This one over here in Business B is an absolute home run. So we're not doing that, we're doing this.'" Breen further explains, "Otherwise if the leader of the business were to make the decision themselves, they would of course do what they think is right for their business. But that's not necessarily right for the company as a whole."

Capital reallocation isn't just about managing new investments and halting others from making them; it's also about who owns what budgets and with what expectations. Some CEOs we spoke to moved resources from the corporate center out to the businesses to give them more empowerment and accountability. Others did the opposite, centralizing for the sake of efficiency and consistency. In either case, without a CEO's deep conviction that such moves are solving for the whole, the mere suggestion of such shifts typically devolves into endless turf wars.

Allianz's Oliver Bäte explains the resistance he experienced when centralizing some functions, as well as the analogies he used to help cut through the office politics: "We grow up with all these kingdoms, that produce their own grain, have their own cows, have their own machinery, build their own highways, and so on. So the leaders of your businesses say, 'If you take all these resources away from me, I don't rule a kingdom anymore. I'm not going to be anything more than a sales outlet.'

"That is totally the wrong analogy," he continues. "The better way to think about it is like the Mercedes-Benz team in Formula 1.

You have two champions. You have Lewis Hamilton, who is a world champion race car driver, which is the heads of the business units. And you have the makers of the car, which is Mercedes, that's the role of the central functions. Lewis Hamilton doesn't design tires, steering wheels, the chassis, or the engine. But he still has to drive in Shanghai, Monte Carlo, and so on. And he has to finish the race first. That's the power of solving for Allianz as a whole," says Bäte. "You [the business head] tell us what car you need to win the race, and we [the center] will bring it to you, built on a world-class platform."

Bäte's analogy was compelling. Allianz has since moved from 132 local and regional data centers down to six strategic ones, and from three dozen data networks globally down to one Allianz Global Network, gaining a significant cost advantage in the process. It also meant that when the COVID-19 global pandemic crisis hit in 2020, Allianz was able to quickly equip its people and enable remote working, a tremendous achievement for a company with offices in over seventy countries around the world.

Manage by Milestones (Not Annual Budgets)

"I get so frustrated," confesses Jamie Dimon, CEO of JPMorgan Chase (JPMC), "with business leaders who say they didn't make an investment because it wasn't in their budget. You have to say, 'I want to do X. I want to add branches, I want to go to the cloud. I need to be competitive.' You want to spend $500 million? Recommend it. Show me why. I may ask a million questions before the ultimate decision, but if it's a good idea, we'll do it. We can change what is planned in the budget."

In essence, Dimon's approach is never to let an annual budget cycle get in the way of making good business decisions. At various points in his career Dimon even went so far as to have his leaders sign a one-page document saying, "I, [fill in your name], have asked for everything I need to be the best in my business and be the best in the world at what I do." That way, as Dimon states, "No one can hide behind excuses."

Dimon's streamlined method helps him deal with the volatility of the business environment. A Brexit vote, a sudden oil price decline, a regional conflict, a financial meltdown—all can provide corporations with opportunities if they can move quickly enough to reallocate their assets. During the global financial crisis of 2008, for instance, Dimon received a call from the US government asking him if JPMC could save the New York City investment bank Bear Stearns, which held large amounts of troubled, mortgage-backed securities and faced sudden bankruptcy.

As Dimon recalls: "I spoke to Bear Stearns on a Thursday night, and I called my board on Friday and told them what was going on—that the government has asked us to look at this as an acquisition. I told the board, 'I'm not going to do it if it puts us at risk. It's got to make sense for shareholders.' I took my directors through all the things that mitigated the risk, which included the [acquisition] price, by the way. We did a weekend of due diligence—we worked on it for fifteen hours a day. We went through all the mortgages Bear Stearns owned, all the loans they had, all their trading books, all their litigation, all their HR policies, so it was really extensive due diligence." The next day Dimon bought Bear Stearns for a heavily discounted $2 a share (which was ultimately raised to $10 a share), and JPMC's people moved in and started operating the firm's trading desks and mortgage operations, busily managing risk.

Dimon's ability to allocate capital quickly and wisely paid off for JPMC, which became the largest and one of the most profitable banks in the United States, and the seventh largest in the world, with total assets exceeding $3 trillion. It didn't hurt the bank's long-term financial performance that Dimon also had the foresight right ahead of the 2008 financial crisis to unload more than $12 billion in risky subprime mortgages—another timely and bold asset allocation move.

But if the capital reallocation process isn't based on a corporate calendar, what is it based on? The best CEOs use performance milestones. They release additional tranches of investment only when there is strong evidence that previous tranches are yielding results. Each milestone forces periodic debate over whether to continue or not. Dupont CEO Ed Breen describes how it works at his company: "We've got metrics around every big program. We ask the question of where we are on cost. We regularly ask whether we still think we're getting the right return on the program. This way we can track every program and see how it's doing, and we always do a postmortem one year after the project is completed."

Closely monitoring investments on a milestone-driven basis, however, doesn't mean that budgets should be constantly moved around. As long as the big moves still make sense, the milestones are being met, and the actions taken are delivering results for the company, the best CEOs stay the course. Gil Shwed, the Israeli founder and CEO of Check Point, the largest pure-play cybersecurity company in the world, holds full-day, off-site meetings once a month to make sure his resources are in the right place. "Even if those meetings don't end in big decisions to invest in new areas or make operational changes, they still act as an important discipline to keep us up to speed." During similar reviews at Alphabet, CEO Sundar Pichai reports, "I look for two things—how we did against our top priorities and whether we did something that feels like a point of inflection. It's important to have the reserves to quickly move things around and adapt."

Kill as Much as You Create

Talking about resource allocation in broad terms risks oversimplifying the choices facing CEOs. In reality, allocation comprises four fundamental activities: seeding, nurturing, pruning, and harvesting. Seeding is entering new business areas, whether through an acquisition or an organic start-up investment. Nurturing involves building up an existing business through investments, including acquisitions that strengthen the original business. Pruning takes resources away from an existing business, either by giving some of its annual capital allocation to others or by putting part of the business up for sale. Finally, harvesting is selling or spinning off whole businesses that no longer fit a company's portfolio.

Our research found that there's little overall difference between the seeding and harvesting behavior of the best CEOs and the rest. This isn't surprising: Seeding involves giving money to new business opportunities—something that's rarely resisted. And while harvesting is difficult, it most often occurs as a result of a business unit's sustained underperformance, which is difficult to ignore. We found, however, that the best nurtured and pruned their business nearly three times more often than the rest. Together, these two functions represent half of all corporate reallocation activity in the best companies.[23] Both tasks are difficult because they often involve taking resources from one business unit and giving them to another. What's more, the better a company is at encouraging seeding, the more important these two activities become—nurturing to ensure the success of new initiatives and pruning to eliminate branches that won't ever bear fruit.

When Nancy McKinstry became CEO of Wolters Kluwer in 2003, the Dutch global publisher was struggling to adapt to the internet age. Revenues and profits were flat, and it lacked a digital strategy. By her own admission, McKinstry was a bold choice for the role given these circumstances—she was the company's first female and the first non-Dutch CEO, though she had developed a deep understanding of the business while serving as leader of its North American business. At the time, Wolters Kluwer was primarily a print publisher of materials catering to tax, legal, and health care professionals. McKinstry knew her customers increasingly wanted their information in digital format, which allowed them to wade through masses of information more quickly and easily, and they wanted expert solutions that improved productivity.

First, McKinstry seeded the new digital publishing businesses through acquisitions while at the same time harvesting businesses that didn't fit the digital profile she was looking for. Since she took the helm, McKinstry has, over the course of ten years, sold off $1 billion of low-potential assets, while acquiring about $1.5 billion worth of new companies that fit her digital strategy.

But it was her nurturing and pruning of the company's portfolio that in the end made her strategy work. To nurture her portfolio, she reinvested each year roughly 8 to 10 percent of the company's revenues into new and enhanced solutions—even during the global financial crisis and COVID-19 pandemic. To ensure these investment dollars were used wisely, she built an internal total shareholder return model and extended it down to her fifty business units. "The numbers told us," says McKinstry, "how much shareholder value a business unit created in the last three years, and then we'd compare it to the new three-year plan we're considering. The model helped the entire organization understand how value creation occurs." Armed with this information McKinstry could see clearly which businesses were nascent, high-growth, mature, or declining, and allocate investments accordingly. The data-driven approach meant, says McKinstry, "that our leaders knew we are investing in the right places."

All that nurturing and pruning paid off. When McKinstry started, 75 percent of the business was print. Today, less than 10 percent is. And the company has a thriving expert solutions business. Since she took over as CEO, the company's stock has risen more than fivefold.

Many leaders set up rituals to ensure the difficult act of pruning becomes a way of life. At Alphabet, Sundar Pichai regularly reflects on advice from his mentor Bill Campbell, a three-time CEO—at Claris, Intuit, and GO Corporation—and influential coach to several technology industry leaders. "Bill used to ask me every Monday, 'What ties did you break last week?' Organizations can be stuck if you don't break ties. For example, we had Play Music and YouTube Music—similar music products. At some point, somebody has to make a decision; it unlocks so many resources. Asking leaders questions and breaking ties are ways of empowering people. And it's equally important that my leaders are breaking ties on their teams as well."

DSM's Feike Sijbesma set up a "Hall of Failures" where the company organized funerals for failed projects. The idea was to show that trying and failing would be honored as long as lessons were learned and shared, much in the same way that a traditional "Hall of Fame" celebrates successes. These corporate funerals also made it clear that no more resources would be allocated to the effort—that the projects were dead. As part of the ritual, it was customary to give a speech with technicians from other divisions in attendance in order to cross-pollinate what was learned.

One such funeral turned out to be a rebirth. A multiyear R&D project for the company's picture frame glass business had flopped. Engineers had created a glass coating that took all the photons from incoming light and pushed them directly through the glass onto the painting or photograph, making the glass fully transparent with absolutely no reflection. Unfortunately, the technology was prohibitively expensive, and the only market for this glass was museums, which was too small for DSM's purposes.

As the project eulogy was being given, one of the technicians from a different unit raised his hand, intrigued by the technology he was hearing about for the first time. "If I'm understanding the chemistry behind the coating, what would happen if you applied it to solar panels? Wouldn't this give them more photons to absorb than otherwise and therefore increase efficiency?" Sijbesma turned to his chief innovation officer and both looked incredulously at each other: serendipity. It was a simple yet brilliant idea that hadn't been considered by the sales department, which had fixated on the picture frame market.

The project was resurrected, and testing showed that the coating gave solar panels a 5 to 10 percent power boost. From there the growth of DSM's antireflective coatings business was nurtured by funds freed up by other products and projects pruned by the "Hall of Failures." Today the coating is installed on many solar panels worldwide.

While the tactics differ, the almost religious zeal for pruning and nurturing that McKinstry and Sijbesma implemented is shared by other top CEOs. Valeo's Jacques Aschenbroich pruned investments in what were previously considered core products to nurture its carbon emission reduction technologies and advanced driver assistance systems businesses. Adidas's Kasper Rørsted pruned inventory from retail partners to nurture its online channel. Israel Discount Bank's Lilach Asher-Topilsky drew resources from her international operations to bolster the pursuit of domestic opportunities.

We didn't find a single excellent CEO who felt they'd somehow been too active in reallocating resources. Majid Al Futtaim's Alain Bejjani sums up why: "Resource reallocation is easier said than done because many organizations are anchored in existing commitments, expectations, and realities that are often outside their control." Boldness is required to break through, which involves acting like an outsider—free of political and historical shackles.

The best resource allocators justify every investment from

scratch by starting with a zero base. They make it clear that the good of the whole company will be put ahead of any one area. They manage less by annual budgets and more by performance milestones, making resource allocation a continuous (not cyclical) process. Lastly, they kill off as much as they start through thoughtful pruning and harvesting.

In this chapter we've talked about resource allocation mostly in financial terms. As you'd expect, the best consider a corporation's resources to extend far beyond capital and operational expenditure. The broader talent pool is also vital, as is where leadership time and energy are focused. These "resources" will be covered fully in the following chapters.

● ● ●

At this point we hope it's clear how the mindset of "be bold" propels the best CEOs to take radically different direction-setting actions in the face of the business world's ever-increasing volatility, uncertainty, complexity, and ambiguity. Below is a summary of the bold actions that characterize excellence in setting direction for a company—actions that our research shows make it more than six times more probable to become a top quintile performer.

Setting the Direction: What separates the best from the rest

Mindset: Be Bold	
Vision practice:	**Reframe the Game**
	◈ Find and amplify intersections
	◈ Make it about more than money
	◈ Look back to look forward
	◈ Involve a broad group of leaders
Strategy practice:	**Make Big Moves Early and Often**
	◈ Be an exceptional futurist
	◈ Keep an eye on the downsides
	◈ Act like an owner
	◈ Regularly apply "heart paddles"
Resource allocation practice:	**Act Like an Outsider**
	◈ Start with a zero base
	◈ Solve for the whole
	◈ Manage by milestones
	◈ Kill as much as you create

If you run a small business or a nonprofit, these lessons in boldness likely still apply in many ways. Ask yourself: Are you pursuing a direction that (1) fills an unmet need, (2) uses your unique capabilities, (3) is driven by a noble purpose, and (4) can be monetized (if that's relevant to your situation)? Have you involved a group of people in shaping the vision and who are therefore emotionally invested in wanting to help you? Are you taking actions that are unquestionably big "needle movers"? Have you redirected time, energy, talent, and finances away from lower priority pursuits toward taking these actions? For most, answering these questions in the affirmative will undoubtedly increase the odds of achieving breakthrough success.

ORGANIZATION ALIGNMENT MINDSET

Treat the Soft Stuff as the Hard Stuff

When dealing with people, remember you are not dealing with creatures of logic, but creatures of emotion.

—Dale Carnegie

Once a CEO sets a direction for the company's future, the probability that the plan will become reality is low. Many studies, including our own research, conclude that only one in three strategies is successfully implemented. The reasons for failure are rooted in the reality that change is rarely an intellectual problem, it's an emotional one. The "soft stuff"—issues related to people and culture—account for the vast majority (72 percent) of the barriers to success.[24]

This finding is hardly revelatory. It's precisely what management guru Peter Drucker was referring to over fifty years ago when he purportedly said, "Culture eats strategy for breakfast." Most CEOs understand this and readily acknowledge that the soft stuff is hard to get right. Accordingly, they ask their chief human resources officer (CHRO) to ensure there's a good plan in place to handle the organization and talent-related changes needed to execute the strategy. These CEOs, however, generally don't expect the same level of robustness and coherence in people-related plans as, for example, the CFO might provide in laying out a financial plan—after all, this is the soft stuff.

The best CEOs *don't* follow this pattern. They don't just acknowledge that the soft stuff is hard, they vow to treat the soft stuff as the hard stuff. And they make sure that every senior leader, not just the CHRO, owns the people-related implications of the strategy. KBC's Johan Thijs puts it thusly: "You have to fix both sides as the CEO: The easy part is technical; the difficult part is people. You might fix the technical issues: finding capital, liquidity, profitability, and so forth. But over time if you can't solve the mindset issues, you'll go back on the same route because the mindset is going to drive you again over a cliff."

The impact of choosing a "treat the soft stuff as the hard stuff" mindset and taking the actions it calls for is dramatic: The odds of a strategy being successfully executed more than double from 30 to 79 percent, and the impact of that execution is 1.8 times greater.[25] These differences in performance are driven by the best CEOs taking radically different approaches with respect to each of the three sub-elements involved in aligning an organization: culture, organizational design, and talent.

CHAPTER 4

Culture Practice
Find the One Thing

Culture is coded wisdom.
—Wangari Maathai

In a poignant scene in the Hollywood blockbuster comedy *City Slickers*, Curly (a weathered, tough old cowboy played by Jack Palance) laughs at the "citified" confusion about life displayed by Mitch (a Manhattan yuppie played by Billy Crystal). Then Curly offers his wisdom: "It all comes down to one thing. You focus on that, and everything else don't mean s#&t." Mitch, still confused, asks him what that one thing is. Curly responds, "That's what you have to find out." Later in the film, Mitch finds out his "one thing" when a life-threatening situation clarifies that what really matters to him are his wife and kids. In that instant, his troubles with his career and reaching middle age—previously considered monumental and insurmountable—melt away.

We could easily imagine any of the best CEOs we spoke to uttering Curly's very same advice to a new CEO when it comes to culture change. Perhaps the starkest example of a focus on "the one thing" is Paul O'Neill's experience while he was CEO of aluminum producer Alcoa (O'Neill went on to serve as the seventy-second US secretary of treasury). When he took the company's reins it was in a state of decline. Investors were worried about profit margins and revenue projections. In his first address to shareholders, O'Neill famously began, "I want to talk to you about worker safety"—confident that higher revenues and lower cost would be a by-product. When grilled by investors on inventory levels and plant utilization, his response was simple: "If you want to understand how Alcoa is doing, you need to look at our workplace safety figures. If we bring our injury rates down, it won't be because of cheerleading or the nonsense you sometimes hear from other CEOs. It will be because the individuals at this company have agreed to become part of something important: They've devoted themselves to creating a habit of excellence."

Although investors hurried to sell the stock when he laid out his safety culture–centric plan, within a year the company was delivering record profits. When he retired thirteen years later, net income had increased fivefold. O'Neill's logic was straightforward: "I knew I had to transform Alcoa, but you can't order people to change. That's not how the brain works. So I decided I was going to start by focusing on one thing. If I could start disrupting habits around one thing, it would spread to the entire company."[26]

When it came to cultural focus, the CEOs we interviewed were laserlike in the same way O'Neill was. Aon's Greg Case is a good example. When he took over the global broker in 2005, it was operated as a federation of acquisitions. Leaders were protective of their client relationships and looked to solve for their individual P&Ls. "Our team inherited a wonderful set of assets from a truly iconic founder, but everyone viewed themselves as an individual entrepreneur, everybody wanted to do their own thing, and we'd all underperform as a result," recalls Case. The "one thing" that would make the biggest difference was what he dubbed "Aon United"—the idea that if Aon's employees put its clients at the center of all they did and supported each other and worked together as a global firm on their clients' behalf, they'd gain and retain more of their clients' business and be able to innovate and scale faster to meet client needs. Although Case describes the journey as a "difficult and challenging path that took a decade," it's been a fruitful one. Aon has grown from a collection of acquisitions with a $6 billion market capitalization into a unified firm valued at over $50 billion as of early 2020.

O'Neill's safety culture and Case's "Aon United" are but two of dozens of examples we could have detailed. At Lockheed Martin, Marillyn Hewson's relentless focus was "Innovation with Purpose," a rallying cry that encouraged unwavering customer focus while developing leading-edge products and services. At Netflix, Reed Hastings consistently emphasizes a culture of "Freedom and Responsibility" that uniquely maximizes both empowerment and accountability in ways other organizations envy. Mastercard's Ajay Banga relentlessly reinforces the importance of the company's "Decency Quotient" (DQ). As he describes, "DQ allowed me to encapsulate many behavioral traits in one phrase. The phrase is flexible enough to allow interpretations, so it applies to different individuals but doesn't allow for misinterpretation."

Some will question the wisdom of having such a narrow focus. What about all of the values statements and leadership models that HR creates with their multiple dimensions? Aren't those important as well? Yes they are, but the best CEOs invariably dwell on the elements that will make the biggest difference and encapsulate those in a pithy word or phrase that they consistently invoke. Ana Botín, who oversees two hundred thousand employees at Banco Santander, routinely drives home her company's cultural mantra through a single phrase: "Simple, Personal, Fair." "Those three words are where you turn when there is no rule book," she says. "I believe in rules and process and governance as much as anybody, but you cannot write everything in a book. Say you have a customer who is ninety-two years old and cannot access their account. The rule says one thing, but if you want to be fair and personal, maybe you go to their house and help them in person. The principles explain how we are different from other competitors, because we do things this way."

At Esquel, CEO Marjorie Yang relentlessly communicates the singular idea of "eCulture" to her employees. Few recall instantly what the five "e"s are—ethics, environment, exploration, excellence, and education—but all understand the essence of what she is referring to. At KBC, Johan Thijs evangelizes the company's PEARL culture—an acronym for "Performance, Empowerment, Accountability, Responsiveness, and Local embeddedness." "Everybody knows it," says Thijs. "If you don't agree with it, the only thing you have to ask yourself is, 'What am I doing here?'" At Sony, former CEO Kazuo Hirai focused in on the word "*Kando*," which in Japanese means to "wow" people. "It boiled down to a simple message, applicable to 110,000 employees, motivating them to put in an extra 10 percent effort: 'Whether you work for the entertainment company, electronics, financial services, or any-thing in between, your job is to provide *kando*, that wow experi-ence, to our customers and consumers around the world.'"

So how do the best CEOs determine what their "one thing" is? Unlike what happened to Mitch in *City Slickers*, it fortunately doesn't require a life-threatening situation. It does require put-ting rigor and discipline into the process, however. Satya Nadella's approach at Microsoft is archetypal. He began by commissioning a small cross-functional team to conduct a deep diagnostic, speaking to experts, senior leaders, VPs, and numerous focus groups to learn about their experience, the culture they desired, what they were passionate about preserving from their history, and what needed to be left behind. With this broad input, a "culture cabinet" made up of seventeen leaders from across Microsoft, chaired by Nadella himself, worked to boil the input down to a vital few themes. In the end, Nadella decided to adopt a "growth mindset," inspired by the research of Stanford psychologist Carol Dweck, who emphasized the importance of learning from mistakes and from others versus trying to prove oneself correct over and over. The company's his-tory of taking on bold technological challenges and giving back to the world would be retained, but the highly individualistic and internally competitive culture that feared failure and struggled to collaborate were attributes that would be shed.

Finding the one thing, as important as it is, means nothing if the culture doesn't actually shift to embrace it. So what role do the best CEOs play in making the desired culture change happen? They . . .

    . . . reshape the work environment
    . . . make it personal
    . . . make it meaningful
    . . . measure what matters

Reshape the Work Environment

Imagine you're at a chamber music recital on Saturday and a sport-ing event on Sunday. As the musicians play one of Mozart's string quartets, you sit silently, rapt in concentration. At the conclusion, you and the audience offer genteel applause. In the final moments of the sporting event—when it's clear your team will win—you leap to your feet, yelling and waving and jumping up and down. You haven't changed; you're the same person with the same feelings, values, and needs. But your environment has, and so has your mindset about how best to express your appreciation and enjoyment.

So what shapes an employee's work environment? There are four primary influencers. It's the stories that are told and the questions that are asked. It's the formal mechanisms that govern how work gets done (structure, processes, systems, incentives). It's the role modeling employees observe (from the CEO, senior team, and others they consider influential). Finally, it's the extent to which people have confidence in their ability to behave in desired ways. The best CEOs demand that culture change efforts address each of these four shapers of environment.

In pursuit of his cultural goal of "Aon United," Greg Case continually reinforces the Aon United narrative in quarterly earnings announcements, emphasizing it as one of the firm's competitive advantages. He also drove home the message of excellence through teamwork by landing a sponsorship with the Manchester United football club.

He's also made a number of changes to the firm's formal mechanisms. He standardized a client service model that had previously been left to local leadership. Operations were consolidated to gain synergies. Senior leaders' compensation was tied to a single, firm-level P&L. What was once an umbrella for sixty sub-brands became a single global brand: Aon. Leaders are explicitly expected to spend a day a week helping colleagues outside of their own area to succeed.

Aware of his role model status, Case virtually never uses "I, me, or my" but instead favors "we, us, and ours" and is quick to give others credit when good things happen. He reinforces the teamwork mantra of "You are either serving a client, or you are helping a colleague serve a client" and spends time working directly with client service teams to ensure the best of the firm is being delivered.

To build skills and confidence, the firm trained over five thousand colleagues in multiday workshops on what it means to "Lead

Aon United," created an online repository of education materials to help colleagues understand the full breadth of the firm, and embedded related skill-building into all management development programs.

On the other side of the world in Thailand, Kan Trakulhoon, former CEO of the Siam Cement Group, wanted to create an "Open and Challenge" culture of innovation in the country's largest and oldest cement and building material company. To do so, he focused on the same four workplace influencers. As for storytelling, after taking the top job in 2006, he went factory to factory (visiting seventy sites in total) sharing his "Go Regional" strategy and the importance of fostering a culture of innovation to enable it. He then told the company's story to every new recruit as part of its month long orientation program

For formal mechanisms, he moved R&D centers next to the plants and had researchers working on teams with those in the factories. He reinvented the incentive system to value deep expertise and created career paths for specialists. He adjusted targets to emphasize the importance of higher value-added products and doubled the spend on R&D every year.

When it came to role modeling, Trakulhoon moved in the opposite direction of the Thai national culture of "keeping face" (not pointing out errors in public) and formality by talking openly about his failures, making his plant visits completely informal affairs, and asking everyone to call him Pi Kan ("Pi" is a friendly, informal term for older brother) instead of sir or president.

To increase confidence and skills, he worked with INSEAD business school to create a leadership training program bringing leaders together across tenures for five days a month of classwork for five months to learn cutting-edge approaches to fostering innovation. He also required leaders to gain global experience to expose them to new ideas and ways of thinking. Trakulhoon's drive to create an "Open and Challenge" culture of innovation was successful. By the time he stepped down from the CEO role in 2016 the company's market cap had increased from $8 billion to $16 billion and employee numbers from twenty-four thousand to fifty-four thousand employees.

As both the Aon and Siam Cement experiences show, the holistic nature of what's required to shift culture quickly and permanently makes it imperative that the CEO—the only one who sits across all the activity happening in the organization—has the understanding and conviction to reshape the work environment consistent with the cultural "one thing" that needs to be unlocked. Once the most important work is identified, much of it can be delegated and performance managed. Regarding some aspects, however, the best CEOs take action themselves, as we'll discuss below.

Make It Personal

Virtually everyone to whom we spoke was surprised by how much their role modeling mattered. DBS's Piyush Gupta shares, "When you're CEO, you've got to realize that every time you say or do something, it's got a massive consequential effect. The whole company pivots." On one hand, this means leaders need to be careful and thoughtful lest they send unintended messages through half-baked ideas or comments. On the other hand, this dynamic creates a huge opportunity to shape the culture—something that the best CEOs do with great acumen.

Many leaders try to follow the well-known aphorism, "Be the change you want to see in the world." At face value, this is exactly right. In practice, however, it isn't enough. On one hand, most aren't aware of just how much they fall short. Like all humans, CEOs are prone to what psychology refers to as "optimism bias." To illustrate, we once asked a CEO how much time he spent managing other people's egos. His response was 20 to 30 percent of the time. We then asked what percent of time people spent managing his ego, and there was silence. Beyond the anecdote, the research is clear: When CEOs are asked if they act as a role model for desired behavior changes, a full 86 percent say yes, whereas only 53 percent of their direct reports concur.[27] As John Akehurst, former CEO of Woodside Petroleum, reflected, "It took a lot of effort for me to recognize that I, as the chief executive, am entirely responsible for the culture of the organization . . . I had an amazing insight into how dysfunctional my behavior was [and] what an impact it had on other people."

A more constructive orientation to role modeling reminds us of a different aphorism: "For things to change, first I must change." This way of thinking suggests that no matter how good I am (or think I am) at being a role model, I also have a responsibility to personally change, which is also what I'm asking all other employees to do. Brad Smith embodied this approach as he drove a cultural focus on design thinking and experimentation at Intuit. "We had to shift our mindsets," says Smith, "to treat success and failure the same way—as an opportunity to learn. I began to very publicly talk about mistakes I'd made. I began to publish my performance reviews on the glass window of my office. I even sent emails out to all employees saying, 'Here is my written performance review from the board. These are the three things I'm working on, and I need your help. So when I'm visiting your office, if you see me do this, please correct me.'"

Smith's willingness to be vulnerable motivated others to follow. "My leadership team soon began to publish their performance reviews. Throughout the organization, people began to admit mistakes or say, 'Here is what I'm working on.' It created this culture of continuous improvement where we were willing to give each other feedback—not in the form of criticism, but to constructively work on things we knew weren't good enough. It encouraged people to run experiments and admit when they didn't work."

While Smith's actions were well planned, the best CEOs look for any opportunity to act as a role model in a "for things to change, first I must change" manner. When he was eight months into his tenure, Microsoft's Satya Nadella gave the keynote speech at an annual event for women in tech. During the Question and Answer (Q&A) he was asked what advice he had for women seeking a pay raise who aren't comfortable asking for one. He advised patience and "knowing and having faith that the system will actually give you the right raises as you go along."

His comments went viral, provoking outrage. He was mocked publicly, charged with being ignorant of well-documented gender pay gaps, and questioned about his stated commitment to diversity. Instead of waiting for the furor to settle or defending his actions, he emailed his employees to tell them, "I answered that question completely wrong." He proceeded to change himself by exploring his own biases and asked his executive team to do the same. Head of Human Resources (HR) Kathleen Hogan recalled: "I became more committed to Satya, not less. He didn't blame anybody. He owned it. He came out to the entire company and he said, 'We're going to learn and we're going to get a lot smarter.'" Nadella said of the experience, "I was determined to use the incident to demonstrate what a growth mindset looks like under pressure." He succeeded, and in so doing helped Microsoft succeed.

Make It Meaningful

The best CEOs are willing to take meaningful actions, often in the face of resistance, that signal just how serious they are about culture change. Shiseido—one of the world's top cosmetic companies with a roster of prestige brands that includes Shiseido, Clé de Peau Beauté, NARS, bareMinerals, Laura Mercier, and Drunk Elephant—provides a case in point. When he took over the CEO role in 2014, Masahiko Uotani was a surprising choice because he was the first leader tapped from outside the company in its 142-year history (1872–2014). Having studied at Columbia Business School and then spent his career rising through the ranks of the Coca-Cola Company, Uotani believed deeply that differences in gender, age, nationality, and culture are immaterial in business—and, in fact, the more diverse a company is, the more creative it can be.

Once inside, Uotani found Shiseido's culture to be very Japan-centric. Although Uotani strongly believed in Shiseido's Japanese heritage, he felt that the company needed more cosmopolitan thinking to drive aggressive global growth. As part of that movement, he made the decision to designate English the official language at the Tokyo headquarters. Explains Uotani: "I was looking to create a diversity of talent and culture. It used to be that if I transferred someone from New York or Paris to Tokyo—and if everything we did here was in Japanese—that person wouldn't fit in. To create a truly global organization, we need people who aren't necessarily Japanese. Think of it as a hybrid culture."

Uotani encountered resistance from middle managers who didn't understand the need for the change. To obtain their buy-in, he kept sharing the company's mission to become more diverse and how that would lead to more international growth. Uotani also offered his employees English lessons: Three thousand employees accepted his offer. "Being bilingual," he told them, "allows the people at our headquarters to communicate better with other parts of the world and also enriches their lives by giving them a wider scope of thinking." Today, Uotani oversees forty-eight thousand people. In 2017, the company was able to achieve its 2020 goal of 1 trillion yen in annual sales three years ahead of schedule, and it has reported a compounded annual growth rate of 9 percent. In the first six years of his tenure, Uotani has positioned his company as a major global player, while building on Shiseido's Japanese heritage.

At DBS, Piyush Gupta made a move early to encourage risk taking that became company folklore. In 2012, the company's ATMs were hacked by card skimmers. When Gupta investigated why DBS was susceptible to such a breach, the problem was traced to a decision made by a junior operations colleague. Asked why he chose that course of action, the colleague said, "Because the way the card protector works increases the cycle time by ten to twelve seconds. We have long queues at our ATMs, so I made the trade-off that reducing cycle time to improve the customer experience was more important than the remote possibility of getting hacked."

When the regulators in Singapore asked Gupta to hold the DBS staff accountable, he refused to do it. He assured them that he'd make certain customers were made whole and that he'd take steps to improve security. About the colleague who caused the problem, though, Gupta said, "In fact, I'm going to give the person an award, because this is exactly what I'm trying to create at DBS— the capacity to use your head and think and make choices." It cost DBS a few million dollars to make their customers whole, but for Gupta that was a small price to pay to truly convince his employees that he had their backs when they took risks—as long as the gambles weren't so big as to put the franchise in jeopardy.

Sometimes simply renaming something can have deep reverberations inside a culture. As part of his turnaround strategy, Toby Cosgrove, the former CEO of the Cleveland Clinic, one of the world's leading nonprofit medical centers, wanted to improve things for his patients at the Clinic. "When you go to a hospital," asks Cosgrove, "what is the physical experience? Well, all of the senses, essentially what you see, what you smell, what you taste, what you hear are all involved." Cosgrove redesigned the rooms to let in more natural light, improved the quality of food served, and even had his patients' gowns designed by Diane von Furstenberg. The biggest impact, however, was to give a badge to every one of his forty thousand employees—from doctors to orderlies to janitors—which said: "I am a caregiver." Recalls Cosgrove, "We changed everybody's identity, and now everybody is referred to as not an employee, but a Cleveland Clinic Caregiver. And all those things improved the patient experience. They improved the buy-in from the employees, and patient satisfaction went up as well. It really came down to that business of putting the patients first."

Cosgrove got a lot of pushback for handing out the badges. The doctors said, "*We're* the caregivers." "No," the CEO said. "You can't do it without somebody in supplies bringing you your instruments or your bandages or whatever you need. We're all in this game together, everybody's a caregiver." Over the first five years of Cosgrove's tenure, the Cleveland Clinic went from ranking last in patient experience among large American hospitals to first.

Delphi's Rod O'Neal would show his top managers around the world a video of a honey badger. "I don't know if you've ever seen a honey badger, but that is one badass animal," he says. "It basically does what it needs to do. Everything runs away from it, even lions. I told my team that we need to be honey badgers when we go up against the competition." The video went viral. After that, when he'd walk through Delphi's facilities, be it in the United States, China, Brazil, or elsewhere, he often saw a picture of a honey badger in someone's office. "You communicate not only when you say, 'Let's go do this,' but when you can describe a journey and put romance behind it," he says.

Even small gestures can have tremendous impact. At McDonald's, for example, employees to this day tell the tale of founder Ray Kroc picking up litter in restaurant parking lots—emphasizing the importance of a culture of cleanliness. Hewlett-Packard's cofounder Bill Hewlett became the stuff of legend when taking a bolt cutter to a lock on a supply room door to signify the importance of trust and openness between management and frontline staff. Esquel's Marjorie Yang had a wall at one of the fashion company's youngest facilities torn down because some bricks were laid incorrectly. Why? To convey to the workers, as she puts it: "that we are looking for quality, nothing else will do." Stories of these actions spread quickly, carrying powerful cultural messages with them.

Marc Casper, the CEO of Thermo Fisher Scientific, which serves the scientific community with advanced equipment and software, was at one point visiting his office in Japan. At the time, the company was trying to clean up many of its legacy brands. The new branding effort was aimed at letting its customers know that Thermo Fisher could now help them significantly scale their operations. As Casper recalls: "Walking through the site, I took off the wall a poster from our old branding campaign and threw it away. People thought I was a lunatic. I'd just flown thirteen hours and was tearing decorations off the wall. But people talked about why I'd done that—why the branding initiative was important, what we were trying to accomplish and why the execution was important to me personally. That dialogue accelerated what we needed to do, and not just in Japan: Around the world, people in every site were asking themselves if they'd made only superficial changes or the substantive changes that our senior executives want. That builds culture."

In getting the word out to a diverse audience, it helps to have a handful of highly memorable and instructive phrases that sit beneath the governing principle of the "one thing." Walmart's founder, Sam Walton, famously enshrined the company's customer service aspiration into its "10-foot rule": Whenever an employee is within ten feet of a customer, they're expected to look them in the eye, smile, and ask, "How can I help you?" At Microsoft, the growth mindset that Satya Nadella aspired to was communicated on the one hand by making Carol Dweck's book *Mindset* mandatory reading for his lieutenants. For the masses, however, the book had to be distilled down into something understandable, memorable, and meaningful. A simple turn of phrase was chosen as Nadella implored his employees to shift from being "know-it-alls" to "learn-it-alls." With those six words, risk aversion and office politics immediately started to decline.

Frank Blake, the former CEO of home supply retailer Home

Depot, uses handwritten notes to convey to the organization that he cares. "I spent a lot of time talking to people about the power of handwritten notes," he says. "And I'd write two hundred notes— every Sunday. We had a structure where the stores would roll up their great customer service stories. They'd go to the district. The district would send them to the region, and the region would send them to me. And I'd write these handwritten notes saying, 'Dear Joe or Jane, I understand that you did this.' I always was specific. 'I understand this. You're awesome. You did this, you're awesome, I love you, Frank.' This was probably the thing I was most passionate about."

A less obvious but extremely powerful tool we've seen CEOs use is turning their cultural themes into questions. At Siam Cement, Kan Trakulhoon used this approach to bolster his culture of innovation. As he visited various sites, he always made it a point while on the shop floor to ask, "What are you working on to improve your process and your productivity?" He recalls what happened when he started doing so: "The foreman I asked got frightened. He froze and couldn't speak." Trakulhoon, a believer in the Buddhist philosophy of *metta* (loving-kindness), put his hand on the foreman's shoulder and assured him it was safe to answer, whatever the answer was. When he came back for his next visit, however, you can bet everyone on the shop floor was ready with an impressive answer.

Measure What Matters

Albert Einstein reputedly had a poster in his office that declared, "Not everything that counts can be counted, and not everything than can be counted, counts." Culture has long been grouped into the realm of those things that can't be counted. In keeping with the mindset of putting equal rigor and discipline into the soft stuff as into business performance, excellent CEOs look for ways to measure cultural change.

Every day at Microsoft, for example, groups of employees are briefly surveyed via a single pop-up question on their computers. In the early stages of the culture change effort they were asked if they were aware of the "growth mindset" that Satya Nadella sought to build. They were later asked the extent to which leaders exhibited this mindset. Such an approach has the multilayered benefit of keeping culture change front and center in employees' minds as well as ensuring that areas of success and failure can be scaled, learned from, and, if necessary, remedied.

Caterpillar former CEO Jim Owens uses a survey-based approach to measure culture on a regular basis. "After all," says Owens, "how do you expect employees to help you deliver on your goals and move you toward your vision if they don't understand what that vision is? If they don't understand what their unit has to do to contribute to achieving that vision? If they don't feel that their manager lives those values day in and day out? If they wouldn't recommend it as a place to work to a friend or colleague?" Although the industry benchmark for Caterpillar's survey was positive feedback from 65 percent of the employees, that didn't seem right to Owens, who set his goal at 90 percent. "How can you be a great company," argues Owens, "unless at least ninety percent of the people understand what you want to do, what role they have to play in helping you get there, and are enthusiastic about you as an employer?"

Over the last seven years of his stint as CEO, Owens improved that number every year. By the end of 2009—which was shattered by the financial crisis—Caterpillar earned an 82 percent approval rating. "People were rolling up their sleeves," says Owens, "and thinking about how I can make this company better."

Employee surveys only work if the results are followed up on vigorously—and doing so starts at the top. Sandy Cutler, the former CEO of Eaton, the power management company, is a big believer in employee surveys, never missing a year. Although the surveys were voluntary, Cutler achieved a 96 percent participation rate in 175 countries and in 37 languages. "The most important number we have in our company, out of all the hundreds of numbers we have," he says, "is our employee survey participation number. As long as that's high, that's telling me that people feel it's worthwhile: They're expressing their opinions on what we're doing well and what we're not doing well. And if you see that number start to drop, that means we're not getting back to you, we're not solving the issues you're bringing up."

To deal with issues raised by the employee surveys, Cutler would get a group of employees together, say, "Here's something that's been highlighted. We want volunteers: Work on this and bring recommendations back." At one of Eaton's sites, the survey came up with terrible scores. Cutler replaced every manager at the plant, and said to his new managers, "This has got real consequences to it. You're expected to lead your people, not to let them just feel like they're unattended and have no leadership." He gave the process real teeth.

Having robust ways to measure a culture can also help in gauging whether mergers and acquisitions will be successful. Maurice Lévy of Publicis ended up walking away from a potential merger with Omnicom that would have created the world's biggest advertising group, in large part due to concerns about the significant differences in corporate cultures and management philosophies. Netflix's Reed Hastings describes how the uniqueness of its culture has ruled out a lot of potential deals: "The positives of having a strong and unique culture are many. The hidden negatives of M&A become quite challenging."

Measurement systems go beyond employee surveys. At Johan Thijs's KBC the "Accountability" element of his PEARL culture translates to everyone having a scorecard that includes four elements. "I give a framework of all the parameters that everyone in the company is accountable for: capital, liquidity, profitability, and people; people includes shareholders, society, customers, and employees," he explains. "They're all equally important." At KBC, how well one adheres to the company's culture can make or break a promotion. "Everyone who is put forward for a manager's position is screened by an external company on Performance, Empowerment, Accountability, Responsiveness, and Local embeddedness," he says. "If you don't pass that test, you can't make it to management, and this happens on a regular basis."

Culture can be a hard topic to get one's head around. It's so broad that, in the words of McKinsey & Company's former managing director Marvin Bower, it can be described simply as, "the way we do things around here." That's why the best CEOs home in on "one thing" culturally that will make the biggest difference to business performance. By taking such a laserlike approach, they can rigorously reshape the employee work environment and measure progress in a disciplined way. And the best CEOs reinforce the effort by showing, through actions and words, that they can change themselves.

Getting the culture right is but the first leg of a three-legged stool used to support an organization's delivery of vision and strategy. Mindful of management expert Arthur W. Jones's observation, "Organizations are perfectly designed to get the results that they get," we turn next to organization design.

CHAPTER 5

Organization Design Practice
Solve for "Stagility"

Design is intelligence made visible.
—Alina Wheeler

When the first skyscrapers were built in the late nineteenth and early twentieth centuries, they were solid structures that wouldn't budge an inch in high winds. As developers built higher and higher towers, however, architects faced a daunting challenge—how to survive the increasingly tumultuous winds at each new height. The solution? Build structures that were both strong and flexible. Designers added lighter, more pliable structural beams, softened the corners of higher floors to reduce wind resistance, installed huge hanging dampers that swung to counteract the force of the wind and even left entire floors open to let the wind rush through and reduce stress on the structures. Today's skyscrapers are strong enough to withstand strong winds and earthquakes not because of their rigidity, but because of their flexibility. They can bend as much as three feet.

In the same way, the rigidly hierarchical organizational structures that were built during the early twentieth century with the advent of mass production through job specialization worked well when organizations were relatively small and national, and the external environment changed relatively slowly and predictably. As organizations have become larger and more global and face even fiercer winds of change in the form of complex stakeholder demands, technology advances and disruptions, digitization and democratization of information, and an ever-escalating war for talent, the rigidity of the hierarchy has become a liability. Just like master architects, the best CEOs have found ways to build flexibility into their organization's design while maintaining strong structural integrity.

In her study of what differentiates high versus low growth among large companies, Columbia Business School professor Rita Gunther McGrath describes this dynamic: "On the one hand, they [high-growth large companies] are built for innovation, are good at experimentation, and can move on a dime. On the other hand, they're extremely stable, [the] strategy and organization structure stay consistent [and the] culture is strong and unchanging."[28] Our research supports McGrath's conclusion: Organizations that have both stable and agile elements are three times more likely to be high-performing than those that are agile but lack stable operating disciplines, and more than four times more likely to be high performing than those that are stable, but lack agile elements. Stability and agility aren't a trade-off to be made; both should be present just as in a modern high-rise building—hence, our coining the combination "stagility."

One of the most famous examples of stagility in organization design dates back to 1943 when Lockheed Martin established its Skunk Works teams to drive a radically new approach to the development and manufacture of aircraft. Engineers, technicians, and aviators were brought together in a shed in the California desert, united by clarity of purpose and empowered to get things done. And they did, designing and building the XP-80, the first jet fighter in the United States Army Air Forces, from a standing start to a flying product in just 143 days. Today's analogous constructs include the likes of JPMC's Financial Solutions Lab, Aon's New Ventures Group, and General Mills Worldwide Innovation Network (G-WIN).

Achieving stagility doesn't happen by chance, nor does it happen overnight. Sometimes it doesn't happen at all. Many of the CEOs we spoke to shared that while they'd made progress, they never fully cracked the code. There was, however, a clear pattern of methodically enabling agility anchored by a strong organizational backbone. More specifically, the best CEOs . . .

. . . stop the pendulum swing
. . . emphasize accountability
. . . think helix, not matrix
. . . make "smart" choices

Stop the Pendulum Swing

The Goldilocks principle is derived from a popular nineteenth-century fairy tale of a young girl named Goldilocks who tastes three bowls of porridge and finds she prefers the porridge that is neither too hot nor too cold, but is just the right temperature. The concept of "just the right amount" is what the best leaders look for when confronted with the inevitable CEO-level question of: How centralized should the organization be? By centralizing, a company can improve efficiency and control risk. Decentralizing can increase customer responsiveness and foster innovation. Less skilled CEOs eschew the Goldilocks principle and adopt categorical positions at extreme ends of the spectrum that work against the business over the long term.

When Percy Barnevik was CEO of the Zurich-based power technology and automation company ABB, he saw a huge opportunity to increase accountability and empowerment through a radical decentralization. The idea was to unleash local entrepreneurship by "ripping down bureaucracy" so that employees all over the world could launch new products, change designs, and alter production methods without meddling from headquarters. Barnevik divided ABB into five thousand profit centers. As profits soared, the structure—in the short term—garnered high praise from academics, journalists, management gurus, and shareholders.

On the other end of the spectrum, consider Yahoo!'s former CEO Terry Semel, who reorganized the company to improve the sharing of resources to capture the benefits of scale. He slimmed down the company's forty-four business units to four groups and a product council to capture the benefits of coordination, planning, and sharing of resources across divisions. The public view at the time was that Semel was very much making Yahoo! a "New Age media company."

Fast-forward a few years, however, and these extreme shifts in organization designs were being derided as significant contributors to both ABB's and Yahoo!'s fall. In ABB's case, as one reporter wrote, "the decentralized management structure ended up causing conflicts and communications problems between departments." Dysfunctional competition festered and enormous duplication created massive inefficiencies (by way of example, at the time ABB had 576 different software systems to handle daily chores such as purchasing and project management, sixty different payroll systems, and more than six hundred spreadsheet software programs). In Yahoo!'s case, the company fell further behind its fast-moving technology peers as its highly centralized design led to a lack of accountability and gridlock in decision-making. In the words of an executive who left the company, "The great people leave because there are so many people who think they are in charge, they can't get anything done. The mediocre people stay, as they are protected and not held accountable."[29]

Barnevik's and Semel's actions aren't uncommon. When a CEO sees an organization tilted one way, there's a temptation to tilt the opposite way—and, like the pendulum of a clock, the swing back and forth between the two polarities is perpetuated. The best CEOs rarely make radical swings from one extreme to the other. Their focus is not how centralized the organization should be, it's, in the words of Ken Powell, former CEO of consumer goods giant General Mills, "Where does being central add or create the most value? And what has to be done locally?" Powell continues, "These are really big, important questions that you need to spend real time on as the CEO."

In Powell's case, he learned the lesson of the pendulum swing when he took over as the CEO of Cereal Partners Worldwide (CPW), a joint venture between General Mills and Nestlé. "Nestlé was a very large and quite decentralized global corporation when CPW was created in the late 1980s," he recalls. "Nestlé urged that CPW be designed as a more centrally managed organization with a highly integrated supply chain, and brand positioning and marketing very consistent from country to country. They may have seen CPW as something of a test bed for a more centralized approach to global brand management. And our initial model for the joint venture was indeed a highly centralized organization with an almost command-and-control approach. Many decisions were made at the head office in Lausanne [Switzerland]." The result was dysfunctional, with many disagreements between the headquarters teams, predominantly American marketeers with only limited international experience, and the local managers.

To remedy the situation, Powell gathered his regional and central leaders together and methodically worked through a list of the key activities required to run the business, making decisions jointly as to where the work should be done to create the most value. Any notions that "everything had to be different in a geography" or "the center would run everything" were taken off the table. It worked well, as Powell describes: "There was a commitment from the senior team to figure it out in a pragmatic and honest way for the good of the enterprise." The decisions made helped CPW become one of the largest cereal companies in the world.

These lessons learned were applied to General Mills as the company expanded internationally during Powell's tenure as CEO, with a strong bias toward building local teams and designing clear lines of authority for what would be done locally and what would be done centrally for core global brands like Häagen-Dazs ice cream, Old El Paso Mexican food, and Nature Valley snack products. The Goldilocks answer enabled international growth, innovation, and social engagement, earning Powell recognition as one of *Harvard Business Review*'s Top 100 CEOs and winning him accolades as "America's Most Beloved CEO" by Glassdoor (based on employee ratings).

Emphasize Accountability

Large, global organizations striving for the "just right" balance between centralized efficiencies and local customer responsiveness tend to adopt what's often referred to as a matrix organization structure. "I don't know how you'd do it without a matrix," Duke Energy CEO Lynn Good confirms. "We have complex operations—generation, transmission, and distribution of electricity—spread across a wide geographic area and several utilities. We have functional leaders over the operations, and regulatory and legislative affairs experts leading the regional utilities. Operating well in this matrix is essential to success. There's just no other way to do it."

In a matrix reporting structure, individuals report to more than one supervisor or leader through relationships described as solid-line or dotted-line. A single employee may report to both a functional business leader (e.g., engineering, manufacturing) whose job it is to solve for synergy and standardization and a business unit leader (e.g., a product, geography, or customer-segment owner) whose job it is to ensure the functional capabilities come together in a tailored manner to deliver just the right result for the customer. Corporate staff functions such as Finance, Human Resources (HR), and Technology operate similarly, with a "hard" or "dotted" line reporting structure to a central function leader and one reporting to a business unit leader.

The origins of the matrix go back to the 1960s and President John F. Kennedy's "man on the moon" goal. Project managers were responsible for costs and schedules, and engineering managers were responsible for technological development of the projects. Both reported equally to the general managers. The success of the US space program, which beat President Kennedy's time line by a year while orchestrating a safe moon landing, became a significant catalyst for the widespread adoption of the matrix in the corporate world.[30]

Unfortunately, few organizations experience the "moonshot" potential of the matrix. Instead, most employees working within a matrix experience confusion and frustration as to who makes the decisions. Typically, each of the two leaders that an employee reports to in a matrix sees it in their purview to perform the same set of functions such as: hiring and firing, job assignments, day-to-day prioritization and supervision of work, promotions, evaluations, and incentives. Power struggles often ensue, and committees end up making decisions just to break the deadlock, but in

doing so competing ideas become diluted to the point of ineffectiveness as individuals with little expertise end up weighing in on
every topic.

To cut through the potential gridlock, the best CEOs are relentless in clarifying where ultimate accountability rests. When Ed
Breen took over Dupont, for example, "There were a lot of people
working really hard, but there was a lack of accountability. It was
such a matrixed organization that half the decisions were being
made for the businesses by staffers overseeing centralized functions who weren't thinking in terms of P&Ls or return on invested
capital."

When Breen looked into what went wrong with a capital
project to build a cellulosic ethanol plant in Iowa that was supposed to cost $220 million but ended up at $520 million and still
never worked, he found that twenty-two people had signed off
on the program. "I started asking people 'Well, who really actually made this decision?'" he recalls "And I got eight different
answers." Breen quickly reorganized the company to give more
decision-making authority to his five business unit presidents, supported by a lean corporate center with a clear mandate to focus on
strategy, risk profile, capital allocation, and talent. "If our current
structure made that kind of decision in Iowa, it would've been the
business unit president, our CFO, and me as the CEO who would
be responsible and accountable."

Think Helix, Not Matrix

As we listened closely to how the best CEOs create accountability
within a complex and multidimensional matrix, we realized they
didn't actually think in terms of a matrix at all. It struck us that
a more apt representation is a helix. The idea is inspired by the
distinctive, double-stranded shape of DNA that scientists discovered in the early 1950s. The two long helical (like a corkscrew)
DNA strands are intertwined without touching one another other
than being connected through nucleotide pairs that run between
them—sort of like a twisted ladder, as depicted below.[31]

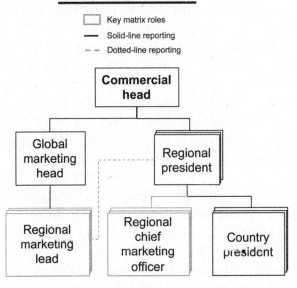

Matrix organization

☐ Key matrix roles
— Solid-line reporting
- - Dotted-line reporting

Commercial head

Global marketing head

Regional president

Regional marketing lead

Regional chief marketing officer

Country president

Helix organization

— Capabilities management: How work gets done
— Value-creation management: What work gets done

No more dotted lines: The helix provides two clear, equal, and parallel lines of accountability

The capabilities manager has the power to hire or fire, and provides the training, tools, and professional development to keep the employee's career on track

The value-creation manager sets the employee's individual goals and objectives, and oversees their day-to-day work

In a helix organization, it's not a "dual hard line" or a "dotted line" reporting structure. Rather, it's a "split hard line" where an employee reports to two different leaders for two different purposes (thus the two intertwined strands). The split hard line construct doesn't apply to every job in an organization, but for roles in complex matrices where sales channel, product, and functional expertise need to come together on behalf of the customer, a helix approach provides an elegant and pragmatic solution.

For an idea of how this works in the real world, consider how Aon's Greg Case restructured his organization. As the company evolved from its federated roots to its current Aon United focus, Case elevated the importance of bringing all of the firm's capability to each of its clients. Historically, power had swung between the geographical and product-line leaders (which, in practice, manifested in constant switching between hard and dotted line roles). To stop the pendulum swing and create clear accountability, Case created a split hard line reporting structure between the two groups. Each of these leaders has a clear, unique, and complementary role (one can't be successful without the other, and both are equally important). Employees report to a geographic leader (e.g., the head of Europe) who owns the primary P&L, local client relationships, and is product-line agnostic. They also report to a product leader (e.g., the head of Commercial Risk) who's responsible for developing world class, innovative products and solutions and building the firm's ability to deliver them to clients.

The geography leader owns the P&L and therefore can decide how many people to hire in a product area. The product leader, given their expertise, will recruit and hire the needed personnel. Once on board, new hires look to the geography leader to place them on a client service team, set their individual goals and objectives, and oversee their day-to-day work. Meanwhile the new hires look to their product leader to provide them with the training, tools, and professional development they need to keep their careers on track.

Westpac's Gail Kelly put in place a similar model at her bank. "I made an extremely bold structural change. Banks are very product-centric, and I kept our products as a center of excellence, but I put the power of the balance sheet into the distribution channels. They became the profit center. I needed a business model where people from those two areas worked together, aligned together, and fought together for the customer—creating both an integrated offering and integrated experience." It wouldn't have happened, however, without her personal involvement as the CEO.

"It worked really well, but you can't just hope it works, you actually have to design who decides what where. Particularly initially," she advises.

At JPMC, Jamie Dimon explains how a helix approach works when it comes to the way corporate staff engage with business units. "I have my management team at the corporate level—my head of HR, my CFO, my general counsel, etc. We set policy for HR, for accounting, for risk, and so on, but other than that, execution is 100 percent the line of business's responsibility. Then from a governance standpoint the corporate team can step into any one of our units and say, 'you can't do this' or 'you can't do that,' but they have to come as a partner. The goal is to do the right thing for the company. As a result they're welcomed as partners by the business leaders."

In the Italian utility Enel's case, while much of the company has more traditional reporting lines, there are 250 critical roles that sit at the intersection of managing assets and customers, and therefore have a split hard line reporting relationship to two bosses. For example, the head of generation in Chile reports to both the head of global generation when it comes to allocating capital between maintenance and growth, and the head of Chile when it comes to customer focus and cash flow. Like Dimon, Enel CEO Francesco Starace emphasizes the importance of placing talent with the right mindsets into such roles. "The real secret to make this work is to put people in the roles who thrive on constructive tension," he describes. "They need the ambition and curiosity; those attributes will push them to ask the right questions and to do more."

To be clear, none of the CEOs we spoke to actually used the word *helix* to describe their organizations. However, given the way they managed, what looked on paper like a traditional matrix was clearly better represented by the helix concept.

Make "Smart" Choices

With a Goldilocks answer to centralization and accountability clear in a more "helix-like" than "matrix-like" manner, the foundation is set to determine what elements of the organization design will be stable and what will be agile. When it comes to making these choices, a smartphone analogy can be helpful. Think of choosing the stable elements as equivalent to choosing the hardware and operating system for your device. These provide a stable base on which you will then put numerous apps (the agile elements) that can be installed, upgraded, and discarded as needed to continually make life easier and better.

At Intuit, Brad Smith describes some of the stable elements of his organization: "We organize first around the customer, and then underneath that, the specific problems for the customer. In practice, that means we have a consumer group and small business group at the top, and underneath that a payments group, for example. That does not change. Then we decide on how to best build the connective tissue as we drive things at scale as a platform company. For example, we have a centralized small business design team that works across that customer's problems."

The agile elements of an organization's design can take many forms. One method is to create temporary teams staffed full-time and given significant autonomy to sprint toward specific outcomes. Smith explains how this was applied at Intuit: "We assigned important strategic questions to teams of three people who hadn't worked with each other—which really built collaboration between business and functions. This really helped us get sharper on our solutions and move faster in important strategic areas."

Another method to increase agility at Intuit was giving all employees 10 percent unstructured time. As Smith puts it, "We had more than 1,800 different experiments going on at any one time. If you had an experiment that proved successful in the eyes of our customers, we would fund your idea for another three months." The result? As Smith shares, "It really helped us bring down the barriers of organization design, because everyone felt empowered to push their ideas out."

Explicitly making choices as to what will be stable and what will be agile is the key to breaking the otherwise predictable cycle of going through large-scale redesigns every couple of years. Instead, high-performing organizations continuously reorganize themselves around a stable core. Their stability makes them as reliable in performance as a high-end smartphone, and their agile apps drive continuous improvement ahead of less flexible competition. Adidas's Herbert Hainer preferred a different analogy, but one that makes the same point: "Before, we'd been a tanker with ten thousand people on it. If you wanted to turn around, it took five hundred miles. Now our fleet includes speedboats."

At KBC, Johan Thijs was very clear on where speedboats were required. "We're going to build a mobile banking and insurance app and it needs to be easy to use—something that customers are delighted about," he told his Belgian Business Unit. "You've got six months and a million Euro to do it," he added. To achieve such a bold aspiration in such a short time frame, Thijs assigned a talented leader and gave them full autonomy to form whatever team they needed. "Forget hierarchy," Thijs told the manager. "You only use those people whom you think add value." For his part, Thijs freed the team of KBC's heavy info-tech bureaucracy. "Work agile and I'll keep management off your back" was his clear message to the team. Less than six months later, the new KBC Mobile app was launched, and less than six months after that it was being called the best and most innovative on the market.

Another agile element Thijs put in place at KBC is Start it @KBC. Launched in 2014, this idea incubator fosters entrepreneurship and thereby unleashes a fleet of speedboats. "We have six hundred people with ideas working there who've established their own companies and who want to grow from a start-up to a resilient, viable company. Among those, we also see real fintechs," observes Thijs. The start-ups present opportunities for KBC to deliver innovation to customers.

Similarly, Enel's Francesco Starace augmented the company's stable organization backbone with a number of agile elements. Dedicated "Innovation Hubs" were opened in different parts of the world. A network of ambassadors within business units connected the hubs to challenges. An energy crowdsourcing platform to harvest ideas externally from an ecosystem of start-ups, Small and Medium-sized Enterprises (SMEs), and universities was created. The "Make It Happen!" program was launched to facilitate the formation of small, cross-functional teams to pursue new ideas. A new division called Enel X was also established to develop new solutions for customers, businesses, and governments in a number of areas such as energy efficiency, storage, and smart lighting. The agile elements of Enel's organization took place under the banner of "Open Innovation," which, as Starace explains, "was a great multiplier for us. In addition to speed it gave us an entrée into different industries."

Alphabet's Sundar Pichai sets up "focus areas" when something important needs to be done outside the traditional product areas such as YouTube, Android, Search, and so on. Each focus area has a team and leader assigned and is empowered with tools to allow them to bypass certain approvals and move faster than the normal organizational processes would allow. "Sometimes you need to design sanctioned ways by which people can break the structures you've set up," says Pichai.

We could fill page after page with company-specific examples of agile organization elements. Most fall into the categories of three buzzwordy contemporary concepts. First, using "team of teams" approaches that delegate authority to numerous teams that are highly empowered to work together fluidly to achieve a big objective. Second, creating resource pools that "flow to work" based on where they can create the most value (versus being constrained by static reporting structures). Third, applying agile methodologies: rapidly iterating products and services by launching a minimum viable product and then getting multiple rounds of customer feedback.

Larry Culp, former CEO of Danaher and now of GE, points out that while the buzzwords are new, the concepts aren't. "When you look at a two-week 'agile sprint' in coding, it doesn't look so different than a week-long Toyota Kaizen event (gathering operators, managers, and owners of a process in one place to map, agree on, and implement improvements to the process). It's all about chunking the work down, getting the right people together, trying something new, and getting something tangible done quickly."

In the 1999 film *The Matrix*, the protagonist, Neo, is offered a choice of two pills: one red, one blue. If he takes the red pill, he'll discover the painful truth that reality is far more complex and demands far more from him than he'd ever imagined. But if he chooses the blue pill, he'll go back to his old life, in blissful ignorance of what is actually occurring. After a moment's thought, he takes the red pill—a choice that marks the beginning of an epic personal journey. In a series of heroic acts, Neo finally frees the human race from a prison: one it had created for itself through its dependence on intelligent machines.

There is a blue pill when it comes to organization design. American writer Charlton Ogburn Jr. described it well: "We tend to meet any new situation by reorganizing; and what a wonderful method for creating the illusion of progress while producing confusion, inefficiency, and demoralization." The facts suggest that there are many leaders who choose this path. A full 70 percent of executives report they've undergone a significant reorganization in the past two years, and the vast majority believe they'll experience another in the next two. Meanwhile, only 23 percent of organization redesigns are reported to have met their objectives and improved performance. Most others are never completed or simply don't meet their objectives, and 10 percent actually have a significant *negative* impact on performance.[32]

The best CEOs take the red pill. It enables them to resist the temptation to swing the pendulum back and forth between centralization and decentralization. It causes them to solve for clear accountability even in complex organization structures, rising above the matrix to reconfigure it as a helix. It prompts them to make smart choices about what the stabile and agile elements of the organization's design are. Although it's a more difficult path, taking the red pill as we've described it increases the odds from 25 to 86 percent of your organization redesign being a success, and very likely it will make your employees feel like they've been freed from a prison.[33]

It's been said that a bad system will beat a good person every time. The organizational alignment topics we've covered so far—culture and organization design—create a good system. Now we turn our sights to how to ensure "good people" work within the system so that the organization is poised for extraordinary execution.

CHAPTER 6

Talent Management Practice

(Don't) Put People First

Judge a fish by its ability to climb a tree and it will spend its whole life believing that it is stupid.
　　—Unknown (often attributed to Albert Einstein)

Some twenty thousand naval recruits each year express interest in joining the Navy SEALs, America's elite fighting organization. Those who sign up know the role requires warriors who can accomplish a mission anywhere in the world, under uncertain circumstances and the toughest of conditions, whether it's sub-zero temperatures, brain-melting desert heat, or immense, boat-swamping waves during a hurricane on the high seas. They're the go-to unit whenever the US government has an especially thorny military, hostage, or terrorist situation.

In the end, only about 250 make it per year. Applicants who are superb physical specimens don't have an edge: Many amazing athletes wash out of the program. Those with the best education are no more likely to make it than those with a high school diploma. Those who eventually win their tridents do so because they meet a very clear set of criteria, the most important being a resolute mind—one that never gives up. The need to test for this trait accounts for the rigor of SEAL training's orientation period, including its notorious "hell week" of cold, wet, brutally difficult challenges on fewer than four hours of sleep a night.

In the same way the Navy leadership first defines the role of a Navy SEAL and then finds recruits who fit the job, the best CEOs know that building a great organization doesn't start with people but, instead, with roles. They first ask themselves what the most important jobs are and define the knowledge, skills, attributes, and experiences needed to get those jobs done.

Doing this isn't as obvious or easy as it might sound. Consider the CEO of an average-performing health care company. When we asked, "Who are your top twenty most talented leaders?" he shared his list with us. We then asked, "What are the twenty most important *roles* in the company?" and he shared that list, though with a speed that suggested he hadn't given that answer nearly as much thought. Finally, we asked, "How many people on the first list are filling roles on the second list?" He went pale. He didn't have to do the math to know that the answer wasn't one that the board or shareholders would be happy to hear.

At the other end of the spectrum, consider how the CEO of private-equity giant Blackstone, Stephen Schwarzman, approached answering the same questions. He, his chief human resources officer (CHRO), and his CFO looked with microscopic precision for what leadership roles in the firm's portfolio of investments drive the most value in terms of revenue, operating margin, capital efficiency, and so on. At one of its companies, for example, the goal was to increase earnings by 60 percent while boosting its price-to-earnings ratio from eight to ten. Their analysis showed there were thirty-seven positions among the company's twelve thousand employees that drove 80 percent of the value. One role actually had the potential to single-handedly swing earnings by 10 percent! Schwarzman and his team then made sure those jobs were filled with leaders fit for the task.[34]

Not all of the excellent CEOs we spoke to embraced such a strict methodology, but all approached the topic of talent with a notably high level of rigor and discipline that enabled them to focus their personal time and energy on the highest impact areas of talent management. As GE CEO Larry Culp states, "Your people decisions are really where all your leverage is. As a CEO, you absolutely have to get those right. And you can't do that at a distance." To make the right people decisions, the best CEOs . . .

. . . clearly define high value roles
. . . don't forget the "left tackles"
. . . find "unusual suspects"
. . . actively build the bench

Clearly Define High Value Roles

We've helped numerous CEOs work with their CHROs and CFOs
to develop a more rigorous understanding of the roles that drive
their company's strategy. In virtually every case, the results have
surprised these executives, who soon came to realize that—contrary
to conventional wisdom—hierarchy and the roles that create the
most value don't always have that much in common. Of the fifty
most valuable roles in a typical corporation, we found that only
10 percent are positions that report directly to a CEO; 60 percent
exist at the next level down; and 20 percent are at the level below
that.[35]

And the last 10 percent? Roles that typically don't exist but
should. The people in these positions work across existing organizational boundaries and/or aim to capitalize on new industry trends. At the Cleveland Clinic, Toby Cosgrove pursued a
patient-centric strategy and, in turn, created a chief experience
officer to better the lives of his patients. That role looked after all
the things that went into the emotional aspect of a patient's care.
"There's HR to look after all of the needs of the employees. But
somebody has to look after the needs of all of our patients and the
intricacies of patient care," he says.

The role brought transparency to the organization, both internally and externally. "One of the things that I'd learned in cardiac
surgery," says Cosgrove, who is a doctor, "is we always looked
at the numbers and were totally transparent about it, whether it
was your mortality rate, or whatever." So he did the same with
patient care by releasing to the public the results of the hospital's
quality-of-care metrics. He also had the chief experience officer
grade and rank each doctor in the hospital, something that wasn't
universally liked. "I was trying to make people realize," says Cosgrove, "that some people did really well, they were well-thought-of

by their patients, and some weren't. And the doctors could find out how to do better."

At Aon, CEO Greg Case created an executive level position to lead its New Ventures Group and to accelerate large-scale innovation in the insurance industry. Duke Energy's Lynn Good added a generation and transmission market transformation officer to ensure successful transition of generation resources from existing technologies to new ones as the company pursues a net zero emissions target. "It was necessary to separate this responsibility from the challenges of day-to-day operations to allow the right strategic focus on this massive transition of energy infrastructure," says Good. At financial services group TIAA, Roger Ferguson created a new chief digital officer role, recognizing that every facet of the company, from interacting with clients to engaging employees, must be approached with a digital lens to be successful. Jamie Dimon recognized that cloud technology would be key to cutting costs and boosting efficiencies, so he created an executive role to run JPMC's cloud services. Ahold Delhaize's Dick Boer added a chief sustainability officer to his team, recognizing the impact of changing sentiment around climate change, and the role of food and health.

Once the most valuable roles are identified, the best CEOs make sure that each is well defined, with a clear description of what work needs to get done and a list of the necessary skills and attributes to succeed. A product leader, for example, may require knowledge and skills related to business development and M&A due diligence. Other requirements could be a global mindset, the ability to make decisions quickly, and great team building skills. The experience needed may include having run a $100 million or more revenue business, having led an integration, and having built and executed a successful sales model.

Aside from role-specific attributes, the best CEOs also have a short list of "must have" characteristics they see as important for all leaders. "Enthusiasm, smarts, flexibility, and results orientation, coupled with clear alignment with the company values" was the list for Gail Kelly at Westpac. Looking back, she says, "If a leader could pass these tests, then I'd move to assess fit for the specific skills the role required." At Itaú Unibanco, Roberto Setúbal looked for "easygoing, open, smart, connected, and innovative" leaders. Santander's Ana Botín looks for "values, empathy, creativity, and collaboration." JPMC's Jamie Dimon made clear what he was *not* looking for: loyalty. "If anyone says to me, 'I'll be loyal to you,' you know what I say to them? 'Please don't. Your loyalty's to the institution, not to me. Your loyalty should be to the customer, not to me. Your loyalty should be to doing the right thing.'"

At KBC, Johan Thijs applied a "must have" criteria of fresh thinking. He explains the unique manner in which he applied it: "Together with my executive committee we defined the top forty positions that were most crucial to making the company work," he explains. He then sorted all of his managers according to their performance and competencies and matched them into the forty roles. "I then filled the boxes with the condition that no one currently in a role could stay in their role," he shares. "As you can imagine, there were no 'sacred cows' anymore. Everything was under debate. We could completely change the company."

As the KBC example shows, by carefully specifying which roles create the most value and what's required to succeed in them, getting the right people into place becomes far easier. Westpac's Gail Kelly explains what can happen otherwise: "Competent executives get moved into roles for which they're not suited and which they don't enjoy. Confidence erodes and performance falls. It's hard to fix."

Don't Forget Your "Left Tackles"

When asked who the highest paid player on an American football team is, most will correctly identify the quarterback, because he executes most of the plays. But when asked to name the second highest paid, people guess running backs or wide receivers, as they work most directly with the quarterback to score the points needed to win. Fans of the movie *The Blind Side,* the story of a homeless teenager who grows up to be a star left tackle in the National Football League, know better. The most valuable person on a football team after the quarterback is the left tackle (or if the quarterback is left-handed, the right tackle), a player who doesn't touch the ball at all. Why? Because they protect the quarterback from getting sacked or even injured by the other team's pass rushers whom he can't see because they're coming at him on his blind side.[36]

In business, the quarterbacks, wide receivers, and running back equivalents are most often thought of as the P&L leaders in a company. Many CEOs feel that they've done the job of identifying the high-value roles simply by listing them. This had been the case at Siam Cement before Kan Trakulhoon took over as CEO in 2006. "At that time there were three things that determined what roles were important," he says. "First was the amount of assets you controlled. Second was the number of people that reported to you. Third was the amount of complexity you had to manage."

The best CEOs dig deeper and ensure enough rigor and discipline is applied to finding the "left tackle" positions that protect and enable value to be created. In Trakulhoon's case, his strategy was to move from commodity to higher value-added products, and that meant roles that had been overlooked by the previous regime became important. The research function was elevated, and its leader was recognized as a "left tackle"—one of the most important people on the team, even though by traditional measures that role had been considered less crucial. Focusing on the R&D role and ensuring it was filled with the best talent enabled Trakulhoon to grow the percent of sales from value-added products from 4 to 35 percent during his tenure.

Flemming Ørnskov, former Shire CEO who went on to become head of the skin care company Galderma, also systematically determines what roles are most important with a keen eye to uncovering the less-obvious left tackles who are key to the company's success (whether their areas of expertise relate to clinical development, analytics, digital, quality, devices, regulatory, and so on). "We also ranked our research programs from one to fifty, so we knew our priorities and ensured the top ones got the most funding, had A-players, and that's where we were spending our leadership time." As part of this process Ørnskov and his team realized a left tackle role wasn't being filled in biologics—products that contain components of living organisms. "It became clear that innovation in dermatology was moving to biologics," he says. "So I had to hire the right leaders in that area."

On taking the reins at GE, Larry Culp laid out the organizational chart and identified the highest value-creating roles. "We determined what were the nonnegotiable A-player slots," he says. By applying an analytic lens, Culp realized that one area where historically it had been fine to have a B-level player was now a left tackle position—the head of supply chain management. "You look today at our business and it's not that we don't have a great product or great people, but if we can't deliver at the right time with the right quality it's going to irritate customers more than ever. We've got to get the day-to-day stuff right."

One left tackle role most CEOs only appreciate after having faced off with the analyst and investor community is the Chief Financial Officer (CFO). IDB's Lilach Asher-Topilsky comments, "It's very important to have the best CFO that you can get. They can take so much of the day-to-day off your shoulders. They become your right-hand person. People sometimes don't understand the importance of a good CFO." Itaú Unibanco's Roberto Setúbal adds, "When I look back over almost twenty years in the role, my CFO was probably the most important person on my team." At Aon, Greg Case ranks bringing Christa Davies into the CFO role among the most important decisions of his tenure. "Christa is a complete partner in the building of Aon," he shares. "We have been at this together from the beginning. Aon is simply not Aon without Christa."

It's only after the best CEOs rigorously define the value-creating roles that they add actual people into the talent management equation—as soon as people are involved, so are politics.

Find the Unusual Suspects

The best CEOs typically see to it that their top thirty to fifty value-creating, protecting, and enabling roles are filled with "best fit" talent both for the short and long term. Yes, this means that a CEO's direct reports aren't necessarily given the freedom to choose their own teams. Instead, the best CEOs see the top echelons of leaders as "enterprise talent." GE's Larry Culp, for example, is very clear with his team that he can veto any new hire who reports to one of his own direct reports. "I call it 'one-over-one,'" he says. "I reserve the right to help you avoid making a bad hire."

Fair warning—done rigorously, this step can be full of surprises. In truth, most CEOs have a "top talent" list that can be counted in the single digits. These usual suspects are considered safe hands—CEOs can entrust them to do things that others can't. These stars sit on just about every standing committee and act as sponsors for most task forces or initiatives, while also having significant leadership responsibilities both internally and externally. Capable and willing, these leaders all too often end up overstretched and far less effective than they'd be if others were able to step up.

The best CEOs put a much more analytic lens on who does what in the organization. To fill the top fifty or so most valuable jobs, they demand that HR provide robust information on the knowledge, skills, attributes, and experiences of, say, the top two to three hundred leaders in the organization. Such an exercise is key to unearthing many new candidates—including some "unusual suspects"—who have the potential to fill the most important positions. The best CEOs also are constantly taking in information to uncover who are potential stars (and to uncover strugglers). GE's Culp explains, "Operating reviews are a great place to take stock: Is someone learning, growing, synthesizing, integrating, and moving forward? Also, while walking around the factory or talking to customers, you're always doing an informal 360 evaluation on your leaders."

With this information, the best CEOs expect that at least five viable candidates will emerge for each of the most valuable roles. Two surprises typically await when this is done with rigor. The first is that as many as 20 to 30 percent of people they previously handpicked to place in priority roles are actually a relatively poor fit. As Westpac's Gail Kelly describes, "I found some trusted and loyal executives were no longer 'in the right role' because the job had changed, and different skills were required. I tackled these situations head-on and early because, quite aside from hampering progress of the business, being indirect or delaying is unfair and disrespectful to the people concerned."

The second surprise of a thorough talent review is that there are far more potential candidates for key roles than most CEOs would have initially conceived. Back to our product leader example: Even though a candidate may not have, say, the desired experience managing a $100 million P&L, they might be stronger when it comes to having a global mindset, making quick decisions, and displaying team building skills, and, therefore, be as good a fit or better for the role. For Shantanu Narayen at Adobe, the process surfaced Gloria Chen, who rose through the ranks in sales and corporate strategy, and—as Narayen's chief of staff—became a candidate to lead the Human Resources function. "You want someone who understands people and strategy. You want someone you can trust one hundred percent. And you want somebody who can push back like crazy if need be," he says. "Gloria may not have experience in HR, but she was all of that."

Among the five or more potential candidates for each critical role, the best CEOs also expect to see multiple diversity lenses applied. At Merck, for example, as CEO Ken Frazier shares, "At the time [before I was the CEO], I was minding my business practicing law in Philadelphia, representing Merck among others. The only reason I'm the CEO of Merck today is that Roy Vagelos, who was CEO then, called me into his office and said, 'I'm two years from retirement. I can't seem to get my colleagues, my white colleagues, to promote any African Americans. Guess what, I'm going to make your career. I'm going to take a lawyer who has all the right raw material. I'm going to bring him inside the company. I'm going to give him a job in the business and I'm going to mentor him.' And on my best day as CEO, I'm simply channeling what Roy taught me."[37]

Herbert Hainer at Adidas felt it was important to ensure the company didn't become insular. As a result, he instituted an overarching rule that for any promotion in the most value-adding roles the question was, "Who is the most qualified person for this job?" whether inside or outside of the company. He also ensured that talent slates weren't limited by age. "It could be that I put a 35-year-old into a high-ranking position, but it could also be a 55-year-old," he says. "It was always about finding the best fit." Adds U.S. Bancorp's former CEO Richard Davis about the benefits of hiring from the outside: "The best way to introduce new thinking is to introduce new thinking."

Build the Bench

Placing the right talent in critical roles is the beginning not the end of the CEO's role in managing talent. Similar to the way in which Ken Frazier described then-CEO Roy Vagelos's role in his success, the best CEOs put real time and energy into coaching, retaining talent, managing performance, and planning for succession for the most valuable roles.

This means spending lots of time with leaders in the most important roles. Brad Smith at Intuit reports, "Thirty percent of my time was coaching and growing our talent in one-on-ones and town hall meetings, and having chats with managers important to the business who aren't my direct reports." Dupont's Ed Breen shares, "We have a system for identifying the promising talent coming up in key roles. I do a mid-year and year-end review of our top talent. I've also spent time every month with talent in key positions that I think are high potential, just meeting one-on-one."

Some CEOs, such as Galderma's Flemming Ørnskov, also ask board members to act as mentors to certain executives where the skill sets and personalities are a good match. Most important, coaching or mentoring provides these talented individuals with the opportunity to truly shape the company and drive impact, to foster a sense of ownership in seeing those projects succeed, and to feel pride in the meaningful contribution they've made.

The best CEOs also become involved in succession planning for key roles. Just as a baseball or soccer club has a "farm" system (teams of younger players that act as feeders into a major league team), the CEO should have a handle on who the up-and-coming stars are and where and when they get the nod to move up a level. At Adidas, as a result of Herbert Hainer's demands to see diverse slates, his team flagged a thirty-five-year-old leader of a Hong Kong–based record company as a potential candidate. Hainer not only hired him for the Chinese marketing role in question, but also mentored him to become the managing director of the Asia-Pacific region two years later. As Hainer reflects, "China was a small business at the time, but it was a key role that was important to our future. When it's that important, I not only got involved as the CEO in picking the talent, but also training them."

During a discussion about the career path of one of major energy player Total's most talented up-and-coming people, the prevailing view in the room was to promote the individual to the head of a region. "I suggested instead that he should head up renewable energy," recalls Total CEO Patrick Pouyanné, "and I saw the surprise this created because the standard career path in Total is to become the head of a major zone." Pouyanné had set a course toward sustainability, and his ambition was to become a leader in renewable energy. He continues, "I needed to put top-level talent on the case, and it was a good fit. CEOs need to spend time on this and make sure the best people get assigned to where the action will be."

The best CEOs also have their head of Human Resources put the processes in place to build a strong bench. Piyush Gupta at DBS shares: "For every job, mine included, we work through what is the slate, who could do the job, who could do the job in three or five years? We then case manage 100-odd people. Who needs to move, what should we move them into, how do we get them the exposure and growth they need to get from point A to point B? It's very well structured." Such an approach opens up space on the bench for up-and-coming talent. Itaú Unibanco's Roberto Setúbal puts it succinctly: "You don't have to carry the people who shouldn't be there." Dupont's Ed Breen describes his process: "We put people into four buckets, and if the ones in the bottom bucket are still there six months later when we do the review, we start to ask, 'Well, why didn't we do something about it?' We have a fairly regimented system that way. I'm just a big believer in having the best team on the field to win."

GE's Larry Culp shares how getting talent right can create a virtuous cycle, as it did for him at his former company Danaher. "The whole philosophy is getting the right people in the right place and coaching them to be great in those roles," he reflects. "It's just a huge part of being a successful CEO. If I have great leaders and they have great teams I can spend my time on capital allocation, doing so in ways that retain the great talent that we're developing. That's how we got the flywheel spinning at Danaher."

The benefits of putting rigor and discipline into talent management are many, and account for why our discussions with the best CEOs were *not* characterized by what otherwise is often cited as a CEO's biggest regret: moving too slowly on low performers in key roles, even when it was clear a change was needed.

Without a data-driven approach to talent, it's easy to see how personnel conversations get bogged down. Myriad social considerations become barriers to action. What about those employees loyal to the executive in question, will they leave? What about the customers who they interact with, how will they respond? Does the board share the same view of their performance? Given their loyalty for many years, will it be seen as heartless to let them go? Do we have a viable successor? And so on.

By clearly defining the talent requirements for the most important value-creating, protecting, and enabling roles (matching them with people with the right skills and attributes), and by building a deep bench of leaders, the politics that otherwise surround personnel issues largely disappear.

JPMC's Jamie Dimon puts a fine point on the issue: "When someone asks me how I can demote a wonderful person, a loyal, 'pillar of society' out of a role where they aren't the best fit, the answer is simple. They're no longer doing a good job. If we were 'loyal' to them by leaving them in the job, we'd be hugely disloyal to everyone else and to the company's clients. That, right there, is the hardest part about talent management."

In this chapter we've dealt with the topic of talent broadly. In the next section we'll home in more specifically on what the best CEOs do to lead their top teams.

• • •

We've now seen how the best CEOs' "treat the soft stuff as the hard stuff" mindset translates into action. It's fair to say that of the CEO's many responsibilities, this is the most difficult to get right, even by the best. Some confessed that they never really felt like they got it as right as they wanted it. Below is a summary of how those who felt successful in doing so brought rigor and discipline to the critical organization-alignment tasks: culture, organization design, and talent management. In doing so, they unlocked more than twice the probability of successful execution and almost twice the magnitude of performance levels achieved.

Aligning the Organization: What separates the best from the rest

Mindset: Treat the Soft Stuff as the Hard Stuff

Culture practice:	**Find the One Thing**
	◆ Reshape the work environment
	◆ Make it personal
	◆ Make it meaningful
	◆ Measure what matters

Organization design practice:	**Solve for "Stagility"**
	◆ Stop the pendulum swing
	◆ Emphasize accountability
	◆ Think helix, not matrix
	◆ Make "smart" choices

Talent management practice:	**(Don't) Put People First**
	◆ Clearly define high value roles
	◆ Don't forget the "left tackles"
	◆ Find unusual suspects
	◆ Actively build the bench

Even if you're not the CEO of a major corporation, in executing your vision and strategy it's important to emphasize the "soft stuff" as much as the "hard stuff." To know if you're doing so, ask yourself: What's the most important behavior change needed to unlock success? To what extent am I personally acting as a role model by telling a deeply compelling story, aligning incentives, and building the confidence and skills of others? Are accountabilities clear, and is work organized in a way that isn't overly rigid but also prevents chaos? Is the best-fit talent in the most important roles? Do I have a reliable way to measure if the "soft stuff" is moving in the right direction, and do I course-correct accordingly? If you do the hard work of getting good answers to these questions, executing your strategy becomes far easier.

MOBILIZING LEADERS MINDSET

Solve for the Team's Psychology

Imagine how hard physics would be if particles could think.

—Murray Gell-Mann

The dynamics of a top executive team can make or break a company. Investors know this—it's why they cite the quality of the top management team as the single most important nonfinancial factor in evaluating a new IPO (initial public offering, in which a private company sells its shares to the public). Their instinct is backed by the data: When a top team works together with a common vision, a company is twice as likely to have above-median financial performance. As leadership expert John Maxwell once said, "Teamwork makes the dream work, but vision becomes a nightmare when the leader has a big dream and a bad team."

Despite the clear benefits, more than half of senior executives report that their company's top team is underperforming. CEOs are often out of touch with this reality: On average, fewer than one-third of CEOs report that they have problems with their teams.[38] This disconnect isn't an intellectual one, but a social one: Individual and institutional biases and awkward group dynamics can diminish the effectiveness of a team. Often, teams consist of opinionated leaders who represent differ-ent perspectives, vie for influence, fight over the allocation of scarce resources, and in some cases compete with one another for the top job. Even though they put on their "I'm here for the team" face in meetings, they're often watching their backs and maneuvering behind closed doors to make sure their agenda—not necessarily that of the company—is being met.

The best CEOs recognize this challenge and acknowledge that it's their leadership that will determine whether their team's work will live up to its potential and propel the company forward. When thinking about how to get the most out of their leaders, many CEOs start with questions such as, "How often should we meet?" and "What should be on the agenda?" The best, however, think less about what the team does together, and more about how the team works together. They obsess with solving for the team's psychology and let the mechanics of coordination and execution follow.

This focus on how the team works together versus what it does together brings to the fore such factors as composition, effectiveness, and operating rhythm. While this section mainly deals with the top team in big corporations, the lessons learned here apply to teams of any size, in any kind of organization.

CHAPTER 7

Team Composition Practice

Create an Ecosystem

The strength of the team is each individual team member. The strength of each member is the team.
—Phil Jackson

Walk through an old-growth forest, and the diversity of trees you'll see can be quite dazzling. Douglas fir, white pine, Aspen, red maple, and oak soar toward the sky, each individually competing with the others for sunlight and space. Or are they? Research suggests that beneath the surface of the soil the trees are actually cooperating (not competing) with each other, with different species acting as a team to maximize the growth of the entire forest. Scientists have discovered that trees and fungi form underground partnerships called mycorrhizae that connect the roots of diverse types of trees to one another to help share carbon, water, and nutrients such as phosphorous and nitrogen.

This research helped explain a puzzling phenomenon—why do cleared forests replanted with a single species like Douglas fir—with no competition for sunlight and space from other species—do more poorly than when the same species is grown amid other types of trees? It turns out that cooperation, not competition, among diverse species fosters sustainable growth.[39] Similarly, in organizational life, a group of high performers only becomes truly high performing if its members are complementary and connected to one another like in old-growth forests, not simply working side by side like replanted Douglas firs.

When in 2014 Lilach Asher-Topilsky became the CEO of IDB, one of Israel's largest banks, she had several dragons to slay. The bank was underperforming financially and falling behind in digitization. Asher-Topilsky knew what she needed to do to bring the bank into the future—she'd compiled a list of thirty bold change initiatives—but after a careful assessment realized that many of her top executives lacked the capability and drive to make the needed changes happen. "It's very hard from the position of the CEO to change something in the organization if you have a person under you who doesn't believe in the change," says Asher-Topilsky. "You can't start managing the people beneath them. So when I thought about which of the management members I was going to replace, I looked at the places in the organization that needed change and which had a manager who didn't believe in this change."

Eventually, Asher-Topilsky ended up switching out roughly half of her top team. Her first big and perhaps most important move was to appoint a new head of human resources (HR), a key position that could unlock the kind of organizational energy she needed to move IDB into the future. She found an insider who understood the culture and history of the bank but also had an outsider's sensibility. The woman she chose was tough enough to deal with big organizations like the labor union that represented many of IDB's employees and smart enough to install hard-nosed HR systems that would help make the workforce more productive. "I needed someone," recalls Asher-Topilsky, "to make sure we had systems in place. A big problem was that almost every employee had a unique employment agreement—not only on wages, but also on work arrangements, for example: 'This employee's allowed to come from nine till three because of this and this and this.'"

By the time Asher-Topilsky left the CEO job at the end of 2019, IDB had become a leader in digital banking, signing partnerships with fintech upstarts including Icount and PayBox, which helped her bank improve payment services and offer more digital products. She also introduced AI to the bank, which allowed IDB to analyze banking transaction data in real time and deliver tailored financial management information to its customers. Under her tenure, the bank's return on equity doubled, its net profits tripled, and IDB paid dividends for the first time in twenty years.

But how exactly do the best CEOs like Asher-Topilsky determine who should be on the team and who shouldn't? They . . .

. . . staff the team with an eye to aptitude and attitude

. . . act fast but fairly regarding those who don't belong

. . . stay connected while keeping their distance

. . . build a leadership coalition beyond their immediate team

Staff for Aptitude and Attitude

As discussed in chapter 3, the right conversation about who should be on the team starts with roles, not people. What kind of senior team will move the company forward? What knowledge and skills are necessary? What experiences are needed? What attributes and attitudes aren't negotiable? What about diversity, equity, and inclusion? Against this backdrop, the best CEOs carefully compose their top team. Adidas's Herbert Hainer, drawing on a European football metaphor, reinforces the importance of thinking about the whole vs. the parts when building a team. "You can't play with only 11 strikers or 11 goalkeepers. You need an excellent goalkeeper, an excellent striker, and excellent supporting players. One of the most important tasks for a CEO is to build a team around them that they can rely on, where there's trust and synergy."

Sony's Kazuo Hirai describes his approach to selecting a management team. "What I basically looked for was expertise and proven ability in the area I was going to ask them to manage, whether it was the TV business, digital imaging, the movie business, PlayStation, what have you." On top of the aptitude, he also looked for attitude. "I looked for demonstrated ability to push back against their bosses and not be afraid to present their ideas and be bold about it. They had to be able to tell their bosses or the CEO that an idea wasn't good. When I got everybody together, I told them that was my expectation."

One aptitude virtually all of the best CEOs look for is the ability to balance the short and long term. GM's Mary Barra explains,

"At first, I thought, 'Just let that person go sell, sell, sell, sell. And that's fine.' Up to a certain level, that's okay. I've come to the conclusion that for the most senior positions, you have to have a person who can execute and drive the results today, but they also have to be looking over the horizon and planning for the future."

When it came to attitudes, being a team player was universally sought by the best CEOs. As IBD's Lilach Asher-Topilsky puts it: "The key was to have people who can understand the joint mission and not just think about their own promotion. That was the most important thing." Alphabet's Sundar Pichai looks at talent at senior levels with the view of "Do I see in them attributes that put the company first? Do they think about our mission and what we are trying to do for our users?" JPMC's Jamie Dimon clarifies further. "Teamwork is often code for 'get along,'" he says, "but teamwork sometimes means standing alone and having the courage to say something. The best team player is the one who puts up their hand and says, 'I don't agree, because I don't think what you're doing is in the best interest of the client or the company.'"

While all the best CEOs valued team members who could manage both the short and long term and who were willing to push back, some had specific attitudes they valued most. Dupont's Ed Breen explains, "For me, the number one thing is passion. Passionate people are infectious in a good way, and people want to be around them. Anyone whose résumé gets to me already has a great education and a great background. I don't have to worry about all that." Cadence Design System's Lip-Bu Tan looked for "transparency, humility, and a learning attitude." For Esquel's Marjorie Yang, "When picking leaders, I look for good quantitative reasoning skills, curiosity, and high emotional intelligence." As it relates to emotional intelligence, Alphabet's Sundar Pichai has grown to value empathy. "Eight years ago, I would not have listed it as a top attribute. But to run an organization today at the scale of Google—with its internal and external engagement demands—requires high levels of interpersonal sophistication."

The overall composition of the team is an important consideration as well. Masahiko Uotani at Shiseido built a management team that included about half of the people who'd been with the company from the beginning and the other half who joined later.

Feike Sijbesma lamented that before he took over DSM, the senior leaders were jokingly addressed as "lady and gentlemen." He made sure his three hundred leaders were comprised of 30 percent women, and his board and top team were 50 percent female. At Ahold Delhaize, Dick Boer created a team where half the members were experienced insiders and half came from the outside. KV Kamath, the former CEO of ICICI, India's largest private bank, strove to increase the number of younger, "in their early thirties" minds on his team.

Having a good attitude combined with the right aptitude isn't just nice to have; it's essential for every member of the team. When it isn't present, the best CEOs take action and while doing so they act fast but fair.

Act Fast but Fair

Aside from the clear-cut cases where a senior leader obviously won't make it or is killing the team dynamic, the best CEOs apply a fair and disciplined approach to give struggling leaders a chance to step up. "Conventional CEO wisdom states that you should move faster on people," Majid Al Futtaim's Alain Bejjani says. "But I think that's a very shortsighted and stubborn view. It's true that you can't make people change—I can barely change my children, let alone members of my team. But you can create an environment that supports people in learning, adapting, and evolving to the extent that they can or want to do so." Intuit's Brad Smith illustrates the point with a sporting analogy: "Any coach who needs to replace all the players isn't as good a coach as they think they are."

Before removing someone from the team, the best CEOs make sure that the following questions can be answered in the affirmative:

Does the team member know exactly what's expected of them:
   i.e., what the agenda is and what jobs need to be done to drive
   that agenda?
Have they been given the needed tools and resources, and a
   chance to build the necessary skills and confidence to use them
   effectively?

Are they surrounded by others (including the CEO) who are
aligned on a common direction and who display the desired
mindsets and behaviors?

Is it clear what the consequences are if they don't get on board
and deliver?

It's surprising how often less adept CEOs can't say "yes" to all
of these questions before acting. Lars Rebien Sørensen, the former CEO of the Danish pharmaceutical company Novo Nordisk,
ensures he can answer in the affirmative. Sørensen, whom the *Harvard Business Review* named the top-ranked CEO in the world
in 2015, was, at one point, pressured to remove a division head
because that business was seen as not scaling up fast enough to
meet market demand. Sørensen, however, was against firing the
leader because he'd concluded that the poor performance was the
result of the company's not investing enough in manufacturing
capacity—resources that would have allowed the division to build
the competencies required to fulfill its mission. With the proper
resources, the head of manufacturing was able to turn around the
situation and keep his job.

To be clear, we're not talking about keeping low performers
or even letting average performers hang around. It's about giving
leaders who have been average under a previous administration an
opportunity to shine in a new environment. DBS Group's Piyush
Gupta describes the evolution of his thinking. "My rule used to
be, if I think somebody has a fifty-fifty chance of making it, I'd
work with them to try and help them get to their potential. But I
changed my benchmarks to: If I think you have a seventy-five percent shot at succeeding, I'll work with you. If it's anything less than
that, I figure bite the bullet and find somebody who has a better
shot at succeeding."

What changed Gupta's mind was a session he had with an executive coach when he was at Citibank in the 1990s. At the time,
he was halfway through one of his typical three-year stints on an
assignment, and the coach put an org chart in front of him and
asked him to identify his A, B, and C players. What Gupta identified surprised him. He had some A players but most of his team
was made up of B and C players. The coach bluntly told him that

he was already halfway through his tenure and he didn't have an A team. When he was transferred in a year or so, he'd leave his successor with at best a B team, and that's not the way to provide an appropriate return to the shareholder. The lesson stuck with him.

Applying a fair process to help a B player become an A player is typically a matter of months, not years. As Lockheed Martin's Marillyn Hewson explains, "You want to test your hypothesis and assess it. But make your changes early because people expect you as a new leader to come in and make change. If you don't, people get comfortable with that, and then if you finally get around to it, it feels to them that all of a sudden you knocked the props out from under them. Then your job is even harder."

Westpac's Gail Kelly reinforces the point from a different perspective: "I've seen it so often where a person has potential and you want them to succeed, but they just aren't getting there. It very rarely gets better if you've put the conditions in place for their success and they aren't succeeding. That's why you want to make those decisions early, because it's best for that person, and it's best for the company. It's the most elegant way of dealing with it, because you can discuss that it's not the right fit. If you let it go on too long, you can't have that discussion."

Aon's Greg Case offers a final piece of advice when it comes to acting fair. "Be mindful of how you think about transitioning a senior leader. Your colleagues watch whether you handle it with compassion or not. It's important to clarify that just because somebody is not going to be on the field going forward does not in any way mean that they're not a great person or haven't made a tremendous contribution in the past. The firm wouldn't be the same without them, and they can take a great deal of pride in what they've helped the firm achieve throughout their tenure. Celebrate successes and celebrate transition."

Stay Connected While Keeping Distance

To ensure that team members become and stay A players, the CEO must play a hands-on role with each individual. Michael Fisher, CEO of the nonprofit Cincinnati Children's Hospital Medical Center (Cincinnati Children's), explains, "You invest time and energy with each, recognizing they're all individuals. Their needs are going to be different, and their strengths and gaps are going to be different. You applaud and cheer them on where they have those strengths and put them in situations where they can most effectively use them. But also give feedback along the way, on some sort of regular cycle—'Here are some things you can do better,' or, 'Here are things we can work on together.' "

Westpac's Gail Kelly describes how she connected with individual team members: "I would ring all of my team at least once a week, most likely later in the afternoons or very early mornings, on the way home or the way to work. I'd encourage them to ring me, too. I built a relationship where their first thought when I'd call wasn't, 'What does she want?' but rather 'It's going to be a chat.' My tack was 'I've noticed this . . .' or 'I'm a bit concerned about what I'm seeing here . . .' or 'By the way, I've heard this.' But it may also be, 'Tell me about,' or, 'What's on your mind,' or, 'Gosh, that's exciting.' My job was to make people be the best that they can be. To do that, I needed to know them, to understand their vulnerabilities, their weaknesses, what they were worrying about."

Adidas's Herbert Hainer points out the benefits of connecting one-on-one with team members. "The top team needs the CEO's time for operational judgment and personal matters," he says. "Sometimes they just want to talk to you and tell you how good they feel or how challenging times seem. If you have enough time for your people and you show you care about them, they pay it back twice and maybe three times. Everyone looks up to you, even if you don't realize it."

Connecting one-on-one doesn't mean making team members feel like family, however. Cincinnati Children's Michael Fisher explains the "distance" aspect of a constructive CEO-subordinate relationship. "You also must recognize that you are their boss. While there's a level of collegiality and familiarity, at the end of the day, your first responsibility is to the institution and making a functional top team." DBS's Piyush Gupta agrees: "If you get too close to everybody, then you wind up not making tough choices and compromising for mediocrity. People need to respect that, finally, you are the boss." Adidas's Kasper Rørsted takes a very black-and-white stance on the issue so as to be able to cleanly enforce needed accountability: "At work, I want to be friendly, but I don't want to make friends. Eventually, I have to be able to make unbiased decisions."

When it comes to conversations with individual team members about their performance, the best CEOs, in the words of Dupont's Ed Breen, "Grade behaviors first—and after that, grade results." JPMC's Jamie Dimon explains why: "You have to acknowledge that failure is okay. There are good mistakes: You argued for it, you thought it through, you talked to the right people, and you were wrong. So you have to allow failure. We don't just look at the profit-and-loss statement. Instead we ask, did you work hard? Did you hire people? Did you train people? Did you do the right thing for the client? Did you help other people? Did you build systems? When we asked you to do something like recruiting, did you help us?"

During evaluations, any feedback should be tailored to the individual. Cincinnati Children's Fisher expounds. "With some people you can say, for example, 'You might want to listen more in these meetings instead of always being the first to offer your opinion and not giving others airtime.' With others you'll need to be more direct: 'You just have to be quiet for the first half hour of the meeting. You're shooting yourself in the foot.'"

Build a Coalition Beyond the Immediate Team

While we've focused thus far in this chapter on the top team in the organization, the best CEOs also create a sense of teamwork with a larger leadership coalition. U.S. Bancorp's Richard Davis explains how he deepens his bench: "I reached out to a remarkable number of employees. Our pyramid had twelve direct reports to the CEO, seventy-six two levels down and 220 three levels down. And I certainly knew everyone by name and found it was important to connect directly with them versus working through the hierarchy. No one was afraid to have me go around them to a direct report to mentor them or expose them to something." Diageo's Ivan Menezes makes a point to have one-on-one catchups with the top eighty people in the organization twice a year. "They are our senior leaders," says Menezes. "We discuss everything, from business, to family, to their development, to how they're doing and how they're feeling. It's unstructured but very valuable."

Engaging leaders further down the pyramid can be done individually, but also should happen as a group or in subgroups. For example, at Duke Energy, Lynn Good describes the approach she took to get closer to the top one hundred at the utility: "I make a concerted effort to spend time with my direct reports, their direct reports, as well as the people who run large operations. I get them together for an hour and a half each month on strategic topics. We get together once a quarter for a longer session. We get together once a year for a day and a half. Timely, transparent communications are important to build trust and confidence among the leadership team."

In addition to meeting with her senior team on a regular basis, GM's Mary Barra meets with her top 230 global leaders as a group more than twice a year. The goal is to ensure everyone's heading in the same direction. "They're good leaders," Barra shares. "Once they understand 'here's the change and why'—and it's very important for them to know, 'Here is why'—they get behind things and keep us moving forward."

Some of the best CEOs create a broader leadership coalition by letting employees a level or two down listen in on selected top team sessions. Brad Smith made this the norm at Intuit: "I broadcast my staff meeting with my twelve direct reports to the top 400 leaders in the company. The 400 would dial in and hear us go through the agenda together, listen to the questions I was asking, and understand the principles we used to make a decision. It began to accelerate our velocity. Everyone learned how to make the right decisions on their own."

CEOs can also broaden their leadership coalition by assigning more junior leaders to work on cross-functional projects. Says Westpac's Gail Kelly: "I reached down into the next levels of the organization and pulled out our very best people from each division, regardless of what they were doing, and put them full-time on a project to define the long-term future of the bank." She continues, "Together we worked through questions: What did we want to be able to say about ourselves? What did we want our customers to say about us, our people to say about us? What's the role we want to play in the community? Let's work now to design the organization we want to be. And then let's start to build pathways from where we are today."

Building a broader leadership coalition not only gives CEOs more leverage in driving the organization forward, but it also puts pressure on the top team members who must respond to the leaders below them whom the CEO has trained to have the same vision about the direction of the company.

When it comes to putting together a team, the best CEOs look for leaders who aren't just interested in being all-stars, but also want and have the skills to build an all-star team. They then put the conditions in place for each team member to be successful, while maintaining enough distance to objectively judge and act on their performance. They also proactively engage leaders beyond their immediate team.

There is one further team construct that the best CEOs have that we haven't talked about here: the formation of a small informal team, sometimes known as a "kitchen cabinet." Such a team typically provides a safe place to discuss highly sensitive issues and provides radically unfiltered feedback. The construct, however, tends to be highly personal, and as such we'll talk more about the value, composition, and use of such a group of informal advisors later when we discuss the CEO's responsibility to manage personal effectiveness.

Thus far we've covered how the best CEOs get the psychology and mechanics right when it comes to their individual team members. As anyone who is a parent with two or more children knows all too well, it's one thing to manage individuals and quite another to manage the complex dynamics existing between them.

CHAPTER 8

Teamwork Practice
Make the Team the Star

Talent wins games, but teamwork and intelligence win championships.

—Michael Jordan

The 1992 US Men's Olympic "Dream Team" squad included some of the greatest players in basketball history: Charles Barkley, Larry Bird, Patrick Ewing, Magic Johnson, Michael Jordan, Scottie Pippen, and Karl Malone. All were consummate professionals with a track record of not only being all-star players but also playing on all-star teams. Yet in their first month of practice, the Dream Team lost to a group of college players by eight points in a scrimmage. In the words of Michael Jordan: "We got killed today, we're out of sync, we have no continuity."[40] Scottie Pippen summarized: "We didn't know how to play with each other."[41]

Lesser known than the outcome of the scrimmage is how the loss came to be. Coach Chuck Daly, who was chosen for his ability to manage personalities and egos, decided not to make any of the adjustments one would have expected as the game went on. "He knew what he was doing," according to assistant coach Mike Krzyzewski, "he threw the game. Not many people would have done it and he did it. From then on, he had a way to say, 'You know, you could lose.' It was brilliant on Chuck's part to orchestrate that."

The psychological wakeup call that coach Daly orchestrated was what the team needed. Any arrogance or complacency was replaced by teamwork and hunger. The next day in training camp the tables were turned as the dream team soundly beat the college players. Fast-forward to the Olympics and the Dream Team scored more than a hundred points in every game and easily took home the gold.[42]

In the corporate world, most teams operate like the Dream Team did in their scrimmage. Only 6 percent of top HR executives, those whose job includes helping to ensure good teamwork takes place, agree with the statement that "Our executive team operates as a well-integrated team." Further, when executives are asked to assess how effectively their top team works together versus its potential, they rate it only a five on a scale of ten.[43] As with the Dream Team's early stumbles, the reason for these challenges is typically less about the individual team members, and more about the dynamics of how the team works together.

DSM's Feike Sijbesma reinforces the point. "Based on my experience, in principle it's right to say you need to have a team with the right people. But the notion that you can fire the weaker people in the team, just hire good people, and now you have a good team is too simple." Instead, he explains, "What really makes the team successful is the way the individuals, whatever their nature, deal with each other. It's not only the bricks but also the cement! That has an even bigger impact on results."

But how hard can it be to get a team of professionals working well together? Very. Group dynamics are complex and full of contradictions, as Dr. Kenwyn Smith and Dr. David Berg argued in their seminal work, *Paradoxes of Group Life*. Here are just three examples: People feel pressure to conform to the group, yet the power of the group comes from leveraging the individuality of its members. A team leader must ask success-oriented people to risk failure. The work of those in power positions is to create the conditions in which others are powerful. Adidas's Herbert Hainer adds to these complex dynamics the fact that: "Executives tend to be alpha leaders and competitive," and it's easy to see why a high-performing top team is not a foregone conclusion, even when it's made up of highly talented individuals.[44]

When Westpac's Gail Kelly took over as CEO, Australia was in the early stages of the global financial crisis, which meant that she couldn't compose her team the way she wanted to. Too many issues needed immediate attention, and the level of uncertainty put a premium on retaining the institutional knowledge and expertise of the old guard. Additionally, she was only the second person to be brought in from outside the company over its two-hundred-year history, and as such, employees viewed her with a degree of skepticism—especially members of her team who felt they, not she, deserved to be CEO. Further, her predecessor had largely dealt with each team member one-on-one, discussing strategic plans for the business units, resource allocation decisions, and key talent decisions individually. The result was that a number of executives around the table habitually operated in a siloed, command-and-control manner.

Without a high degree of team trust and collaboration, Kelly knew progress toward her vision would be stifled, and that making it through the crisis would be far more difficult. She therefore relentlessly built her group of twelve direct reports into a high-performing team through a series of off-sites, having them do the work of the transformation together. The purpose of the top team was clarified, behavioral expectations were set, and trust was built through facilitated sessions that broke down barriers between individuals. Over time, as the company began emerging from the global financial crisis, Kelly found ways to fine-tune the composition of her team. In the end, she attributes a significant portion of her success during her seven years to having placed high demands on teamwork. The results speak for themselves: The value of the company more than doubled from $38 billion to $79 billion, and Kelly herself received multiple accolades for being among the world's best and most influential leaders.

In keeping with how Kelly took on the team dynamics challenge at Westpac, the best CEOs build high performing teams by . . .

- . . . ensuring that their team does work that only it can do
- . . . clearly defining what it means to be a member on the "first team"
- . . . combining dialogue, data, and speed in decision-making
- . . . investing regularly in team building

Do Work That Only the Team Can Do

In his 1958 book *The Pursuit of Progress*, C. Northcote Parkinson described a common way a team can become dysfunctional. He tells the story of an executive team that was gathered to make three investment decisions. First, they discussed the investment for a £10 million nuclear power plant. This decision was approved in two and a half minutes. The next agenda item was to decide which color to paint their bike shed (total cost about £350). After a forty-five-minute discussion, the decision was made. Third, the staff needed a new coffee machine, which would roughly cost £21. The committee discussed this topic for one hour and fifteen minutes and decided to postpone the decision until the next meeting.[45]

The story illustrates what is known as the "law of triviality" (also referred to as the "bike shed effect"), where groups of people have a strong tendency to give disproportionate attention to trivial issues and details—in particular, those the entire group can relate to (and therefore have strong opinions about). The bike shed effect often leads to team members voicing complaints that "we spend too much time in meetings," to which the well-intentioned response is to consolidate meetings. This only exacerbates the problem, however. More ends up packed into less time in a less effective format, making the time spent feel even more senseless. Our research and that of others fully backs up how real these dynamics are. Only 38 percent of CEO direct reports feel their top team is focused on work that truly benefits from a top-of-the-house perspective, and only 35 percent feel the right amount of time is allocated to important topics.[46]

This isn't the case when the best CEOs are at the helm. These leaders make sure that only needle-moving work items are on the agenda. Thermo Fisher Scientific CEO Marc Casper shares his philosophy: "One of the reasons for our success is the 'ruthless prioritization' of what we work on together. We're okay with letting things be mediocre that aren't on our list of priorities. That's perfectly fine. The key to success is that we focus our time and energy on what really matters."

Priority work for the top team typically includes: corporate strategy (priorities, targets, M&A), large-scale allocation of resources, identifying synergies and interdependencies across business units, validating decisions that significantly affect all employees, assuring delivery of company financial targets, providing direction for major company-wide projects, reinforcing the desired company culture (including individual and collective role modeling), and building the company's leadership bench strength (which includes providing feedback to one another).

What teams should *not* focus on are topics that can be done better in individual functions, lines of business, or smaller subsets of the group. For example, quarterly business performance reviews are done with a subset of corporate leaders (e.g., CEO, CFO, and CHRO) and individual businesses, unless there is a cultural reason to combine the reviews into one session. Corporate governance and policy decisions (e.g., risk management controls and processes) are typically taken by a subset of leaders, and those decisions are then shared broadly so that the team can execute against them.

Ecolab's Doug Baker summarizes what's required of the CEO: "My role is making sure the top team does the big things really well. Our job is to focus on what can make the company successful, and what can kill us. All the rest is email."

Define the "First Team" Norms

Once there's clarity on what topics team time will be spent on, the next step is to gain the same degree of clarity on how those topics will be tackled, which starts by establishing the mindset that the top team is every member's "first team." The best CEOs are unequivocal on this issue. This means that everyone is expected to put the company's needs ahead of those of the business unit's or function's. Said another way, the mindset of a top team member is not: "I'm on the team to represent my function or business," but "I'm on the team so I can represent the company to my function or business."

Baker describes how he explained the concept at Ecolab: "My request to all my teammates was that they have one foot in my job and one foot in theirs. So our job here isn't to maximize, for example, Human Resources (HR) effectiveness. HR is here to maximize Ecolab's effectiveness. Their job is to help the company; the company is not here to help HR. That's how it works. Same with the CEO, by the way." U.S. Bancorp's Richard Davis reiterates the idea: "The holy grail is to have twelve people on a management team who are equal voices and equal storytellers. That means they can speak for the team, for the company, not just for themselves." Lockheed Martin's Marillyn Hewson emphasized that the mindset applies to what customers experience as well: "Each member of my top team knows that it's their job to represent the corporation as one and get the right people lined up to serve customers."

The best CEOs are maniacal about this for good reason. Just as we saw in chapter 3 (in the section Solve for the Whole), that emphasizing the good of the entire company over its parts pays dividends when it comes to capital allocation, the same is true for how the company is run. When we analyzed data from over two thousand organizations across one hundred countries looking at the extent to which a top team applies a consistent set of management practices across the entire company, the results showed that those who do so are on average 3.4 times higher performing. The catch, however, is that the performance boost only kicks in at very high levels of consistency, so there can be no half measures when it comes to the first team being the top team.

As we've already seen, many CEOs have a catchphrase to capture the essence of the first team mindset. Marillyn Hewson describes this ethos as being part of "One Lockheed Martin." Similarly, Flemming Ørnskov called it "One Shire," and Sony's Kazuo Hirai rallied his troops around "One Sony." Diageo's Ivan Menezes made it clear that everyone plays for "One Diageo." Jim Owens refers to it as "Team Caterpillar." Likewise, Johan Thijs at KBC uses "Team Blue," in reference to blue being the color under which all the Group's units in all countries operate. Greg Case captures the notion with "Aon United." At Atlas Copco, Ronnie Leten talks about "the Atlas Copco nationality." Allianz's Oliver Bäte emphasizes "moving from multi-local to global." At Publicis, Maurice Lévy promotes "The Power of One." Lilach Asher-Topilsky dubbed IDB's management team "the Fist" because, in her words, "You can't get in the lines between the fingers. Not the board of directors, not the union, not the competitors—not anyone." Bill George at Medtronic used the label "Enterprise leaders" for his executive committee. "They had to help me run Medtronic, because I couldn't run it alone," he says.

Westpac's Gail Kelly describes how rules were put in place to govern her senior team: "We developed a behavior charter that became absolutely written in steel for us. We had it with us at all of our meetings. We referred to it often and reviewed our behaviors against it." The content of the behavioral charter included items such as, "If any of us is unhappy about something, we are going to put our hands up and say it. If we have a problem, we're going to talk about it soon and ideally face-to-face. We're not going to let our general managers fight it out for us as proxies. We will never undermine someone behind their back. If we as a team agree on something, even if as an individual you didn't agree with it in the meeting, and even if it's not the path you would've chosen, you will back it anyway." The impact, as Kelly describes, was that "It really helped diminish the politics. It doesn't eliminate it totally, but it cuts down on it, because people were accountable to this team as their first team."

Caterpillar's Jim Owens shares a norm that's important to set early in a CEO's tenure and that helps get people to be more candid in meetings: "Interestingly, when you become CEO, one of the things you learn right away is that everybody thinks you're suddenly much smarter. When you attend a meeting and express an opinion, people line up on your side. Early in my tenure, I purposefully said: 'Look. I have great respect for everyone here. I want to be part of this debate but remember that I don't have all the answers. If you don't vigorously disagree with me when you feel like you should, shame on you. And shame on me because that means I'm not very effective.'"

Having established the first team mindset, the next step the best CEOs take is to make sure their teams understand how decisions will be made. While methods vary, all emphasize data, dialogue, and speed.

Combine Data, Dialogue, and Speed

"In God we trust, all others bring data" is a famous quote often attributed to management scientist W. Edwards Deming. The quote espoused his fundamental philosophy that data measurement and analysis are essential to making good management decisions. The best CEOs adhere to this mantra. Brad Smith describes a method he used to ensure decisions were data-driven at Intuit: "Our decision-making principles insist on evidence. One of the mottos at Intuit is, 'Because of (blank), I believe we should do (blank).' If it's not based in evidence, it's an opinion, and we discount it. By pushing for evidence-based assertions instead of opinions, we've been able to sharpen our decision-making."

Smith also recognized the importance of dialogue, which is a hallmark of the best CEOs. As TIAA's Roger Ferguson told us: "It's certainly true that numbers don't lie. But also numbers don't necessarily tell you exactly what they mean, which is why dialogue is awfully important." The importance of data *and* dialogue is backed by the research. In a cross-industry study of thousands of major decisions made over five years (including ones made on new product investments, M&A, capital expenditures), managers were asked to report on the quality and detail of the data analysis. Did they build a detailed financial model or do sensitivity analysis? They were also asked if the dialogue was robust. Did the right participants engage in high-quality debate? It turns out that engaging in dialogue was more correlated to good decision-making than data—by a factor of six.[47]

Dialogue only works, however, if the team members are free of bias. The most common bias is groupthink: our tendency to back an idea based on how favorably we believe others will view that decision. Another is the confirmation bias, where one accepts information that confirms one's beliefs and resists any information to the contrary. A third prevalent bias is the optimism bias: the assumption and expectation that the best possible outcome will emerge. The best CEOs proactively mitigate the impact of such biases.

DBS uses an approach it refers to as the "Wreckoon." CEO

Piyush Gupta explains its origins and intent: "Netflix has something called the Chaos Monkey that they use in programming. Once they create a program, they unleash the Chaos Monkey in the program to try and mess it up. It stress-tests the program. We stole that idea and created 'Wreckoon' where we stress-test our thinking in meetings." In practice, a picture of a racoon shows up periodically in DBS's discussion documents, and when it does, it prompts the group to stop and reflect on questions such as: What are we not thinking about but should be? What could be wrong with the path we're going down? What would have to be true for this to be a bad decision? Gupta explains the benefits of this exercise: "You can tell people to dissent, but when you create a small mnemonic, people remember, and it becomes easier. You start to see it happen more in practice, and decision-making gets better as a result."

Sometimes good dialogue is inhibited simply by having the CEO in the room. As Ecolab's Doug Baker explains, "Especially over time, as people start to perceive you as a successful CEO, your views are given too much weight. What you suggest as a thought-starter, they can take as a directive." To mitigate the risk, Baker explains that, "You have to leave the room at times. Say, 'Why don't you all talk about this for a little bit?' If I'm there, I might stifle the conversation, or they may not want to say anything bad about what they think is my idea."

Combining dialogue and data in decision-making is straightforward in concept, but, too often, is far from a panacea in practice. Why? Without the right balance, swift decision-making can be hindered and action can grind to a halt. Teams can quickly descend into analysis paralysis: the perpetual desire to see more and more data before a decision is made. Another potential affliction: what might be called a "consensus coma" in which there are seemingly endless rounds of group meetings, allowing for everyone, even those not qualified to do so, to weigh in.

To avoid this outcome, Intuit's Brad Smith used a clever technique. "We also used a tool called DACI for decision-making: 'D' is the driver, 'A' is the approver/accountability, 'C' is the contributor, and 'I' is everyone who should be informed." In his model, every discrete decision had only one driver (the person who writes the six-page memo). There could be no more than two approvers. There could be no more than five contributors prior to the decision, so experts had to be picked wisely. And everybody involved was owed an answer, as well as anyone involved in the execution of the decision. As Smith shares, "The approver is responsible for articulating up front the principles they're using to make the decision. For example, this is going to be a cost decision, or a quality decision. The approver also picks the date the decision would be made, even if all the data is not available."

Smith's comment on the timing of a decision is vital. Lockheed Martin's Marillyn Hewson explains why: "For the big decisions you have to make, you're never going to have all of the information or consensus you want. If you get hung up waiting for more data, you may lose the opportunity. You trust in your team and the experience they have, and you pull the trigger and make decisions." ICICI's KV Kamath went so far as to create a "90-day rule" that said, "if we do anything, we do it in 90 days or less, or we don't do it at all."

Discipline is a must to get the most out of team meetings. At DBS, Piyush Gupta created a mechanism called MOJO to ensure meetings were productive. The "MO" stands for the Meeting Owner who makes sure the objectives of the meeting are clear, the right attendees and information are present, and that the discussion is well organized and led. The "JO" is the Joyful Observer, whose role is to critique the meeting. According to Gupta, "the fact you have someone sitting there empowered to say, 'Hey, this is how the meeting is going, this worked, this didn't work, this isn't getting to the point' made a massive difference."

DBS also created a simple tool to enable every meeting to be evaluated afterward by the participants, the results of which are shared with the meeting owner, a technique common in organizations led by the best CEOs. Brad Smith describes the mechanism used at Intuit to guarantee time was being well spent: "We had participants indicate on a zero-to-ten scale whether they'd recommend a meeting to a colleague. Was it valuable? After diagnosing the low-scoring ones, we sometimes fixed them but mostly decided that they weren't necessary."

Invest in Team Building

Courage is often required to pursue team building in the face of the inevitable naysayers. As GM's Mary Barra concedes, "When we started to explicitly focus on building a high-performing leadership team, people were saying, 'Mary's making us do therapy.' I'd say, 'No, I'm not, I'm just investing in your leadership and in this team.'" In the end, however, it's worth it. As Barra, who applied at GM all the team-building approaches discussed in this chapter, puts it: "To a person today if you asked, 'What is one of the reasons why we've been able to drive success?' they'd say it's because of our high-performance teamwork."

Virtually every CEO we spoke to reported similar experiences with team building. When Westpac's Gail Kelly decided to bring her team together for their first two-day off-site, many eyes rolled when she announced that they'd have a facilitator work with the group on "team dynamics." Kelly would have none of it, however, as she knew what was needed. "There were sessions where people got to speak about what made them tick, what made them anxious. I did it, too," she recalls. "I'm prepared to be very vulnerable, and asked others to do the same. We developed a little book called *The Story of Us*, and each one of us had a page about what strengths we had, and what things we are working on. What's our personal vision? Not just the vision for the company, but what's your own vision? What really drives you as an individual? It really helped build trust."

Kelly describes how the off-site kicked off a journey that continuously improved teamwork: "With every new person who came on board later, we had them do *The Story of Us*. At the same time, I started to do 360-degree reviews with my top team, and I included myself. We'd sit in a big circle, literally, and talk about our feedback. It required a lot of trust, and a lot of mental preparedness to be vulnerable and open. I also got our general managers, the people below us, the very senior and respected executives, to come and tell us as a team what we needed to do better. And we said to them, 'Right, we've got some improvements to make, here's what we're going to do to be better.' It really worked for us."

Her experience may feel "soft" to those who haven't built their teams using such techniques, but Kelly's not alone. Virtually all of the best CEOs carve out team time to specifically reflect on how to improve the ways in which they'll all work together. Over the past decade, we've asked more than five thousand executives to think about their "peak experience" as a team member and to write down the word or words that describe that environment. The results are remarkably consistent and reveal three key dimensions of great teamwork. The first is alignment on direction—a shared belief about what the company is striving toward and the role of the team in getting there. The second is high-quality interaction, characterized by trust, open communication, and a willingness to embrace conflict. The third is a strong sense of renewal, meaning an environment in which team members become energized because they feel they can take risks, innovate, learn from outside ideas, and achieve something that matters—often against the odds. Research shows that for every 20 percent improvement on these dimensions, team productivity on average doubles.[48]

Many teams benefit, as Gail Kelly's did at Westpac, from having an executive coach or some other impartial facilitator lead discussions related to three dimensions of team performance. Piyush Gupta shares his experience at DBS: "We had the Authentic Leadership Institute come and spend a couple days with us doing Organizational Behavior kind of work. It was cathartic. We all looked deep into ourselves and said, 'What are we about? And what's our purpose? And what makes us tick? And how do we align the company?'" The two days was only the start, as Gupta explains, "We've now done more work like that, where we help each other be better and become better as a team."

Facilitators can also trigger more extreme forms of reflection within the team. As U.S. Bancorp's Richard Davis describes: "An outside facilitator did a very interesting exercise which was, 'I want all of you to rank all twelve members, including yourself, in terms of who you trust the most. Then draw a line above anybody's name who you think falls below the level of trust you would wish to have.' I promised that if anybody in the team came up on the low end, I would share that with them, so that the goal would be not to call out a shortcoming but to indicate to them that I'm going to operate a trust-based team."

Not all team building efforts happen in off-sites. Many CEOs have a "team coach" who periodically joins staff meetings to observe how teams are interacting and provides feedback in real time, often against the backdrop of helping each other better understand the causes of unintended conflict that can emerge in group settings. Cadence's Lip-Bu Tan explains the approach he found to be helpful: "I had a coach help our team. We took the Myers-Briggs personality test, which enabled us to get to know each other a lot better. Who are the more introverted ones? Who is more focused on decision-making? All in all, it's worthwhile to get to know your colleagues and even yourself in this manner."

We don't want to imply that every experience with facilitators or team coaches is a good one. As Ecolab's Doug Baker relays: "A couple years into the job we had another group come in, and I was skeptical about their approach, which was getting people to tell each other what irritated them about one another. I thought, *this is not going to go well.* Sure enough, it did not go well." Despite the bad experience, Baker did what the best CEOs do and resolutely kept investing in teamwork by subsequently bringing in other consultants to help his people continuously improve.

As we've seen, the best CEOs combine a series of facilitated off-sites, team and individual coaching, and reflective exercises to improve teamwork. As teams become higher performing, taking time to reflect on working norms becomes a habit. After making a major decision, for example, many of the best CEOs will carve out an extra thirty minutes with their team to reflect on their decision-making. For example, did team members feel in synch from the outset regarding what they were trying to achieve? Did they feel excited about the conclusions once reached? If not, why? Did they feel as if they'd brought out the best in one another? The answers to such questions provide a postmortem opportunity for the team to learn together, and often trust deepens regardless of the answers.

Simple measures such as spending social time together can also improve team dynamics. "That was very important for our bonding as an executive team," says Cadence's Lip-Bu Tan. "We got to know what made each other tick, know about each other's families, and we were able to better care for each other as a result." DBS's Piyush Gupta agrees, capturing the thought playfully: "I'm a big believer in off-sites and parties. I'd much rather spend money on those things than give cash bonuses because I think the value you get from getting people together and the memories and sense of camaraderie you create is a lot more important."

A common analogy is that managers are thermometers, and leaders are thermostats. Managers react to their environment, deal with the here and now, and measure and report results. Leaders influence their environment. They alter people's beliefs and expectations. They cause action, they don't just measure it. They are continually working toward a goal. When it comes to teamwork, the best CEOs are without question thermostats.

To promote ever-increasing levels of teamwork, the best CEOs tend to four areas that most managers leave to others. First, they ensure that their team's time is focused on the work that only it can do together. Second, they're serious about the top team being every team member's first team. Next, in top-level decision-making they stay in the triangle formed by data, dialogue, and speed. Finally, they invest regularly in team building, often using a facilitator or team coach to enable more rapid progress.

CHAPTER 9

Operating Rhythm Practice

Get into a Groove

The best way to learn is through the powerful force of rhythm.

—Wolfgang Amadeus Mozart

The Tour de France is one of the world's most grueling sporting events. Over three summer weeks, about twenty teams with eight riders each push themselves to the limit, pedaling through two thousand miles of terrain including the breath-stealing hills of the French Alps. What wins the race, however, has as much to do with what happens leading up to the race as during those arduous climbs in the mountains.

Preparations start only a few months after the riders cross the finish line on Avenue des Champs-Élysées, once the remaining races on the annual pro-cycling world tour have been completed. The riders and their coaches know that over their long training season there'll be a strict rhythm to the way the team works out for the upcoming race. First the coaches make an outline of how they want to set up training for the season, and then the process starts with a low-intensity focus on aerobic activity. Later on in October or November when the route is announced, they fine-tune the selection of the team members and their plans. Five months out, the intensity and tempo ramp up. Three months out, they shift to race-specific training, and then the week before the competition, they taper down, riding only an hour or so a day or even taking a day off. The entire process is mapped out, race-by-race, for each rider based on their role, responsibilities, and capabilities—all specifically designed to maximize their performance when it matters.[49]

In the corporate world, coming out on top similarly requires organizing the year to ensure the right work gets done, at the right time, by the right people. While some would argue that matters of process can be handled by others outside of the C-suite, the best CEOs proactively shape the operating rhythm of their team to drive the company's strategy forward. Once that sequence and cadence are determined, they then keep it disciplined, even when the ride is grueling.

When a CEO creates a clear and effective operating rhythm, every member of the top team can synch the rhythm of their specific area with that of the company as a whole. Galderma's Flemming Ørnskov explains, "When people know there's an organizational rhythm, it allows them to be more efficient. They know where in the organization to go to get decisions—and which body makes which decisions." It's also what enables the CEO to keep all of the various plates spinning. "Creating the right operating structure for my team that is intense and focused enables me both to best leverage the great people that work for me and ensure I have the right amount of time outside of meetings to think, meet with customers or other stakeholders, take time off, exercise, etc." In short, he adds, "It means we don't spend time in meetings that aren't relevant."

Ørnskov and his team at Shire grew the company from a $5 billion business in 2013 into one of biopharma's most prominent rare disease players with $15 billion in revenue in just five years. He improved the company's margin from 36 to 44 percent and then sold the company to Takeda for an impressive $62 billion. After the sale of Shire, Ørnskov took the CEO role in Nestlé's $10 billion skin care spin-out, Galderma. On arriving at his new company in 2019, Ørnskov found an operating rhythm that was "not coordinated, not clear on its processes, and not quite sure of prioritization," he says. One of Ørnskov's early orders of business was to tailor the company's operating model to a new strategy.

To put in place a new model at Galderma, Ørnskov asked himself,

"Where do I need to be involved, and what are the decision-making bodies I need to create?" Since the strategy had performance, platform, and growth elements, he established a committee for each. "I have what I call an In-line Committee," he shares, "which is where one day a month I discuss performance with all the relevant P&L owners." He also put together a monthly innovation committee to focus on future growth drivers. "I call that Pipeline," says Ørnskov. A third body, the Corporate Committee, also meets monthly: "I get together with the corporate staff and we discuss capital allocation and investment as well as people-related and operational issues, always focusing on creating a lean and efficient company platform."

Once the committees have all met, Ørnskov gets his full team together to keep everyone on the same page. "It structures my month very clearly," he reports. "I have three days I need to focus on these things. Then when I've been through that, I have a half day with the executive committee where we gather, summarize, and implement the things covered on the other three days." The result, according to Ørnskov, is that, "The decision-making bodies are crystal clear for all issues, whether performance, platform, or growth-related. Once you get that rhythm and predictability into the organization things can move quickly."

Not every CEO does what Ørnskov does, but all of the best have just as clearly defined operating rhythms that are purpose-built for their organization. Associated with these are four clear roles and responsibilities . . .

> . . . setting the template and tempo for how the organization is run
> . . . connecting the dots between various decision-making bodies
> . . . acting like an orchestra conductor
> . . . demanding disciplined execution

Set the Template and Tempo

Larry Culp, who has been a "CEO of CEOs" at both Danaher and GE and who himself has been the CEO of a business unit, knows that those reporting to him want great freedom. "I've seen a lot of my peers who end up running portfolios," he says, "giving their business unit CEOs a lot of room because that's what they always wanted when they were in the role. Then someone surprises them, and not in a good way, and they start to think differently." For Culp, as for the best company CEOs, the key is to have a regular rhythm of reviews covering organizational, operational, and strategic issues.

Although every company's operating rhythm is unique, there are many commonalities among those used by the most successful CEOs. For example, there's usually a check-in with the senior team as a group, typically weekly. JPMC's Jamie Dimon explains how he uses his Monday morning meeting with his management team, which forms the foundation of his operating rhythm. "In that meeting, there's no agenda because it's my team's responsibility to bring their issues to the table. Everything's got to be on the table. It could be a client issue; it could be someone wants permission to do something; it could be they want a bunch of people to interview someone for a job; it could be a risk issue. If you work for me, you can't say, 'Well, you didn't bring it up.' I walk in with my list every Monday and I expect others to have theirs."

At Dupont (and Tyco and GI before that), Ed Breen holds a similar hour-long Monday morning staff meeting to ensure the team is on the same page. To get the most out of it, Breen uses a red flag (challenges)/green flag (things to celebrate) system. "It's a very quick around-the-horn sharing of what your red flags and your green flags are. The only time I'll ever get upset with you is if you're not telling me the red flags. If there's something we need to hear: It's not going well, you're not going to meet your forecast, you have a legal issue, or there's a factory you're concerned about—whatever it is, we need to hear it. Usually someone on the team can help."

It may seem odd to some that the best CEOs hold weekly meetings based primarily on an "around the horn" update regarding what's working and what's not. Such a check-in, however, plays a vital role, and sometimes can be even a matter of life or death. When GM's Mary Barra took over as CEO, one of her early orders of business was to look into the ignition switch recalls that were implicated in a number of fatal crashes. (We'll discuss this event and how it was handled in more depth later in the book.) Reflecting on the crisis, Barra shares, "The big learning I had from the ignition switch issue was that, had we understood the situation when we first had symptoms, it would have been a much smaller problem. By the time we were done with it, it was a multi-billon-dollar problem with a tragic outcome for some of our customers." As a result, Barra says, "I ask my team, 'When is the best time to solve a problem?' I always say, 'The minute you know you have one.' Problems don't get smaller on their own."

Beyond the weekly meeting, most great CEOs conduct a more formal monthly senior team meeting. At Valeo, for example, Jacques Aschenbroich brings his team together for four or five hours. The agenda reviews progress against strategic, operational, and organizational issues, as well as trends in the external environment. At Lockheed Martin, such meetings were a full day. "I brought everybody in, and we generally would have a dinner, so there was team-building time together as well," Marillyn Hewson shares. "The primary focus was on the strategy of the business, but the topics would vary based on what we needed to address— M&A targets, cross-functional initiatives, diversity and inclusion, or taking cost out, driving margin improvement . . . it was about the top-of-house kinds of things."

For many CEOs, Hewson's format of having a day-long session and a dinner together is reserved for quarterly meetings which are, in the words of JPMC's Jamie Dimon, typically reserved for "big issues that don't tend to change monthly—like cybersecurity." In advance of such intense sessions, it's common for relevant subgroups to roll up their sleeves regarding specific topics so that they can be covered more quickly in the larger group.

The last aspect of the annual operating rhythm is a multiday off-site for the top team. Every July, for example, Dimon holds a four-day strategy off-site for the JPMC top team where he asks, "What are the most important questions facing the company?" The topics range from business expansion plans to technology strategies to HR policies to leadership training. They also discuss whether the operating rhythm is serving the company well. "What do we think is a waste of time, what is not; we really lay it all out on the table," says Dimon. In the end, he points out, "It's a big deal for us; a whole bunch of to-dos come out of it that we then follow up on in the other meetings during the year."

At most high-performing companies, the CEO and senior team host a broader group of often hundreds of executives for a two- or three-day senior leadership conference. Ken Chenault, former CEO of American Express, brought together a group of two hundred leaders annually. At these sessions he articulated what he referred to as the "headlines" he'd like to read about the company in twelve months' time, in the context of the company's multiyear objectives. "Part of what you want to do is manage constructive tension between the short term and the long term and be clear on the trade-offs that need to be made," he says. Chenault also always brought in outside speakers to give leaders a perspective on the marketplace, world affairs, and customer views. As he puts it, "I wanted to bring in a lot of different points of view so people could gauge how we were doing, where we stood from a competitive standpoint, and what we did and didn't do well."

Most operating rhythms also include meetings between the CEO and individual business units and functions. They occur quarterly, at minimum, the purpose being to review performance against plans. Ajay Banga describes how these sessions work at Mastercard: "I do quarterly operating reviews with every business. My operating rhythm is that if you're not performing, it will be a longer operating review, we'll dig into what's going on. If you're growing market share and growing on the priorities we agreed to in the KPIs [Key Performance Indicators], it'll be a very short review. Most people don't want a long operating review with me." GE's Larry Culp shares an experience where he knew he was getting the tone right in regular business reviews: "I was on the way to the airport with the leader of the business," says Culp, "and he said to me 'I really feel you're invested in our success. You want to help. And it's our role to get the full benefit of your experience and perspectives.'" Culp earned that feeling from his business leaders over time by engaging consistently and substantively, and not playing "gotcha."

Quarterly business reviews aren't the only time that CEOs will meet with their top team members. Regularly scheduled one-on-one meetings are also part of the mix. For some CEOs these take place weekly, others every fortnight, and still others monthly. Time spent with each team member depends on how well they're performing and how much the CEO can help. As TIAA's Roger Ferguson observes, "The CEO is a bit of a player/coach. I have an obligation to put myself in the play where I have some comparative advantage based on my background, skill set, or network, but I don't try and play in other places." In those areas, he says, "I coached and held people accountable, but I'd be less involved and trust I'd hired the right people."

Westpac's Gail Kelly describes her overall takeaway with respect to setting a tempo: "It's very important early on for a new CEO to dive into getting various pieces of the organization to sync. Don't just leave it to chance." It sounds sensible, but should a CEO really play a hands-on role in determining the weekly, monthly, quarterly, and annual meetings with individuals, committees, the team as a whole, and the top two hundred? Kelly's view is strongly affirmative. "You have to get into that level of detail, you can't just hope it happens—it won't," she says. "You have to ensure the charters are right for each forum and be clear where the decision-making lies. The effectiveness of the strategy depends on these things being clear and aligned." Itaú Unibanco's Roberto Setúbal adds that doing so isn't a one-time event early in a CEO's tenure. "As we grew, I started creating more processes to better organize the way decisions were made so that actions were driven in a way that felt natural," he shares. "Importantly, all this process must evolve with the times." Said another way, it's important to not let a groove become a rut.

Connect the Dots

Once the tempo is set, the CEO must bear down to ensure not only that the operating rhythm works, but that the management processes are effective. First and foremost is playing the role of chief dot-connector. As Ecolab's Doug Baker puts it, "You sit in this job, and you have the broadest view of what's going on in the company. You need to make sure that your leadership team has that view, too. It's like being in the crow's nest. You can just see farther because you're higher up, so it's important to make sure everyone has the advantage of that perspective."

What kind of things *don't* other people see? Some common examples are how finance can push executives to agree to both "base" and "stretch" targets in the budgeting process; meanwhile at year's end HR treats meeting the stretch target as the basis for compensation. Once this happens, executives learn to consistently "sandbag" their targets—setting expectations low so that they're sure to exceed anticipated results. Another common disconnect is between well-intentioned product development managers who obtain fast-track funding from finance to take advantage of time-sensitive market opportunities, only to have the technology group force the project to sit in a long queue, while the requests from risk managers for documentation slow things down even further. The criteria for promotions from one level to the next can also create challenges when they disproportionately reward delivery of short-term results versus execution of sustainable long-term strategies.

If the CEO is not making the gears mesh together, dysfunctions quickly become hardwired. "One of the things we've paid close attention to," says Majid Al Futtaim's Alain Bejjani, "is that our people management processes are congruent with our financial management processes. This includes resource allocation, budgeting, mapping talent to value, and so on. When we talk about succession planning, are we considering the budgeting and resourcing implications? When we look at business cases, are we considering the human capital component as well? Consistent and sustained excellence cannot be achieved if it's only happenstance that sees the right teams connecting at the right time."

Gil Shwed cofounded the information technology security company Check Point Software Technologies in 1993 and took it public in 1996. By 2020, it was selling its products in eighty-eight countries and had a market capitalization of $18.8 billion. One of the company's core products for over twenty-five years has provided employees with secure remote access to corporate servers. Shwed shares how he had to be the chief dot-connector when Check Point recently acquired another company whose product gives employees remote access to a corporation's systems using newly developed cloud technology.

"Our internal discussions about the new company were initially about marketing," he shared. "How do we sell the product? What do we name it? What does the website look like?" After a few meetings focused on those types of questions, Shwed moved into dot-connecting mode. He relays the rest of the story: "'Everything you presented is right,' I told the team working on the integration, 'from the price to the validation against the competition. But how does this new product work with the product we already have? You can't tell a customer, 'I have product "A" that's doing remote access, and I have product "B" that's also doing remote access. You choose.'" The leaders in the room hadn't ever thought about that vital question. They then took a step back and rethought how to unify the message, product, and technology. Shwed's intervention reflected what he sees as one of his important learnings as his company grew: "When you have a big company, everybody thinks about their own corner. My job is to think how these things fit into a bigger picture, how all the pieces of the puzzle fit together."

Fair warning, however, that being the dot-connector isn't glamorous. As Microsoft's Satya Nadella reflects, "People say the job is lonely. I realized that it's an information asymmetry problem. Nobody who works for you sees what you see. And nobody you work for sees what you see. That's the fundamental problem of a CEO, which is you see it all, and nobody else around you sees it, so you can get very frustrated." Even so, remaining calm and keeping your antennae up are vital. Cincinnati Children's Michael Fisher brings it home: "The CEO role is one of the few places where processes come together for the benefit of the whole institution. I don't have the granular knowledge in each area to get too much in the weeds, but as the CEO I try to make sure I understand the key assumptions, that the right people are involved, and that the downstream effects are considered before a decision is made. It's important those decisions not be made independently."

Conduct the Orchestra

Along with connecting dots, the best CEOs also play the role of an orchestra conductor amid the day-to-day operating rhythm of the company. U.S. Bancorp's Richard Davis explains the metaphor: "You go to a classical concert," he says, "and if you arrive early, the orchestra is warming up. And it's a very unpleasant noise because they're all doing their own flourishes. Suddenly, they stop. And then out of stage right comes a human being holding nothing more than a stick who then stands and takes a bow for nothing they've done. Yet he or she puts his stick in the air, and beautiful music follows. At the end, the first applause is directed at the conductor who then acknowledges the performers. Not one time did the conductor actually play an instrument, but he or she earned respect from the orchestra for knowing when to have different instruments come in and play louder or softer.

"A good CEO," continues Davis, "will sit back and be the conductor and enjoy the music themselves and not get so caught up in how they look or whether it's going well, but just love it. Like a conductor, I would find myself in any part of the day trying to find places where I could literally step back and be proud of the decisions that were made in that meeting or humbled that I could create this. And the less I talked, the more I felt like I'd done something well. And then, on occasion, I'd find we were so far off-base that I'd make it more of a teaching moment."

Similarly, Alphabet's Sundar Pichai describes good leadership as often "getting out of the way if things are working well, thanking people for doing a good job, and actually not leaving your footprint at all." Netflix's Reed Hastings shares his view of the orchestrator role: "You need to build the decision-making muscles throughout the organization, so that the leader makes fewer decisions. I've said before, 'A perfect quarter for me would be one where I've made no decisions.' I haven't yet had that. Every quarter, I've had to make some decisions, but that's the goal. My approach has always been building muscle, trying to teach principles, so that I can do less. Not because I don't like it, but because the impact is longer lasting."

The importance of the kind of muscle building Hastings refers to isn't always obvious until the end of one's CEO tenure—as LEGO's Jørgen Vig Knudstorp learned. "When I stepped down initially, the company fell apart a bit," he confesses. "I was fortunate to find an outsider who, relatively quickly, came in not as my immediate successor, but the number two after me. What people have shared with me is that I was so involved with everything that, the moment I left, it became clear that there were a lot of things I'd been doing to keep the company together that no one had noticed. So when you pulled me out of the equation, the company collapsed a bit. That's not best in class!"

Ultimately, the way a CEO conducts should evolve with each phase the business is in. "During the turnaround phase of the company," says Best Buy's Hubert Joly, "the CEO needs to be quite heavy-handed in orchestrating. That doesn't mean the CEO does everything. My role was to orchestrate the process, and I was making a lot of the decisions. In the next phase we didn't abandon discipline, but I did push decision-making down so we could take risks and unleash our potential. We encouraged this by distributing 'Get out of jail free' cards to all the officers at Best Buy. It was a way of saying that if you fail for the right reasons, it's okay. You can use one of these cards."

Demand Disciplined Execution

The best conductors listen closely to every note from every instrument, and if anything is out of time or out of tune, they act on it. Doing the equivalent as a CEO requires that a disciplined approach be taken to the meetings that determine the operating rhythm. As GE's Larry Culp puts it, "Even people with general manager or business unit CEO titles often have been trained to talk about the financial numbers as opposed to really understanding operationally how you actually deliver those numbers and the organizational piece that enables you to do so. That's a lot of what you're doing in an operating review, teaching them how to manage and lead as opposed to report."

For the best CEOs, a disciplined approach starts with having the right information beyond the high-level financials. JPMC's Jamie Dimon explains, "There are commonalities to good leaders. It starts with a very basic thing, which is the discipline of analytics. I see people who just don't do the basics right, who don't understand the details on pricing, products, distribution, variable cost, and fixed cost. It's like flying an airplane without all the equipment. The first job is to look at the facts. Circulate one set of numbers. And it's not just financials. I have to remind people, 'They're not just financial reviews, they're business reviews.' "

Dimon continues, "No matter the issue, I'm going to expect that you will have already looked at our peers: what Goldman Sachs does, what Morgan Stanley does, and what Bank of America does. I shouldn't have to ask whether you've looked at what our peers are doing, what the best practices are, and anything like that. A lot of companies don't do this, and they really don't know what their competitors are doing. They're just guessing. We do a real deep dive." Ahold Delhaize's Dick Boer reinforces the point: "I quickly realized during my tenure that we didn't have the granularity of information we needed for decision-making. There was a lot of information in the business, but we were seeing only aggregated numbers." Boer and his team came to the conclusion that, "If we don't have the right data, we'll never have the opportunity to tackle the real performance issues."

The best CEOs ensure that granular data is comparable across the organization's various units. As Caterpillar's Jim Owens relates: "We had a lot of cowboy types in our leadership at the plants. Each plant did things a little differently, and manufacturing had an engrained culture. So, we challenged the traditional way of thinking by introducing a global, Toyota-type production system with common metrics, process tools, and management systems. We customized it as the Caterpillar Production System. Under our new protocol, everyone needed to complete, measure, and report tasks in a specific way."

Beyond ensuring the right information is available, the best CEOs also demand discipline in how meetings are conducted. JPMC's Jamie Dimon explains, "Very rarely do I allow a presentation. It's all pre-reads and recommendations. We prepare in advance so that we're using meeting time to make decisions." Another key aspect of a disciplined approach is setting expectations for attendance. DuPont's Ed Breen put it succinctly: "Unless you're in the hospital or something, you're there." Westpac's Gail Kelly explains how it's not just physical presence that's demanded, but mental and emotional as well: "Those were meetings that you couldn't cancel, nor send a delegate. You had to be there in person and you had to be prepared," she says. "I didn't let anyone look at their mobile phones or go in and out of meetings. We pushed ourselves to talk about difficult subjects in those meetings and that meant everyone had to be engaged. We literally had a toy elephant sitting on a side table—the elephant in the room. Whenever there was tension, we'd put the elephant in the middle of the conference table and say, 'All right, there's an elephant in the room. Let's talk about the elephant in the room.'"

Discipline also applies to the CEO themselves. As Dimon explains, "I always read the reports, so I'm completely engaged. I read a tremendous amount over the weekends and I make a list of questions. 'Why are we losing money in a certain area? How come we spoke about adding 500 bankers and we've only added 100? Why is our attrition fifteen percent and not eight percent? I'm usually a little frustrated—why didn't someone ask this question before I did?" To mitigate the risk that his questions create a flurry of unhelpful analysis after a meeting, Dimon adds, "I tell everyone they're not allowed to do an exercise just for me. They should do this analysis to run their business. If you think my question is a complete waste of time, you are required to tell me that, too."

While in an ideal world the CEO can spend their time conducting the orchestra versus playing an instrument, the real world dictates that there are times a CEO needs to roll up their sleeves and get involved more deeply. We've previously alluded to this in talking about Ajay Banga's quarterly reviews at Mastercard and Roger Ferguson's "player/coach" thinking at TIAA-CREF. GM's Mary Barra explains how she thinks about where to go deep: "In areas that are running well with great leaders who understand the vision, they're going to get a lot of independence. In areas that we're transforming, I'm more involved. I'm making sure the organization moves with them and works to remove roadblocks."

For Kasper Rørsted at Adidas, the approach is similar. "Where things are going well, I'm not really interested in interfering. In those areas the conversation is about where we're going, whether we're hitting milestones, and strategic implications," he says. "But where things aren't going well, then I have very operational-related reviews with the relevant people where we dig down where the

problems are. We'll figure out a plan and I'll hold them accountable to deliver on it."

Going deep into troubled areas is yet another example of the discipline the best CEOs have. Galderma's Flemming Ørnskov drives
home the point as it relates to a company's operating rhythm: "I
really prepare for meetings, and make sure the agenda is tight and
focused. I read the pre-reads, I think about it, I start and finish
meetings on time. All meetings start and end with a recap of action
items and follow-ups. And I think that discipline is something people observe. I also have the discipline to say no to a lot of things
that shareholders aren't paying me to do; I don't run to meetings,
internal or external, that are irrelevant. I don't measure success
by the number of keynote speeches made at industry gatherings."

Some 2,500 years ago, Chinese military strategist Sun Tzu wrote
in *The Art of War*, "Strategy without tactics is the slowest route
to victory. Tactics without strategy is the noise before defeat."[50] A
well-designed operating rhythm connects strategy and tactics in a
synchronous way that allows the company to execute efficiently
and the CEO to know what's happening and to get involved where
it matters most.

Getting it right isn't easy, however, as JPMC's Jamie Dimon
reinforces: "Most companies don't execute well. This is about
execution and getting disciplined, like it's exercise. It's about getting to the specifics, looking at the right measures and making the
right decisions." In keeping with Dimon's observation, the best
CEOs put their companies in a groove by setting the template
and tempo for how the organization is run, connecting the dots
between decision-making bodies, playing an orchestrating role,
and demanding disciplined execution of the strategy.

•   •   •

As we've seen, the best CEOs place heavy emphasis on solving for the team's psychology and let the mechanics of coordination and execution follow. Below is a summary of how doing so translates into three main dimensions of mobilizing the leadership team—composition, effectiveness, and operating rhythm. As we shared at the beginning of this section, the rewards are tangible: With the right mindset and applying the related practices at this level, a company is twice as likely to achieve above-median financial performance.

Mobilizing through Leaders: What separates the best from the rest

Mindset: Solve for the Team's Psychology	
Team composition practice:	**Create an Ecosystem**
	⬢ Staff for aptitude and attitude
	⬢ Act fast but fair
	⬢ Stay connected while keeping distance
	⬢ Build a coalition beyond the team
Teamwork practice:	**Make the Team the Star**
	⬢ Do work only the team can do
	⬢ Define "first team" norms
	⬢ Combine data, dialogue, and speed
	⬢ Invest in team building
Operating rhythm practice:	**Get into a Groove**
	⬢ Set the template and tempo
	⬢ Connect the dots
	⬢ Conduct the orchestra
	⬢ Demand disciplined execution

Even if you're not a CEO, solving for the psychology of your team is a clear pathway to great performance. Ask yourself: Does every one of my team members have the right aptitude and attitude? If not, are you courageously acting fast but fair to remediate the situation? If an outsider came in, would they keep this team—and if not, does it mean you've grown too close? Does the team do only the work that it can do when it meets, or is team time spent on low-priority things that could be done outside the room? Is your team the "first team" for all who are on it? (And if not, why not?) Are discussions characterized by both data and dialogue, and do decisions get made in a timely manner? Are you investing methodically in team building? Have you created an efficient and effective annual operating rhythm of meetings? Do you connect dots for people, orchestrate the right interactions, and roll up your sleeves as needed to ensure progress is being made in priority areas?

The mindsets we've covered thus far related to direction-setting, aligning the organization, and mobilizing leaders are all in areas many leaders are familiar with, even if they're not the chief executive. We now turn to, as GE's Larry Culp put it, "those relationships that are unique to the CEO role that can make or break you"—the interactions with the board and the many external stakeholders who need to be managed.

BOARD ENGAGEMENT MINDSET

Help Directors Help the Business

Be strong enough to stand alone, smart enough to know when you need help, and brave enough to ask for it.

—Ziad K. Abdelnour

Engaging with the board is one of the most daunting challenges that CEOs face. Why? Directors are at the pinnacle of governance—the CEO's boss. That said, the board is like no boss an executive has ever had. As Ecolab's Doug Baker explains: "Our synapses are designed for one boss. Our whole career, we have had one boss. And now all of a sudden, you've got thirteen versions of a boss." GE's Larry Culp adds, "Oh, and by the way, they don't come to work every day, like all your other bosses did."

To further complicate matters, it's not the CEO's role to determine who is on their board and how it operates. When Intuit's Brad Smith asked one of his mentors, A. G. Lafley, a former CEO of Procter & Gamble, for advice on how to manage the board, the response was unambiguous: "Young man, first of all, you don't manage the board. They manage you." Even when a CEO also holds the board chair title, as is the case in almost half of the S&P 500, there is almost always a lead independent director appointed who is then responsible for most board matters. In short, the job of the board chair (or lead independent director) is to run the board and the job of the CEO is to run the organization.

Left to their own devices, however, boards rarely add great value to the organizations they govern. Only 30 percent of board members report that they serve on boards whose processes are effective,[51] and nearly half of executives observe that their board's performance falls short.[52] The best CEOs don't tolerate these outcomes. Instead, they eschew the traditional mindset of "my role is to help the board fulfill its fiduciary duties" in favor of a mindset of "my role is to help directors help the business." This isn't to say the former isn't essential, but excellent CEOs also play a proactive role in helping build a board with the right skills, making sure members' time is used to the greatest possible effect, and ensuring the boardroom is open, transparent, and effective. In short, the best CEOs help the board chair run the board so that the directors can help the CEO run the business. As Ecolab's Doug Baker shares, "The board is a great tool to help the business succeed, if you know how to invite them in."

Although board models differ due to ownership structures and a mix of practices in various parts of the world, the ways in which the best CEOs put into practice the "help directors help the business" mindset are fairly common across the three key dimensions of board engagement: relationships, capabilities, and meeting effectiveness.

CHAPTER 10

Board Relationships Practice
Build a Foundation of Trust

Money is the currency of transactions. Trust is the currency of interactions.

—Rachel Botsman

On March 4, 1933, the US economy had, for all intents and purposes, shut down. Thousands of the nation's banks were closed after repeated panics. Roughly a quarter of the labor force was out of work. On this day Franklin D. Roosevelt made his first inaugural address to the American people. "The only thing we have to fear is fear itself," he famously asserted. One speech, however, wasn't enough to convince the populace that they should be confident in him or his plans. Roosevelt subsequently invented his fireside radio chats. On March 12, he opened his first chat with, "My friends, I want to talk for a few minutes with the people of the United States about banking . . ." He was ruthlessly honest in his outlook, sharing openly, "Only a foolish optimist can deny the dark realities of the moment."

The candor of Roosevelt's fireside chats played an important role in building trust between the governed and their governors, which gave him the flexibility to try different remedies for the Great Depression—with the understanding that many might fail. A letter to Roosevelt from Mildred Goldstein from Joliet, Illinois, just after his first fireside chat is revealing: "You are the first president to come into our homes; to make us feel you are working for us; to let us know what you are doing. Until last night, to me, the president of the United States was merely a legend. A picture to look at. A newspaper item. But you are real. I know your voice; what you are trying to do. Give radio credit. But to you goes the greater credit for your courage to use it as you have."[53]

Like Roosevelt, the best CEOs find ways to create trust between themselves and the board (who are surrogates for the company's shareholders). At Mastercard, when Ajay Banga shared his aspiration to refocus on cash instead of electronic payments (the "kill cash" vision we described in chapter 1), "there was pin-drop silence," he recalls. It was a *calculated* risk, however, since going into the meeting he had a sense of what each individual board member's attitude was, having met with them beforehand. "Two very credible board members were strongly in favor about where the company could go and, in me, found a willing partner," Banga shares. "They spoke up and said, 'best idea we've heard in a long time.' That changed the course of the conversation."

Not that it was smooth sailing from there. "We battled for the next couple of years about what was the best way of going after cash. I encouraged the openness. We had very vigorous discussions where some board members would literally stand up and thump the table. And that's fine, that's their job. That evening the same board member, over a drink, would say, 'At least you listen.' " Along the way, Banga made mistakes as well. "I made an acquisition in e-commerce that turned out to be a waste of money." Instead of being a setback to trust, however, it accelerated it. "When that happened," Banga recalls, "I told them what I'd done, what went wrong, and what I'd learned from it. That kept them on my side. They said, 'He's willing to share when he makes an error.' "

After a few years, it became clear Banga was doing a lot more right than wrong. "The year I joined, Mastercard had three percent revenue growth, and Visa was growing at eight percent," he reveals. "For the last five years, we've grown faster than Visa most quarters. That gives you credibility that no board will question." Today he describes his board as, "Very collegial, everybody gets along. There's transparency. There's fairness."

The best CEOs create the same virtuous cycle that Banga created: By building trust early he had the flexibility to make bold moves that improved performance, which, in turn, deepened trust. Beyond reliably doing what they say they'll do, excellent CEOs build and maintain trust with the boards by . . .

. . . choosing radical transparency
. . . building a strong relationship with the board chair
. . . reaching out to individual directors
. . . exposing the board to management

Choose Radical Transparency

Given that boards only meet periodically, it's tempting for CEOs to work around them or keep things "under the radar" when it comes to handling tough issues. A CEO might get wind of a key executive who has pushed the edge of ethical boundaries. That executive might be someone who is hard to replace quickly, and ideally the company would like to remediate the situation and retain the person. The facts might be fuzzy and open to interpretation. So why tell the board? One might imagine similarly complex scenarios involving mergers and acquisitions, regulatory compliance issues, customer complaints, and so on.

"When in doubt, share," advises GE's Larry Culp. Excellent CEOs know that it will cost them to keep the board in the dark in such situations. Consider how the ethics of the example we just cited could play out if the CEO chose not to mention anything to the board, and later it came to light that laws had been broken. The CEO's own ethics would very likely be seen as equally compromised.

Consider how Equity Group's James Mwangi got ahead of a sensitive problem.[54] One day he received a letter signed by six women who said they believed there was sexual harassment in the organization. He knew the only way to give them confidence to come forward was to go public. So he informed the board, and issued a press release saying that he'd received these accusations and that in sixty days he'd tell the general public the results of an investigation. He created a team of six women from middle management to hear the complaints. Within two weeks, sixteen women came forward. Within four weeks, the disciplinary process kicked in, and six people were terminated. "Since we dealt with the issue decisively by terminating the six, that issue has never arisen again," says Mwangi. "We lost a popular manager, who'd been a skilled coach and mentor, but he became the symbol of what Equity should not be."

For the best CEOs, the benefit of such openness isn't just about mitigating the downside, as in our ethics example; it's about creating upside for the business. TIAA's Roger Ferguson shares some of the immediate benefits: "I describe it as radical transparency. The worst that can happen is the board makes judgments I don't agree with. When they share those judgments, we can have a good conversation." Best Buy's Hubert Joly points out that even bad news can give way to constructive input: "With the board, I was completely transparent on good news and bad news. I had this principle that bad news needs to travel as fast, and probably faster, than good news. And so, the minute you're transparent with your board, it makes them comfortable. And then you can ask for their help."

Cincinnati Children's Michael Fisher shares how being open doesn't pay off just in the moment, but also over time. "I share things early. It may be on an investment topic or a challenging situation with someone on the management team. When the issue becomes ripe, and I need to make a decision, I'm never coming at them cold turkey. The board has been brought along the way, and already offered input where necessary." Diageo's Ivan Menezes starts the board's annual off-site with a list of seven or so things that are going well, matched by an equal number that *aren't* going well. "Integrity and courage are important characteristics for a board, because decisions aren't easy," says Menezes. "I keep it real with them and often focus the agenda on what's not going well. That builds trust and helps the board understand and get behind you when you really need it—when the times get tough." Esquel Group's Marjorie Yang confirms the trust-building impact that CEO transparency has in her role serving on other company's boards: "I've been on boards where I've really appreciated the CEO sharing their concerns. As a board member, you buy in a lot more when you know that there's no secret being kept from you."

Practicing radical transparency isn't a burden for the best CEOs, it comes naturally and is a force for good. Cadence's Lip-Bu Tan explains, "My board is comfortable because I always look out for the shareholders. I have confidence in myself and am doing what I believe to be the right things for the company." In that context, he continues, "Creating a transparent culture makes things easier for me. When management wants to push for a decision, it's no surprise for the board. They already know what we're trying to do. The board works with me."

Strengthen the CEO/Board Chair Relationship

Being open doesn't mean overwhelming the board with information but it does mean sharing the news they need to hear, good or bad. The best place to start is with the board chair or lead director. As we've discussed, the chair or lead director runs the board, which means if they're aligned with the CEO, they can shut down red herrings and ensure the real issues are focused on, and at the right level. They also can and should be a mentor and advisor to the CEO on all matters. JPMC's Jamie Dimon gives a window into the dynamic: "My lead director would come down at the end of every meeting with a handwritten note for me, to give me four or five pieces of feedback. 'The board wants this,' or, 'We're a little concerned about that,' or whatever the issue is."

Westpac's Gail Kelly describes how she doesn't leave anything to chance in her relationship with the chair. "The role of the CEO is to make the board members' jobs easier, not more difficult. That starts with forming a great relationship with the chairman," she says. "I can't overemphasize how important it is. I always saw it as *my* job to make sure the relationship's great, not the chairman's job." During her tenure at Westpac, Kelly had two different chairs and tailored her approach accordingly to build a strong relationship with each.

Kelly's first chair, the one who appointed her, spent a lot of time in the office and had few other corporate commitments. This lent itself to frequent informal discussions. "We talked about the financial crisis, or about the government, or other current events," she shares. "He was a very wise head with a breadth of expertise. I found those discussions really valuable in helping shape my thinking, and they also helped create a strong, trusted relationship between us." During the course of the conversations, Kelly also briefed him on what was happening in the business, and helped him shape the board agenda and materials, ensuring they were as crisp and relevant as possible for upcoming discussions.

With her second chair, Kelly tailored her approach differently. He was a professional chairman who sat on many boards and had an extremely busy agenda outside the company. "I was very respectful of his time," Kelly shares. "We got into a pattern of every Friday, regardless of where he or I was, I'd ring him. It wasn't an informal, free-flowing discussion like I had with the previous chairman. I had my agenda of issues we needed to tackle. For example, if I had a meeting with the prime minister I'd debrief him on it. We also had conversations like, 'I'm just a little worried about X, I'm not sure it's going to go well.'" As with her first chair, Kelly established a great relationship with her second chair. "Even though we've both left the bank," she shares, "today, sometimes I'll ring him on a Friday afternoon, and he'll say, 'Oh, Gail, the Friday afternoon meeting.' It's a lovely thing."

Many of the best CEOs use their chair or lead director as a sounding board to sharpen their thinking. Total's Patrick Pouyanné meets regularly with his lead director who came from outside the oil industry. "Her role is very helpful to me," he shares. "She's an external mirror. She's not inside the company but is very good at absorbing information, listening, and problem-solving." When Pouyanné shares his rationale for proposing an acquisition or making a capital investment decision he can test how his argument comes across. "It makes me clarify more, review the analysis more deeply, and find the best words. If I can't do that, it means the decision isn't robust; there's more to clarify. It keeps you honest with yourself." Assa Abloy's former CEO Johan Molin, who went on to become chairman of Swedish engineering company Sandvik, confirms that board chairs welcome such conversations: "Beyond making sure we have the right CEO, my role is only as a sparring partner," he says. "I talk to the present CEO every other week for a few hours. It's conversational, I'm not trying to take over."

To get the chair/CEO relationship right, the best CEOs make the relationship they're looking for explicit. Early in his tenure DSM's Feike Sijbesma discussed with his chair the nature of their relationship: "Please, challenge as well as support me." He continues, "To do that, we realized we needed trust and openness between us. You can't support if you don't trust people, and you can't listen to criticisms if you aren't sure about the real agenda behind it."

As part of creating that mutual trust, Sijbesma and his chair of the supervisory board took time to evaluate meetings, especially the less easy ones. "In the beginning, we needed to get used to this," recalls Sijbesma. "Sometimes after a difficult board meeting, one of us would say 'Let's not reopen that box again. We took care of the issue.' But then we persisted: 'No, let's try to understand what happened.' It helped enormously to create mutual respect and trust. While it sounds simple, that type of openness in a chair/CEO relationship isn't common."

The value of having a strong relationship with the board chair can't be overstated. When David Thodey took over as CEO of the Australian telecom Telstra in 2014, he had a problem on his hands. This formerly government-owned cell and landline operator was the biggest in the country but had a poor reputation for customer service. The first thing Thodey did was present a paper to his board outlining how he wanted to make Telstra the most trusted company not just in Australia but in the world. A number of the directors pushed back against Thodey's customer-driven strategy, thinking it too amorphous. And, for a while at least, it looked like those dissenting directors might be right. Telstra had to issue two profit warnings in Thodey's first six months, and its stock was dropping fast. One board member said to the new CEO: "Well David, if you don't get this right, we're going have to look at options."

To gain time to implement his strategy, Thodey reached out to his lead director and worked hard to win her trust. He met with her on a weekly basis to keep her informed on how the new initiative was doing. "She was very clear about her expectations," recalls Thodey. "She was very firm but also an incredibly capable and caring executive at the same time. She stepped into that gap between the board and myself, and I think acted as an advocate for what I was doing. But she also brought back to me concerns from the board. So there was a very open and honest discussion."

One factor that built trust between Thodey and his chair was that the two were able to agree on which metrics he'd share with her and the board to show progress. "Trust is not about charisma or friendship. Trust is based on delivery," says Thodey. "My job was to come back and say, 'Here are the results—good and bad—and what I'm going to do about it.'" The milestones Thodey used to win over the rest of the board were customer churn in mobile, which he reduced from 18 percent to 9 percent, and the number of times the company had to interact with a customer to install broadband, which dropped from fifteen times to eight. Thanks to those moves and others, Telstra's return on capital rose some 23 percent during his tenure.

Reach Out to Individual Directors

Although the best CEOs spend disproportionate amounts of time with their board chair or lead director, they also invest in building relationships with all of the other board members. "The board's not monolithic," GE's Larry Culp explains. "You have ten or twelve individuals who have their own unique views. You need to manage the individuals, not just the collective."

Those that excel make it their mission to get to know each director personally—understanding their world view, priorities, communications preferences, and what specific talents they bring to the table. They also use time with individuals to shape their thinking, as Ahold Delhaize's Dick Boer explains: "I spent a lot of time with individual board directors so that they felt heard and had a chance to give their opinion. I also shared my vision and started taking them along on the journey of the strategic framework I was building. These open conversations later allowed me to use their input in a constructive way."

Building individual relationships is particularly important early in the tenure of a CEO, as Aon's Greg Case explains: "Spend more time, substantial amounts of time, early on as a new CEO. It's absolutely essential that your board understands you, and you understand them individually. It builds trust and transparency. I wish I'd spent more time early on." Caterpillar's Jim Owens shares the underlying mindset: "I recognized that it wasn't my board. The board was there when I took over. After all, they hired me! But the board was the two previous CEOs'." He continues, "So, for the first six to nine months, I personally met with each board member at their place of business, took time to have dinner, got to know them a little better, and talked about the business in depth."

In unfortunate situations where a former CEO has become the chair and wants to continue controlling the company, building individual relationships becomes make-or-break. Doug Baker at Ecolab learned the hard way. "It took me a while to figure it out," he says. "My predecessor stayed on the board way too long and I felt he undermined me on a few things." Baker had never served on a board before, and his board experience amounted to nothing more than having sat through a few board presentations as a more junior executive. "I finally realized the problem was me," he shares. "I had to start reaching out to other board members instead of just talking to the chairman, who was my predecessor." As Baker sees it, "Getting on top of board dynamics is one of the real challenges for the CEO early on. There's informal power and formal power, and in boards it's the informal power you really have to understand." The informal power Baker is referring to relates to the differing levels of influence wielded by individual board members, alliances between them, and other agendas that may be at play beyond those overtly stated.

Typically, the best CEOs make the rounds of all board members once or twice a year. Dupont's Ed Breen advises, "In between board meetings, schedule work calls to board members so that by the time a half a year goes by, you've talked to every board member one-on-one for half an hour outside of a board meeting. Let them ask any question they want. Some are a little shyer than others. You want them to speak openly with you and help you, and the way you get that is to be open and honest with them." Mary Barra at GM visits every one of her board members on their "home turf" at least once a year: "We have a conversation for at least an hour, generally two. I ask a few questions about the company and the board and how we can do better."

Checking in more than once or twice a year is generally considered too much. As Intuit's Brad Smith puts it, "Directors don't want to be a check-the-box exercise. People are busy." Some directors should be called on more often, however. Smith continues, "Each director comes with a different set of skills and experiences, so use your directors as you need them, and know there's no greater honor for a board member than to be called and asked for help offline." Atlas Copco's Ronnie Leten reinforces this: "Even if you have ten board members, it's impossible to have the same type of relationship with each. Some are sitting on the board because they're financial gurus, others will be very strong in certain segments of the market, and so on. So you'll bounce ideas off certain people more than others depending on your needs."

While interacting with individual board members, the best CEOs always keep a sober perspective on the nature of the relationship. As Galderma's Flemming Ørnskov shares, "They're not your friends. They're there on behalf of shareholders or owners to make sure you're the right person at any given time and that you perform your best." He adds, "Any CEO who thinks there's something casual about a board has misunderstood the situation. I would recommend always being prepared and not throwing around a lot of casual remarks." U.S. Bancorp's Richard Davis puts the advice succinctly: "The board is your boss. You don't make buddies with your boss. Just don't."

Expose the Board to Management

Trust can also be built by ensuring the board has direct access to management. The best CEOs agree with Ecolab's Doug Baker's statement: "I want the board to have a relationship with management." As a result, the executive team typically plays an active role in board meetings. "I do very little of the presentation," says TIAA's Roger Ferguson. "Other executives do a lot of it." This approach isn't without potential downside, however. Other executives are typically not as thick-skinned as the CEO when it comes to board questioning. "My board pushes back a lot," Ferguson shares. "So my role is to help my colleagues understand that it doesn't mean they aren't supportive of our work. It simply means they're doing their job." Another risk is that other executives won't present what's needed as well as the CEO might. To mitigate that, the best CEOs spend real time coaching their people to succeed in front of the board. As Assa Abloy's Johan Molin describes, "I gave advice like: 'This is perhaps too detailed. You can aggregate your material into some bigger themes or takeaway,' and so on, so that they're sharing at the right level."

Given the risks, why don't the best CEOs just run all the board meetings themselves? Because doing so would be a red flag for the board. "One day every two months or every quarter is the board's time to observe you," observes Galderma's Flemming Ørnskov. "This is where they see how you act, including how you act with your colleagues. Who do you bring to the board? Are you promoting a diverse group of people? If someone speaks, are you listening or talking over them? Is it you talking all the time? Is your team talking? Are you positive even when you have areas needing improvement, or are you constantly negative about your team? All these behaviors matter."

There's also additional upside for CEOs in connecting management with the board as it can save significant time and energy. "I was able to hand off a number of board activities to my management team members," reports IDB's Lilach Asher-Topilsky. "We had different committees, for example a risk committee, a strategy committee, a technology committee. So I had my top managers— my CRO [Chief Risk Officer], CFO, and my CIO [Chief Information Officer]—spend time with the relevant board committee chairs and come to the committee meetings. I wanted them to have the same relationship with them that I had with the chairman of the board. After a few months, I didn't have to join any of the committee meetings, they just let me know if they needed me for any specific issues. Most of the time they did it themselves."

Beyond presentations during the board meeting itself, the best CEOs create other opportunities to further expose the board to the company's managers. U.S. Bancorp's Richard Davis shares his method: "We do something that we call a gallery walk. It involves cocktails where the senior leadership team is in the room with a few of their direct reports. The board's role is to move between little groups of three or four, almost as if it's speed dating. In each group the senior leader talks for a few minutes, bragging about their direct reports. Now, as a board member, I not only know the head of compliance, but I also get to meet her top three people. And because we're not watching them make a presentation there's no nervousness or lost time; they're just having a cocktail and talking about themselves."

Another approach is to have management and the board do site visits together, something General Mills' Ken Powell did frequently. "It created the opportunity to learn together and for the board to hold a dinner at an annual conference where each board member sits at a table with ten managers. We don't discuss beforehand what they should say, and I don't control what kind of questions the board members will ask," he explains. Patrick Pouyanné at Total adds a slightly different twist by having board members in groups of three each interview four executives plus one or two future members of the executive committee. "This exercise, which they really enjoyed, was of course partly about making sure they were aligned with the strategy and getting to know our leaders, but it was also about board members getting to know each other. That's why I insisted that the interviews be done in groups of three."

Again and again, we noted that the best CEOs generally give directors broad access to management. As DBS's Piyush Gupta shares, "The board, to me, is a partner, and they can talk to anyone in my management team. I believe the free flow of information is helpful for complete alignment." This access often comes with some caveats, however. On the management front, Intuit's Brad Smith told his leaders, "You can interact with any board member. You don't have to go through me. But be really clear about how they can be helpful and honor the fact that they have full-time gigs outside, even if fully retired." Westpac's Gail Kelly asked her executives to let her or her chief of staff know if something emerged out of any board member engagement that would be important to be aware of. Some CEOs prefer to have board members' advice run through them, though they'll always encourage board members to meet with management to collect impressions.

• • •

The adage "trust arrives on foot and leaves on horseback" applies to all relationships. When it comes to board relationships, the best CEOs find ways to make it arrive on horseback, and never leave. They do so by choosing to be radically transparent with the board on the good, the bad, and the ugly, establishing individual relationships (with a focus on the board chair), and exposing the board to management.

We've now discussed how CEOs establish and maintain a foundation of trust with individual directors. As trust builds, so does a chief executive's ability to help the board add value to the business.

CHAPTER 11

Board Capabilities Practice
Tap the Wisdom of Elders

I can do things you cannot. You can do things I cannot. Together we can do great things.

—Mother Teresa

In the feudal system of the Middle Ages, as much as 75 percent of England's population lived as serfs—experiencing conditions close to slavery. On May 25, 1200, King John (of Robin Hood and Magna Carta fame) "freed" a small group of people living near the North Sea by granting them one of the oldest royal "corporation" charters in England's history. The charter gave the newly freed population of the town of Ipswich the ability to elect its officials. On June 29, the town assembled in the churchyard of St. Mary's Tower and elected the leadership positions decreed by the king: two bailiffs who acted as the executive officers, and four officials representing the king's interests.

What happened next wasn't part of the charter and had little precedent. After completing voting, the townsfolk decided that, as chronicled by the town clerk, "henceforth there should be in the said borough twelve sworn chief portmen" that "have full power, for themselves and for the whole town, to govern and maintain the said borough and all its liberties, to render judgments of the town and also to keep, ordain, and do in the said borough whatever should be done for the well-being and honor of the said town." In doing so, Ipswich had just created the first documented board of directors in England.[55]

While the specific motives of Ipswich's citizens weren't recorded, many historians speculate that it was a combination of not every-one having the right knowledge or judgment to govern a town and the impracticability of having all citizens attend town assemblies—which bears some similarity to the reasons underpinning today's corporate governance structures. Indeed, the example set by Ipswich and other townships significantly influenced the governance models created by early trading companies, which themselves became models on which modern-day corporations are based. The best CEOs, just like the residents of Ipswich, proactively work to ensure their boards collectively have the knowledge and judgment to help their corporations flourish.

Jamie Dimon's experience taking over Bank One in the spring of 2000 is illustrative. The press at the time published accounts of the contentious board meeting that led to Dimon's selection, during which the acting CEO, who was still favored by a number of board members, adamantly opposed Dimon's appointment. Also well-known was the tumultuous infighting between factions at Bank One and those at First Chicago (the two banks had merged two years earlier, which led to Dimon's being called in to take the CEO job).

As Dimon recalls, he was at the time receiving a chorus of advice from family and friends about taking the job. "You shouldn't go there, it's totally messed up," was the refrain, sung against a back-drop that included job offers on the table from Amazon and firms in Silicon Valley. Having taken more than a year off since he'd acrimoniously split with his former employer, Citigroup, Dimon had thought long and hard about what he wanted to do with his life. His heart was in financial services, and Bank One with all of its challenges was a great opportunity to really make a difference.

Dimon had already decided that the company's twenty-two-member board—half from First Chicago and half from the original Bank One—was too big a group to make decisions efficiently. Plus, the members disliked one another and, distracted by the infighting, allowed duplicate processes, redundant software systems, and office politics to fester. Many of the directors didn't believe an outsider could ever understand the concerns of the company or move the culture.[56]

In his first board meeting, Dimon addressed the group: "Just so you know, I'm going to do the right thing for this company. I'm going to tell you the whole truth and nothing but the truth to the best of my ability every time. I'm not going to make many promises, because I can't. I'm just going to tell you what I think, why I think it, and if I'm wrong, I'm going to confess that, too." He continued to describe how he'd run the bank, paused, then stated directly, "But the really important thing to me is, I need your help. I don't care about your previous loyalties to Bank One and First Chicago. You guys have been fighting that merger for years. I never want to hear those two names again. What I want is the right thing for the company going forward, and the right thing for our clients, and that's all we should be thinking about."

Dimon quickly persuaded the board to cut its membership from twenty-two members to fourteen. "We did it through a fair process, looking at criteria that would ensure we had the right diverse experiences and capabilities so we kept those who could contribute the most value going forward. I told the board, 'I can't tell you what to do, but we all know this is the right thing to do.' Their response was, 'Jamie, you're dead right.' " Dimon continued to win the trust of the board as they guided and supported his recommendations, including pushing through tough decisions like increasing loan-loss reserves and slashing the company's dividend, which eventually resulted in Bank One building a "fortress" balance sheet.

By 2004, profitability had soared, and the stock was up 80 percent since Dimon took over. The turnaround paved the way for a landmark $58 billion merger with JPMC, creating the second largest financial services institution at the time, behind Citigroup.

Although Dimon's Bank One experience is an extreme one, all boards need at least some fine-tuning over time. The best CEOs are clear on how much change is needed and they influence shifts by . . .

   . . . explicitly delineating the roles of the board and management
   . . . specifying the desired profile of directors
   . . . educating the group
   . . . encouraging the board to continuously renew itself

Delineate the Roles

Conceptually, there's rarely any disagreement on the role of the board in public companies. A board is an independent governance mechanism representing the owners (in other words the shareholders, most of whom are not directly involved in the company) and hence is accountable to them, not the CEO. The management team on the other hand, led by the CEO, is accountable to the board and responsible for running the company. As Cadence's Lip-Bu Tan describes, "The board has three primary functions: One is succession planning—hire and fire the CEO—and the second is to approve the strategy of the company—where we want to be five or ten years from now. Third is to monitor and manage risks through the audit, governance, and compensation committees."

It sounds straightforward. What all this means in practice, however, is always contentious. CEOs and their teams are often touchy about what they see as interference by directors. Weighty boards with years of experience are used to getting their way and are frequently frustrated because their advice is ignored. Poorly managed, the relationship between the CEO and the board can devolve into a loss of trust and paralyzing ineffectiveness. The best CEOs, however, work with their boards to defuse tensions at the outset. Methods include clearly defining the board's role and establishing well-understood boundaries.

U.S. Bancorp's Richard Davis explains why the latter is vital: "It's critical to understand that the board will operate at the level you bring them to," he says. "If you bring them to the weeds, they will operate in the weeds." Serving on many boards, Davis has seen the movie play out from both sides. "In my years as an outside board member, I've seen a situation where, before every board meeting, the CEO called every director to ask what was on their mind. That's a terrible idea." Instead, he explains, "You should leverage the board where you as CEO think it's most beneficial." Davis therefore advises, "Be clear about the role you want them to play. Start with the lead director or chairman, given that they manage the board, not you. But it's up to you alone to establish what your relationship with the board should be."

The question then is: What role do the best CEOs suggest their board play? American Express's Ken Chenault shares what the role *shouldn't* be: "One of the worst things you can do as a CEO is have a passive board that simply consents to what you want to do and doesn't engage." Like Davis, Chenault has been on both sides of the fence. "I've been in situations on some other boards where it became clear management felt the board, or some members of the board, didn't get it. It's debilitating to an organization when someone gives a very informed presentation and there's really no engagement as a result. Over time that has an impact on the resolve and confidence of management."

As for what the role of the board *should* be, Shiseido's Masahiko Uotani cites a potent analogy (offered by a board member who was a university professor and former lawyer): "He said to me, 'Uotani-san, you have to understand that corporate governance is like the Japanese Shinkansen—the bullet train. We appointed you as CEO. As CEO, you are running this company; you need autonomy; you need empowerment. Obviously, you want to really do what you think is right. You can't go back to the board asking for their approval for small decisions each time, or you're going to lack speed and it's not fun for you as a CEO. You need to go 300 kilometers per hour, very fast. However, the Japanese Shinkansen can be stopped in a minute when it's necessary. So, if we find you doing something completely wrong we're going to stop you in a minute.' "

The best CEOs all describe this same "Shinkansen" idea, albeit each in different ways. As Netflix's Reed Hastings explains, "We don't want the board formulating strategy, because if they're wrong, it's fatal. Because then they're not the judge, right? . . . If it's their strategy, they can't be impartial. You want the board to really understand what the management team's doing, and you want them to be a good judge of the results and to make the changes necessary to hold them accountable." Andrew Wilson at Electronic Arts similarly reveals that the healthy dynamic he and his board have is rooted in a shared understanding of the role. "Boards aren't there to provide direction," says Wilson. "They're there to provide perspective. Given the diversity of backgrounds and opinions of board members, the feedback itself is going to have conflict. Our role as a management team is to take that feedback and use it to make the best decisions we can with the information available. The board's role, once they've provided their perspective, is to support us."

Microsoft's Satya Nadella similarly instructs his board members: "Your job is to pass judgment on my judgment. That's what your job really is. So don't go around thinking you're going to somehow understand everything that we're doing." At Intuit, Brad Smith believed, "the role of the board in corporate strategy is to make sure the company has one, and it's not a bad one. Nose in, hands out. If board members want to start moving around the button on the homepage, that's not the board's role." When onboarding new board members, Best Buy's Hubert Joly made it a point to let them know, "I absolutely want your input, but let's be clear: My job is not to do everything you say." Such agreements are often formalized in an annual discussion between the board and management, and some CEOs even ask for a written letter of understanding setting out the roles of each party.

Beyond defining the relationship between the board and the CEO, the best also set ground rules in areas that are likely to be contentious. Jamie Dimon, for example, has an explicit agreement with the JPMC board when it comes to mergers and acquisitions. "To not get sideways with the board I immediately put a procedure in place about acquisitions," he explains. "CEOs can get fired because they have merger talks and don't inform the board. At the same time, loose lips sink ships, and so I'm clear with the board that if I'm having very preliminary conversations that are the equivalent of getting to know someone, I'm not going to tell them. If it ever gets a little more serious, I'm going to make a phone call to the lead director to let them know where we are in the process. I'll let the lead director decide whether to call a board meeting or not. I'll never surprise them."

Of course, some areas are reserved strictly for the board. As Dimon shares, "Without the CEO in the room, they should talk about succession, about CEO compensation, about how the full board functions. And if and when there's a crisis, they need to make sure the processes are in place to determine whether the CEO has done anything wrong."

Specify the Desired Profile

In some ancient Greek city states, a council of elders was elected by voice vote of the people, with the winners determined by a group of men in a separate building who'd judge which shouts were the loudest without knowing which candidate received each shout.[57] In modern-day governance in most legal systems, the process is less noisy but not dissimilar. The ultimate appointment and removal of directors is voted on by the shareholders. The board or a nominating subcommittee of the board selects candidates for the director's job. Most important for CEOs, the board typically seeks input from management for such nominations. The best CEOs don't wait to be asked—they actively assert what skills and experience are needed to help drive the business forward.

At TIAA, Roger Ferguson shares, "We wanted more digital skills, asset-management skills, retail-advisory skills, and diversity so we made those changes. Today we have someone on the board whom we can turn to who has expertise in almost every one of the things we're trying to do, and that's a very beneficial place to be." Nancy McKinstry transitioned Wolters Kluwer's all-Dutch board to one in which the majority of seats are held by other nationalities. She also brought in tech talent and people with experience as customers of the company's legal, tax, and health care businesses. "The goal was that the board would reflect the company, and to some extent, reflect our customers," she says. Hubert Joly at Best Buy brought on board members with expertise in the strategically important health space. Santander's Ana Botín sought more international representation to reflect the nature of her multinational bank. At the Equity Group, James Mwangi made sure four of his nine directors were women because "they're a major inspiration to young women in the bank of how far they can go." And the list goes on.

One tool to facilitate getting the right directors in place is a board matrix. Intuit's Brad Smith explains, "We adopted some systematic ways to influence the board's makeup, without doing the board's job. One tool is the capability matrix. It lists across the top the skills and domains needed on the board to deliver our strategy of being a platform company in the cloud with design thinking. Down below, it lists every director's name." The tool comes to life, Smith shares, "by having directors self-assess whether they bring that skill or experience in the room. Then we actually draw circles around the gaps to identify the capabilities we need." At GM, "We have a board skills matrix we evaluate every year," Mary Barra describes. "As the company evolves, we adjust the matrix methodically, updating it for the skills we need over the next five years." In addition to the matrix itself, such evaluations also ensure board composition requirements include cultural, gender, race, and geographic considerations.

When Eaton CEO Sandy Cutler was the chair of the corporate governance task force at the Business Roundtable in the early 2000s, he pushed hard for companies to adopt a skills matrix. At the time, a majority of companies in the S&P 500 actually had a minority of independent directors. Cutler affirms that synching up the matrix with the strategic planning process is a positive—that it forces the key question: "In light of the challenges and the opportunities that lie in front of the company what skills do we need on this board? Not backward-looking, but forward-looking."

CEOs without formal boards are often well advised to put together an outside advisory board applying many of the same approaches discussed above. In his role before taking the reins at Cincinnati Children's, Michael Fisher was the CEO of Premier Manufacturing Support Services, a supplier to the global automotive industry (the firm was eventually sold to ServiceMaster). "I put together an outside advisory board of a retired COO, an HR executive, a successful entrepreneur, an accomplished sales and marketing executive, and a labor economist. We couldn't afford to hire those people yet, but we needed their expertise and experience to tap into the potential of the company."

Educate the Group

Getting the right members onto the board is important, but to be impactful, as Netflix's Reed Hastings puts it, "The board really needs to understand the business, and helping them to do so is something that a CEO should feel it's their duty to do—board members need to know the market, the opportunity, the threats, the internal players, the external."

Research shows only 10 percent of board members feel they have a solid understanding of the dynamics of the industries in which their companies operate, and only 21 percent feel they fully understand how their business creates value.[58] Even when board members do understand the industry, they're often looking in the rearview mirror, assuming that what was successful over the past twenty years will be the same in the next twenty, which is rarely true. To remedy these challenges, boards need to spend time educating themselves on what's happening inside and outside the company. Excellent CEOs shape what this education should look like, and help the board add value to the business.

In 2013, DBS's Piyush Gupta decided that his bank had to get ahead of the digital transformation that was happening in the business world. Inspired by a conversation he'd had with Alibaba founder Jack Ma about the power of big data, AI, and analytics, Gupta wanted to make DBS the Alibaba of the banking sector— a technology company that delivers financial services, not vice versa. In August of that year he took his board to South Korea for two days because the banks there were doing some advanced experiments with digital. They also visited the T.um technology museum, which was created by SK Telecom to show how society will use technology in the future, and they made stops at big technology companies like Samsung to see what they were doing.

With the educational visit still fresh in their minds, Gupta presented his new strategic plan to the group: "This is what I want to do. I think we should invest a lot more money in technology and try to build our own technology stack." The board listened to him, and then said: "If you do all of the stuff you're telling us you'll do next year, does that enable you to catch up to Alibaba?" Gupta smiled and said, "Not really. Alibaba is ten years ahead of us. It's going to take a long, long time." So the board said, "Look, in that case, you won't achieve your vision. We suggest you try to be more ambitious and bolder." The board then gave Gupta hundreds of millions more to invest in technology on top of the nearly $1 billion the company was already spending. Says Gupta: "The board signaled that it was willing to make a big bet on the way we thought the company should go. The check was a tremendous vote of faith that galvanized the company that we could go out and do it."

Another way CEOs broaden their board's horizons is to hold meetings at different locations and plan educational events around the meeting. General Mills' Ken Powell points out, "Our board traveled to Shanghai, Paris, and so on, and we'd visit plants and get to understand local regulatory matters, consumer preferences, economics, and other issues that impact the business. Travel not only helps the board better understand the business, but it also helps cement relationships."

Continuing education needn't require travel, however. Cincinnati Children's Michael Fisher describes the closer-to-home technique he employed: "When I became CEO, we started to bring in outside dinner speakers who addressed the board quarterly, and that has been enormously valuable. We've brought in CEOs from other health systems, big health insurers, big industry partners, and big customers. We've even had investment bankers in to give a broader view on the health care industry. It has really elevated the board members' understanding and knowledge, because we shouldn't expect them to know our business as well as we do."

A good orientation program for new board members can also be a powerful education tool. Establishing such not only grounds new board members in topics like changing technology, emerging risks, rising competitors, and shifting macroeconomic scenarios, but also provides a formal introduction to what it means to be an effective board member at the company by reinforcing the roles and expectations. While this may sound obvious, the fact of the matter is that only 33 percent of board members report they feel they received a "sufficient induction" when they took on the job.[59] The best CEOs don't let this happen.

Shell's Peter Voser takes his board members to offshore platforms, gas-to-liquids plants, and refineries as part of their onboarding. "Let's face it, most people have no clue what an oil company actually does," Voser shares. "We brought in technicians who explain how flying robots 2,500 meters under the ocean would fix some hole, and board members would be startled. 'I didn't know we did this!' they'd say. The board needs to understand that the risks of not being able to do that maintenance are vast, as we saw with the Deepwater Horizon. They also need to internalize that the business, to a large extent, is a probabilities game when it comes to exploration. You're maybe 60 percent successful, and you're happy with that. Those who come from a retail business or industrial business can find it hard to accept. You need to spend time on that."

Encourage Renewal

Given the importance of good governance, many find it surprising to hear that only 32 percent of directors report they regularly engage in formal evaluations of their performance, and a paltry 23 percent say their chair invites them to give feedback on whether a meeting was well run or not.[60] Without such feedback, managing the performance of the board becomes challenging. A full 82 percent of executives think at least one member of their company's board should be replaced, citing reasons such as diminishing performance due to advanced age, serving on too many boards, and reluctance to challenge management.[61] Term and age limits can help, but even with those guardrails in place it's easy for boards to become bloated and stale. Mastercard's Ajay Banga drives home the point: "You must agree on cycling people off at some frequency. Otherwise, they stay on and if people have been there for fourteen, eighteen, twenty-two years it doesn't work."

Top CEOs encourage the chair to regularly evaluate board performance. Brad Smith describes how the process works at Intuit: "The board has an annual evaluation process run by an outside counsel. We all fill out the same forms that ask questions like: 'How do you think the committees are performing? How do you think the board overall is performing? What areas can be made better?' We also do anonymous 360 feedback. That gives us insight into questions such as: 'What does this particular board member bring that is highly relevant to the company and advancing our cause? What is the one thing that would make this board member even more effective? Are there any superstars and any laggards?' That process has actually led us to discussions about replacing directors."

Sometimes it helps to bring in a facilitator to work on the dynamics of the board, but this requires everyone who's participating to have a very mature perspective. Best Buy's Hubert Joly explains: "We'd invite an outside consultant to do an assessment of the CEO and board's effectiveness. The first time we did this, the consultant had all these suggestions for how the board could improve. My first reaction was, as a recovering arrogant leader, 'Who are these people? The company was performing great, we should be saying thank you and congratulations to each other.' It took me one or two weeks to make peace with that, and realize that what I was getting wasn't feedback but 'feedforward'—things we can work on to be even better in the future. It takes enormous courage to listen to the criticism and say, yes, of course we can do better. In the end, however, it's a very energizing process."

Like any team, a board is ideally made up of individuals with the right skills and will to win. Unlike most teams, however, the members of boards typically spend less than 10 percent of their time working together.[62] The best CEOs not only work with their board chairs or lead directors to get the right people on the team—they also put the conditions in place for collective success by explicitly delineating the role of the board vis-à-vis management, specifying the board member profiles that will best help the business, proactively educating the group, and finding ways to encourage the board to continually renew itself.

Beyond establishing a baseline of trust and influencing the right board composition, there's one more vital step in helping directors help the business—making the most of board meetings themselves.

CHAPTER 12

Board Meetings Practice

Focus on the Future

Don't let yesterday take up too much of today.
—Will Rogers

Like most aspiring comedians, Jim Carrey early in his career was broke, and his prospects looked dim. One day in 1990, he wrote a $10 million check to himself and dated it five years into the future. He carried that check in his wallet at all times and looked at it every morning, thinking about what he'd have to do and how hard he'd have to work to earn $10 million. Almost five years after he wrote that check to himself, he learned that he'd made $10 million from the hit movie *Dumb and Dumber*.[63]

Carrey knew that having a clear intention, and focusing where one places their attention, leads to superior outcomes. Majid Al Futtaim's Alain Bejjani shares how the same is true for boards: "Management plays a very important role in guiding the board to elicit the best out of them," he says. "How do you engage them in a way where they can be more than just a great tool for oversight?" Underlying Bejjani's question is the recognition that the intrinsic nature of governance is about preventing bad things from happening from a risk and reputation standpoint. "When the mindset of the board is to prevent you from failing, the discussions tend to focus on failure," he observes. "It's important to focus on the future. That will help capture opportunity, drive growth, and take the company forward, instead of just managing risk."

In keeping with this approach, the best CEOs ensure that time spent in the boardroom doesn't become consumed with, as DBS's

Piyush Gupta puts it, "the board being a policeman on top of the business." Instead they consider the board meetings an opportunity to tap into the wisdom of a group of smart people with similar interests or, as Mastercard's Ajay Banga viewed it, "The best expert consultants you can get; they're dying to do anything for you."

American Express's Ken Chenault deftly used his board to help shape the future. "There was a really good exchange of ideas," he recalls, reflecting on how the board helped shape the strategy to rethink the company's card and payment products as service platforms. While pursuing a substantial re-engineering effort to drive cost savings, for example, his board pushed him to simultaneously make major investments in future growth. When the September 11 terrorist attacks on the United States happened in 2001, certain directors such as former US secretary of state Henry Kissinger proved invaluable by sharing their thoughts about what might happen next. "He was able to provide a global context that was very helpful to us in working through the implications of it all," Chenault recalls.

Companies hold board meetings anywhere from four to ten times a year, and for those meetings to be productive and forward-looking, the best CEOs . . .

   . . . start with a private session
   . . . promote a forward-looking agenda
   . . . walk in board members' shoes
   . . . let the board run itself

Start with a Private Session

When Feike Sijbesma took over DSM in 2007, there was a slot for "any other business" scheduled at the end of every board meeting's agenda. He asked his chairman if that session could be moved to the beginning of the agenda instead. Some were confused and responded, "You want to talk about other business—everything that is left—before we even start with anything?" Sijbesma responded in the affirmative, and then made a further request of his chair: "I'd like you to ask me, at the beginning of every meeting, this one question: 'Feike, besides what's on the agenda and what approvals we need to take, what is going on in your mind? What are you most excited or concerned about?' " Sijbesma's final request was, "Other than that, there should be no other formal structure for the discussion and no prepared presentation materials. Let's call it highlights and lowlights."

The rationale behind Sijbesma's request was twofold. First, to be able to set the context for what the board would hear during the course of the board meeting so that they could orient themselves to the discussions to come in the most helpful ways. Second, to be able to put topics on the radar that weren't yet ready for a decision and therefore not on the agenda. "We tried that, and it went very well," Sijbesma reports. "We talked over an hour about everything, and it became the norm in every board meeting. It created further openness and trust between the board and management."

Though Sijbesma's requests seemed novel to his board chair at the time, he was simply asking to do what the best CEOs do. Dupont's Ed Breen shares, "I tell all of the new CEOs I talk with to take the first hour of the board meeting in executive session with just you and the board. No other internal members of the company should be present. Just recently one of them told me it was the best advice—it gives board members a better perspective of what you're dealing with, so they give you better guidance."

The private session is only a success if it's radically transparent, as we described previously. One of the first things that Thermo Fisher Scientific's Marc Casper did when he took the role was to start every board meeting with an executive session. "I focused on what I was worried about and the challenges we were facing," he says. "My sole reason for that was to create a culture of transparency so that directors wouldn't spend their time hunting for problems. We want them to do that, by the way, but we also want them to know that the management team's true inclination is to bring problems to the board. That creates a totally different culture: You earn their trust and they hold you to a high standard. It elevates the dialogue and the impact."

JPMC's Jamie Dimon has been known to take such sessions to the extreme when circumstances demand it. During the financial crisis, for example, he entered a board meeting feeling that any discussion would be a distraction from what he really needed to be doing at that moment. He feared that "like the *Titanic*—we'd be talking about the band while the ship is sinking." Instead of spending the hour sharing what was on his mind, Dimon said to the board, "I have to go to work. We have some real issues we have to deal with urgently. Why don't you come with me?" The board proceeded to get a front-row view of trading desks reporting risk exposures and making recommendations on what to sell and what to hedge.

Beside private sessions, some CEOs directly communicate with the board in other ways. Duke Energy's Lynn Good generally sends a letter to her board every two weeks as issues dictate "so that they're more frequently in the conversation about complex issues." Shiseido's Masahiko Uotani shares, "I'm always sending emails to our board members, sharing what's going on. I don't want them to open their newspaper or newsfeed and see that Shiseido is announcing something they haven't heard about. I'm always trying to give them information in advance." Uotani also enthusiastically writes a seven- to eight-page memo to his board on his flight back to Japan after he travels for rounds of investor meetings.

Promote a Forward-Looking Agenda

After the opening private session, the best CEOs ensure the rest of the board agenda includes forward-looking topics in addition to fiduciary ones. By and large, boards welcome this; more than half of directors say they'd like to dedicate more time to topics that drive company performance such as strategy, organizational health, and talent.[64] Doing so in an effective way is harder than one might think, however. Ahold Delhaize's Dick Boer explains: "Many times, board members forget what you said eight weeks ago at the last meeting. In the interim, you're developing your views on the business and working with the team every day to advance your strategy." Intuit's Brad Smith shares a further complication: "If you aren't clear in telling them where you need their help, they'll give you all kinds of ideas in places you don't want help."

To overcome these challenges, the best CEOs work with the board to create a strategic framework that they've agreed upon and that creates consistency across meetings. At Ahold Delhaize, for example, Boer's framework had six pillars designed to reshape retail and drive growth. The first group of pillars included building customer loyalty, driving innovation, and entering new markets. The second group was focused internally on simplifying the business, fostering corporate responsibility, and developing talent. Boer enthuses, "Once the framework was set, it was much easier to report back to the board—and the feedback I received was more valuable."

Every CEO's strategic framework is different, but as long as they include elements of strategy, culture, and talent, the board agenda will then naturally include the most important forward-looking topics. Not that these topics have to show up in every board meeting, but at the same time they also aren't relegated to once-a-year discussions. Instead, they're typically addressed over three or four board sessions in a time frame that synchs with management's own operating rhythm. "It becomes very easy to prepare for board meetings," GE's Larry Culp explains, "if the cadence and rhythm with the board mirrors how we run the company."

Take strategy, for example. The first session calls for approval of any changes to the overall strategic framework. The next gets sign-off on broad suggestions, followed by a session to select and approve specific options. Further meetings then review progress—not just financial outcomes but also key performance indicators—against the backdrop of changes in the market or competitive landscape. On the topic of talent, the board might discuss in the first meeting the overall talent objectives for the company, in the following they might go over the performance reviews of the top thirty to fifty executives, and in the next the overall plan to improve leadership bench strength. These topics sit side by side on the agenda with fiduciary, continuing board education, and board evaluation (the latter two topics we discussed in chapter 11).

Note that one talent-related topic CEOs often fail to bring up with the board—especially early in their tenure—but should is their own succession planning. While they won't have anything to do with the selection of the next CEO when the time comes, the best CEOs take a leadership role in developing potential candidates. A sitting chief executive has a uniquely broad and deep understanding of the company's strategy and therefore what kind of successor would be the best fit. Practically speaking—and to ensure biases don't distort the process—the CEO, the head of HR, and selected board members should regularly review the criteria for selecting internal candidates, assess or reassess short-listed ones, provide feedback to them, and develop and implement a plan for their developmental needs.

Mastercard's Ajay Banga started having such conversations in the first year of his tenure, and did so every December thereafter. He reveals that the process was as helpful for him as it was the board. "My biggest advice to CEOs is to start early with the attributes of what you believe will make a successful CEO when you're gone," he says. "Don't be nervous about discussing that with the board. Take their feedback. It's actually a way for you to get an appraisal of how you're doing."

Across all forward-looking topics covered in a board meeting, it's a clear best practice to state up front what management is looking for from the board. Brad Smith shares an approach that worked well for him at Intuit: "In every presentation to the board, we included a cover page with an executive summary and a box to the right that outlined the two or three things where we needed their advice. That channeled ninety percent of the board's energy into helping us."

To be effective, such requests for advice need to be genuine, otherwise the conversation won't happen in the most helpful way possible. Best Buy's Hubert Joly recalls how early in his tenure his attitude got in the way: "Earlier in my career, I thought I was very smart, that I could do it on my own, and that reporting to the board was like a dog-and-pony show. I tried to impress them and because of that, they didn't try to change or add anything to what I said. This was victory, right? With age comes more modesty and with experience comes wisdom, and I changed my approach."

Walk in Board Members' Shoes

For a CEO, there's no better way to understand what it means to be a board member than to become a director at another company. Experiencing a board meeting from the other side of the board table is a profound learning experience, allowing one to borrow from what works and avoid what doesn't.

Aon's Greg Case expands: "I joined another board because I wanted to understand the dynamic and develop better pattern recognition. When you're the CEO, you sit in the boardroom, have a nice conversation, and it's really good. And then, eventually, you leave. And then whatever happens after you leave is reported back to you. And there's nothing like being on another board when the CEO leaves, and you witness the conversation. That's a piece of learning that you can't replicate."

Some CEOs, like American Express's Ken Chenault, served on outside boards before they stepped into the role. "The first board I joined was IBM, before I became CEO," Chenault shares. "In a very personal way, serving on a board helped me better understand some of the issues I'd later face as CEO and how to manage them. And, in turn, once I became a CEO, I was able to contribute even more as a board member through my leadership experience."

The best CEOs generally recommend making the choice to sit on one board and doing so in the first couple of years of one's tenure. General Mills' Ken Powell shares why: "My predecessor was on three boards, which was quite common for CEOs during that era and pretty manageable. But given the time demands on today's CEOs, and frankly, the increased time required of directors, I think it's a mistake for CEOs to sit on multiple boards. But one is super valuable. There's nothing like seeing what it looks like from the other side."

Beyond gaining that extra perspective, being a board member for another company also reveals how another firm is run. Duke Energy's Lynn Good explains, "It's interesting to get an inside look at not just the way governance works, but also how strategy works, the way talent works, the way large capital decisions are made, all of which are relevant to my business. When you sit on the board you get a front-row seat."

Let the Board Run Itself

With all that we've discussed in this section about how the best CEOs engage with the board, it would be easy to assume that they spend a lot of their time dealing with the board. In fact, the best CEOs don't. As JPMC's Jamie Dimon relays, "I met a CEO who told me they spent thirty percent of their time with their board. I was like, 'What?' I spend *far* less of my time than that with my board. Of course, by now I know my board quite well, but even early on I couldn't imagine spending that much time, and I can't imagine any board would want me to spend that much time dealing with them."

Aon's Greg Case emphasizes the point: "I'm so fortunate, our board is highly disciplined. They read all the materials. We have issue-focused discussions and never page-flip through a deck, and we do this in only as many board meetings as there needs to be. I've had conversations with some of my counterparts in which they literally spend twenty percent of their time on their board. No. It's better to have four or five high-quality board meetings than a sub-quality ten. It's better to focus on the top issues that matter and let details get discussed in committees. And the CEO doesn't have to go to every committee meeting if you have great executives who are brilliant at running them."

Beyond leaving the nitty-gritty work to committees, the best CEOs also don't engage in governance issues beyond what's been discussed in previous chapters. U.S. Bancorp's Richard Davis emphatically explains, "Never, ever, ever meddle with your board's process. I mean, just never, ever get into it. If the board says, well, what do you think about who should be on this committee, say, 'I'm going to leave that to you.' There's no upside. I say, 'You know what, everybody's qualified. You know your board better than anybody. You make that decision.' It's never, ever smart for the CEO to get in the middle of anything because later on the board might decide you'd showed bias or favoritism. I've seen cases where the CEO answers a well-intended question, but later on, it works against them."

JPMC's Dimon gives a window into the importance of steering

clear of board governance outside of the areas we've discussed: "When the London Whale [a trading problem that led to more than six billion dollars of losses for the bank] happened, it was an example of where I simply told the board, 'You better have a playbook in place to take care of the problem, because I have to be investigated, too. I'll run my own investigation as CEO, but you have to have a separate process to make sure I didn't do anything wrong, and that the board didn't do anything wrong. My job is to fix the problem and analyze it and tell you if we have the problem anywhere else.'"

Even when it comes to succession planning, aside from the role of developing internal candidates described previously, CEOs are well advised to keep at arm's length as much as possible. Ecolab's Doug Baker had his board members interview the candidates and had an outside group do assessments of each. "I wouldn't give them my opinion until they had all the data," recalls Baker. "I wanted them to have the outside assessment and to have the assessment from the other board members who interviewed candidates. I told them that after that, I'd give them my perspective because I didn't want to taint the process. I could live with whatever the final decision was, and I'd fully back it because ultimately it has to be the board's choice. It was how I felt intellectually and it would have been how I behaved no matter what. Emotionally, of course, I wanted it to be my choice. I mean, we're human."

If care isn't taken, board meetings can be spent disproportionately looking at the dashboard and the rearview mirror. The best CEOs ensure that the board's eyes are also trained on the horizon so that their expertise can be fully tapped to navigate the road ahead. They do so by starting meetings with a private session during which they can preview important topics. They also ensure strategy, culture, and talent are on the agenda, not just fiduciary items. Additionally, they experience what it means to be a board member by being a director in another company, gaining a "walking in their shoes" understanding of how boards operate while also acquiring practical insight into how other companies operate. Beyond that, they steer clear of the work of the board for both practical (time investment) and philosophical (ensuring independence) reasons.

• • •

We've now discussed what Best Buy's Hubert Joly calls "the biggest change and challenge" for new CEOs: engaging the board. DBS's Piyush Gupta sums up the mindset that differentiates the best from the rest. "Most people, and most boards actually, think of themselves as governance bodies," he says. "I've had a very different approach. I believed from day one that the board is a partner to the business."

Below is a summary of how the mindset of helping the board help the business translates into three main dimensions that CEOs should influence while engaging the board—capability, relationships, and meetings. Getting board effectiveness right is a high-value endeavor: Research shows that it's strongly correlated with better performance and higher market valuations, and it also acts as a repellent to unwanted activist investors.

Engaging the Board: What separates the best from the rest

Mindset: Help Directors Help the Business

Relationships practice:	Build a Foundation of Trust
	▪ Choose radical transparency
	▪ Strengthen the CEO/board chair relationship
	▪ Reach out to individual directors
	▪ Expose the board to management
Capabilities practice:	**Tap the Wisdom of Elders**
	▪ Delineate the roles
	▪ Specify the desired profile
	▪ Educate the group
	▪ Encourage renewal
Meetings practice:	**Focus on the Future**
	▪ Start with a private session
	▪ Make the agenda forward-looking
	▪ Walk in board members' shoes
	▪ Let the board run itself

Even if you're not a CEO of a big public company, many lessons from those who are still apply. Ask yourself: Who is my independent advisory board (even if informal) that both advises me and holds me accountable for my commitments? What are the skills these people have that are important to me, and are any missing? Are they connected with, and do they understand, my context well enough for their guidance to be relevant? How radically transparent am I with them about where I am and what I need? Do we talk in some depth both about managing risks and capturing opportunities? Whose advisory board am I on and what have I learned as a result?

STAKEHOLDER CONNECTION MINDSET

Start with "Why?"

Everyone's important. Trouble is trying to figure out why.

—Emory R. Frie

While it's hard enough running a business and managing a board, today's CEOs find that they must interact with stakeholder groups more often than they ever could have imagined. As Microsoft's Satya Nadella puts it: "The job is all about customers; it's all about partners; it's all about your employees, your investors, governments. It's all about all of them, all the time." In fact, how well a business performs can be linked to how well a CEO handles such interactions. Research shows that a company's relationships with external stakeholders can influence as much as 30 percent of corporate earnings.[65] Further, stakeholder engagement can impact a company's fortunes significantly and unexpectedly. What happens when a crisis hits varies dramatically based not just on how a leader responds to the situation, but also on what they've done beforehand to build trust and credibility (or not) with various stakeholder groups.

Most CEOs understand this reality, and in turn ask their public relations departments to help them maintain good relationships with stakeholders. The focus is predominately on who to talk to, about what, and when. The best CEOs, however, start with the question of "why?": Why is our company worthy of operating in society? Why are we relevant to each of our stakeholders? Why are each of our stakeholders relevant to us? Why are they choosing to do whatever they might be doing? By deeply understanding the motivations, hopes, and fears of their constituents, excellent CEOs create strong bonds with the outside world that help the business prosper in the long run.

In the chapters that follow, we'll discuss the ways in which a "why?" mindset translates into practice in each of the three dimensions of the role of dealing with stakeholders: embracing social purpose, shaping strong relationships, and leading through moments of truth.

CHAPTER 13

Social Purpose Practice
Impact the Big Picture

Definiteness of purpose is the starting point of all achievement.

— W. Clement Stone

In 1946, Viktor Frankl chronicled his experiences as a prisoner in Nazi concentration camps in his book *Man's Search for Meaning*. Wondering why some prisoners survived and others didn't in an atmosphere of hopelessness and despair, he concluded that those who made it lived with a greater sense of purpose. He recalled some men who walked through the huts comforting others, giving away their last piece of bread. Frankl wrote: "They may have been few in number, but they offer sufficient proof that everything can be taken from a man but one thing: the last of the human freedoms—to choose one's attitude in any given set of circumstances, to choose one's own way."[66]

Just over seventy years later, Frankl's book has sold more than ten million copies, been translated into twenty-four languages, and was named by the US Library of Congress as one of the "ten most influential books" ever written. The reason for its popularity and influence is that it deals with a profound human truth: Having a sense of meaning is essential for surviving and thriving in the world.

But where do humans find meaning at work? Research shows that employees draw on at least five sources of purpose and motivation.[67] The first is *themselves*—their development, their financial and nonfinancial rewards, and their freedom to act. The second is *fellow employees*—feeling a sense of belonging, caring for one another, and doing the right thing for the group. The third is the *company*—achieving industry leadership through creating best practices and beating the competition. The fourth is impact on the *customer*—making life easier and better for them by providing a superior service or product. The fifth and final is their impact on *society*—making the world a better place.

Most people draw meaning from all five sources to some degree but find more motivation from one of the five than the others. Research also shows that in any given population there'll be a roughly equal number of people who gravitate to each of the five as their primary source of energy at work—a fifth are most motivated by their own development, a fifth by their fellow employees, and so forth. CEOs therefore should ensure that their organization has a powerful reason "why?" it does what it does on each of the five dimensions. A speech that talks only about how the company will beat the competition, for example, will connect deeply with only 20 percent of the audience. By articulating each of the five whys, CEOs can tap into the primary motivations of everyone in the company.

Increasingly, the line between social purpose and the other four sources of meaning is blurring. Today, 87 percent of US customers say they will purchase from companies that support issues they care about,[68] and 94 percent of those entering the workforce say that they want to use their talents to benefit a cause.[69] As we've mentioned previously, the rise of social media has also created increased transparency into a company's business practices that enables the general public to hold leaders accountable for social and environmental impact in ways not possible until the twenty-first century.

It's no wonder that in 2019 the Business Roundtable, a lobbying group composed of 181 leading CEOs in the United States whose board included JPMC's Jamie Dimon, GM's Mary Barra, Duke Energy's Lynn Good, and Lockheed Martin's Marillyn Hewson, changed the definition of the "purpose of a corporation" from the decades-old capitalist goal of maximizing profits at any cost to a more holistic goal of looking out for the well-being of everything and everyone the company's actions affect.[70]

The decision made global headlines, and subsequently virtually every CEO of a large company was being asked by their constituents to clarify their social purpose. The best CEOs, however, already had one. Research shows that over the last twenty years companies with a clear social purpose have significantly outperformed the S&P 500.[71] Their superior financial performance was driven by the multiple benefits of stakeholder capitalism. These companies enjoyed increased customer loyalty, better efficiency (through reducing resource usage), motivated employees, a lower cost of capital, and the ability to spot and mitigate risks earlier than others because they were closer to their constituents. Wall Street sees the benefits of such an approach. Sustainable investing has grown eighteenfold since 1995.

Despite all of the evidence that having a social purpose is good business, however, most companies don't make it a practice. While 82 percent of companies affirm the importance of purpose, only 42 percent report that their company's stated "purpose" has much effect.[72] Meanwhile, more than half of consumers think brands aren't as committed to society as they claim and only a third say they trust the brands they buy.[73]

Nairobi-based Equity Group Holding, the largest financial services firm in East and Central Africa with almost a billion-dollar balance sheet and fifteen million customers, is an example of a company that walks the talk. Its social purpose is to change lives, give dignity, and create opportunities for wealth creation. As one of many efforts to fulfill this mission, Equity Bank created the Wings to Fly program that has given full four-year secondary-school scholarships to thirty-six thousand orphans. "That means," says James Mwangi, the CEO since 2005, "that thousands of villages have somebody they can identify with and say, 'That child would have been struggling if it were not for Equity.' And since we've taken responsibility for educating orphans from the community, the community pays us back by supporting us—consuming our products and services. So, the more we share, the more we both live our purpose and improve our profits. It's a symbiotic relationship; I no longer call it corporate social responsibility—I call it shared prosperity."

The best CEOs create the kind of "shared prosperity" that Mwangi describes by . . .

... clarifying their company's societal "why?"
... embedding it into the core of the business
... using strengths to make a difference
... making a stand when it's warranted

Clarify the Societal "Why?"

The notion of an organization having a social purpose is anything but new. On March 8, 1960, Dave Packard, cofounder and later CEO of Hewlett-Packard, addressed HP's training group. "I want to discuss why a company exists in the first place," he began. "In other words, why are we here? I think many people assume, wrongly, that a company exists simply to make money. While this is an important result of a company's existence, we have to go deeper to find our reasons for being." Packard proceeded to share his view that firms exist to "make a contribution to society." He went on to explain how HP had a responsibility to make a major contribution to the advancement of science. "Purpose should not be confused with specific goals or business strategies," he explained. "Whereas you might achieve a goal or complete a strategy, you cannot fulfill a purpose; it's like a guiding star on the horizon—forever pursued but never reached. Yet although purpose itself does not change; it does inspire change. The very fact purpose can never be fully realized means that an organization can never stop stimulating change and progress."[74]

The best CEOs, like Packard, instill a clear sense of social purpose in their organizations. If you ask a Lockheed Martin employee what their job is, according to Marillyn Hewson, "they'll tell you they're not just building airplanes, radars, and missile defense systems—they're helping US and allied forces strengthen global security. They're not just writing software—they're helping governments deliver essential services to millions of citizens. They're not just designing satellites and rockets—they're expanding the boundaries of scientific discovery." At General Mills, shares former CEO Ken Powell, employees are "serving the world with products consumers love." At Flemming Ørnskov's Galderma, employees are, "enhancing the quality of people's lives by focusing on science-based solutions to skin health." All of the best CEOs we spoke to have a similarly clear and compelling articulation of why their company exists and how it adds value to society.

Some companies are founded very explicitly on a social mission such as Patagonia, TOMS, Warby Parker, Seventh Generation, Ben & Jerry's, and so on. Where a company's social identity isn't as overt, excellent CEOs apply many of the same lenses as they do when reframing the vision of the company, which accounts for why many of the best CEOs see the concepts of vision, mission, and purpose as interchangeable. Some find a social intent in their company's origin story that they can elevate, as we saw in chapter 1 with Brad Smith reconnecting with Intuit's "championing of the underdog" founding ethos and Satya Nadella connecting with Microsoft's early ideal of "creating technology so that others can create more technology."

After Henrik Poulsen took over the utility giant Ørsted (formerly named Danish Oil and Natural Gas) in year 2012, he—to the surprise of many—pulled off one of the most dramatic purpose-led corporate transformations in recent history. Growth had stalled at what was Denmark's largest utility, and Poulsen decided he had to find a way to breathe new life into the business. While searching for a new direction, Poulsen and his team asked themselves: "What does the world need, and where does the company excel?"

They believed that their industry was at the brink of a massive transformation away from fossil fuels toward clean energy. "We had to take a stance on whether we genuinely believed that science is right and that the world is eventually going to have to face up to global warming," Poulsen says. He believed it was, and decided, "We'd better get on the right side of it earlier rather than later." The CEO bet that the offshore wind projects in Ørsted's portfolio, a technology that was at the time more expensive than fossil fuel–generated electricity, promised the best opportunity for long-term growth. It was an uneconomic niche, and demand was uncertain, but Poulsen believed he was on the right side of the macrotrend.

In the early days of the transformation, he took a series of bold steps to rid Ørsted of its fossil fuel assets, one of which was to raise capital in 2014 by selling 18 percent of the company to Goldman Sachs's private equity arm. At the time the Danish government owned a majority stake in Ørsted, and Poulsen, who needed capital to make his plan a reality, had tried to raise money from the government and failed. When he announced the Goldman deal, the backlash was fierce. Many Danes believed he was selling out cheap. Sixty-eight percent of the country opposed the sale, and a number of major politicians resigned, including six cabinet members. Yet, Poulsen stuck to his course, using the capital he raised from Goldman to become the global leader in offshore wind after winning a series of projects in the UK, Germany, and elsewhere.

In 2016, Ørsted successfully went public at a valuation of $16 billion, and by the following year had phased out the use of coal, sold off its oil and gas businesses to Ineos for $1 billion, and changed its name from Danish Oil and Natural Gas to Ørsted to reflect a shift to renewable energy. (The company took its new name from Hans Christian Ørsted, the Danish scientist who discovered electromagnetic fields.) Today, 90 percent of the company's energy is produced by renewable resources. Deploying a powerful social mission—climate change—to transform the company paid off. By the time Poulsen retired in 2021, the former Danish utility was ranked the world's most sustainable company, with a market value of more than $80 billion, up ninefold since he took over. Over his tenure he'd grown the firm's offshore wind capacity more than fivefold.

"When I look back over the last eight years," Poulsen reflects, "the deep rooting of purpose in the organization was absolutely critical for us. People fundamentally believed in what we were doing. That all translates into productivity. It translates into execution capacity. And ultimately it drives your competitiveness. And as our conviction grew, the world around us became more and more convinced that we were right. If you have a purpose that is really linked to a fundamental need in the market and it's something people really care about, that's the biggest asset you can have."

Not every company's social purpose can be as obvious as Ørsted's. So how does a CEO know their company's purpose is the right one? A litmus test is whether it has emotional impact (does it inspire employees with a "can we really do this?" challenge?) and whether it makes rational sense (is it symbiotic with the company's vision, strategy, capabilities, culture, and brand?). Galderma's

Flemming Ørnskov shares how he knew he had it right in leading his former biotech company: "I ran into someone who used to work for me at Shire," he shares. "She said to me, 'The thing I'm missing at my new company is that at Shire I always knew why we were doing what we were doing. The purpose was totally clear to me. When I came home, I could talk to my family about rare diseases, how important it is to address them, and how we and I made a contribution."

Embed Purpose into the Core

Some critics roll their eyes at CEOs who talk about social purpose, questioning whether it has any real bearing on how the company operates. They have a point. Given the public pressure to talk about a company's social purpose, many CEOs are increasingly engaging in "woke-washing." That's when a company says it backs a good cause but continues to do harm to vulnerable communities. By contrast, Microsoft's Satya Nadella speaks to what great CEOs aspire to: "Somebody once said that you can only trust people who think, say, and do the same thing. By the same token, you can only trust companies that are thinking, saying, and doing the same thing. That's the consistency you need."

At Ecolab, for example, Doug Baker aimed to make sustainability an *outcome* of growth, not a hobby. "If your approach is, 'My growth creates more pollution, so I buy offsets to neutralize it'—you're in a natural position of conflict," says Baker. "We've tried to remove that friction from the business by engineering our programs to deliver world-class results while using less resources. Therefore, the more we grow, the less water and energy is consumed, which drives a positive impact." Baker has made sustainability not a PR campaign but an integral part of the way Ecolab operates.

Baker's epiphany around purpose came early in his CEO tenure when he was thumbing through the annual report of Medtronic, a medical device maker. "When I read their mission statement, I was blown away," says Baker. "It's a pacemaker company, so its product extends and saves lives. The company would even bring in patients to talk with employees about how Medtronic saved their lives. Those are stirring moments. It made me realize that we had the power at Ecolab to do more. I like the game of business, which is putting points on the board. I think it's a lot of fun. But there's more to life than making money, and you need to capture your team's hearts as well as their minds."

Baker proceeded to get his top team to think more deeply about the company's impact and purpose. At the time the eighty-year-old firm was selling industrial cleansers and food safety products and services by promoting labor savings and cost reduction. After many iterations, Baker and the team chose to ground their purpose in sustainability: making the world cleaner, safer, and healthier, protecting people and vital resources. As a result, he says, "we focused much more on saving water and energy, which created both economic and environmental benefits." Ecolab started engineering its products to be more water and energy efficient and made acquisitions to build its capabilities including Nalco (water treatment) and Champion (energy services).

"My advice," says Baker, "is to not get trapped in this life where you do evil during the day and good from 6:00 p.m. to 7:00 p.m. to try to offset it. It's an unsuccessful model. You'll be found out. It just won't work in the long term. Marrying the two, so that the more we sell, the more water and energy we save, brings your work in line with your values." The advice is worth listening to: Baker grew Ecolab from a roughly $7 billion market capitalization in 2004 to over $60 billion in 2020, placing it among America's top one hundred most valuable firms. Baker himself is ranked in *Harvard Business Review*'s Top 100 CEOs. Just as important, one of the primary metrics driving the organization—how much water is saved by its clients annually—now stands at 206 billion gallons, against a 2030 target of 300 billion gallons.

The best CEOs, like Baker, embed their social purpose into the core operation of their businesses, thereby minimizing the tension between the two. They test their strategy, products and services, supply chain, performance metrics, and incentives to make sure they mesh with their purpose. They also regularly ask themselves, "What would our most critical stakeholders say are areas where we're being hypocritical?" and "What is *not* currently being measured or reported that society will hold us accountable for in the future?"

At Best Buy, Hubert Joly found that testing the company's strategy against its purpose of enriching lives through technology opened up new growth opportunities. "It vastly expanded how we thought about what we could do for customers," he shares. An example is the company's entry into the health care space, capitalizing on the global trend of aging populations and seniors wanting to stay in their homes longer because it's better for them. "So we did a series of acquisitions and now we're able to put sensors in seniors' homes and, using artificial intelligence, monitor their daily activities," Joly says. "Are they eating, drinking, and sleeping well? We have centers that are alerted if any concerns emerge. That service is sold through insurance companies and it's a high-growth opportunity for us. We never would have thought of that if we'd just looked at our business in the traditional way."

Use Strengths to Make a Difference

Even with a clear, compelling, and embedded social purpose, few companies will be doing all they need to be doing to meet the corporate social responsibility (CSR) practices that their stakeholders demand. The most scrutiny typically relates to the CSR risks and business opportunities around environmental, social, and governance factors (ESG). Environmental factors include, among others, energy efficiency, pollution, deforestation, and waste management. Social factors have to do with how people are treated, e.g., diversity and inclusion, working conditions, human rights protection, fair wages, and good community relationships. Governance factors include risk management, executive compensation, donations, political lobbying, tax strategy, transparency, and so on. The best CEOs attend to all these elements and while doing so, look for areas where they can achieve outsized results by leveraging their company's strengths.

In the wake of racial justice demonstrations in America, JPMC is making a $30 billion investment over five years to provide economic opportunity to underserved neighborhoods, especially

Black and Latinx communities. The investment will take the form of mortgage loans, refinancing, equity investments in affordable housing, and small business loans—all muscles that the company can flex powerfully. Jamie Dimon announced the investment by saying, "Systemic racism is a tragic part of America's history. We can do more and do better to break down systems that have propagated racism and widespread economic inequality, especially for Black and Latinx people. It's long past time that society addresses racial inequities in a more tangible, meaningful, and sustainable way."[75]

When the COVID-19 pandemic hit, the best CEOs flexed their company's muscles to help. GM cleared out a plant in Kokomo, Indiana, and replaced machines that made electrical components for cars with an assembly line for manufacturing ventilators. The goal wasn't to make a profit (the ventilators were purchased by the US government at cost), it was to help in the nationwide effort to quadruple the national strategic stockpile. Netflix set up a $100 million relief fund for out-of-work movie and TV production professionals, such as electricians, carpenters, and drivers, many of whom are paid hourly on a project basis. At Cincinnati Children's Hospital, Michael Fisher said to his board of directors, "If the community needs us to repurpose some of our facilities to serve adult patients who are critically ill from COVID-19, I'm prepared to do it."

Using strengths to make a difference on ESG issues doesn't just come into play when there's a crisis. Ken Powell describes his approach at General Mills: "We focused on food security around the world and sustainable agriculture, which made sense for us given our industry. We've done some incredible things around the world in those areas, and if you're a General Mills employee and you're volunteering your time to help a small food start-up in Africa, it's super rewarding, builds loyalty and commitment, and it's an opportunity pretty unique to us."

Similarly, early in his tenure at Novo Nordisk, Lars Rebien Sørensen recognized that the pharmaceutical industry had yet to find an appropriate way of dealing with access to medicine. While companies needed to protect their intellectual property rights, developing countries also needed a cost-effective way to produce medicines for their vulnerable populations. "We ended up deciding to sell insulin to the poorest countries at cost," shares Sørensen. "More important, we created an independent organization called the World Diabetes Foundation. A portion of each vial of insulin we sell goes to the foundation, which uses the funds to build capacity in developing countries." Today, the foundation is the biggest funding agency for chronic disease in the world.

As with social purpose statements, many look at CSR/ESG reports cynically. The best CEOs welcome the scrutiny because they know that purpose is reflected in their company's soul. DSM's Feike Sijbesma explains, "We abandoned our CSR report and integrated all our activities and angles into our annual report. The core of our business needed to make money by contributing to a better world. I wanted purpose, CSR if you want, in the core of our competencies and businesses. This helped sustainability become both our purpose and business model. Sustainability became sustainable." Sijbesma's ethos has landed the company on *Fortune*'s Change the World list three years running for its leadership in corporate sustainability and Sijbesma himself was awarded the UN Humanitarian of the Year award while CEO.

Make a Stand When Warranted

Whether CEOs like it or not, they're very likely to be thrust into the spotlight on the societal issues of the day, even if far removed from the company's social purpose. The best CEOs are prepared to be, and many choose to be proactive. "The reality is that a lot of employees want to see their CEOs front and center on the main topics of the day," Majid Al Futtaim's Alain Bejjani observes. "Societal issues and global challenges are too big for governments to deal with on their own, and engagement between government, business, and civil society is extremely important. CEOs have a significant role to play in driving that narrative and engaging in forums where they can constructively add to the debate. Change starts with words and ideas before they translate into actions."

Ecolab's Doug Baker reflects on the evolution of the CEO role in this regard during his more than fifteen-year tenure: "I think business now understands we have to speak up much more—on issues that we would have chosen not to comment on in the past. Social justice issues, like policing issues for example—I would never have said 'boo' before on those. I would have my opinion; I would have voiced it to friends. But as CEO, I would say to myself, 'Really, it's just not my place. People don't want to hear that from me,' at least that's what I assumed. Now when I speak up, even if it's about negative things that you would have hoped others assumed we were against, the number of people who say, 'We're so happy you took a stand'—it's incredible. It's just a very different time."

Baker's not alone. In early 2021, while Twitter CEO Jack Dorsey and Facebook CEO Mark Zuckerberg made the tough decision to close down US president Donald Trump's Twitter account and Facebook page—to check the spread of falsehoods on social media about the election in which he lost to Joe Biden—many others also took action. American Express, Best Buy, and Mastercard, among others, said they'd no longer make contributions to the 147 members of Congress who voted to challenge election results during a joint session to ratify electoral votes from each of the country's fifty states. Others such as JPMC, Microsoft, and Aon announced they'd pause all political contributions because attempts to subvert election results weren't aligned with their values.

The best CEOs don't confuse their personal passions for their company's principles. It's critical for CEOs to get the views of their senior team, board, and rank-and-file employees on when they should speak as an individual and when as a representative of all the company's constituents and stakeholders. As Intuit's Brad Smith explains: "After the 2016 presidential election, I was under a lot of pressure from people asking me to write a letter to the employees acknowledging how badly some felt after candidate Trump won. I refused and instead said, 'Do me a favor. Plot where all of our offices are and tell me if they're red [Republican-leaning] or blue [Democrat-leaning] states. Plot where every TurboTax customer and QuickBooks customer is.' And guess what—they were in both red and blue states. I may have voted one way, and you may have voted one way, but we're not here to put our personal principles out there."

Smith continues: "What we do have to say is what we stand for.

So we wrote down a set of principles. We simply said, 'We stand by our values. We stand for human rights, civil liberties, and equal protection under the law. We stand for abiding by the laws in all the states and the countries in which we operate. If any of those are violated, we'll take action in the way we see fit, and the first thing we'll try to do is influence the change.' I think many CEOs have not done this, and it's important." Smith shared that handling this messaging was the hardest part of his job for the final three years of his tenure. "It can tear many companies down the middle, because some employees expect you to stand up for certain things and be the leader they envision, while others don't share those same viewpoints," he says. "It's hard, but you have to find a way to navigate it."

Sometimes listening matters more than speaking. "You have to be comfortable having an uncomfortable conversation," Smith says. "Open up a town hall with, 'I don't know how to handle this. How can we help? What can we do? What do you need?' Give people a chance to be part of the solution." U.S. Bancorp's Richard Davis did precisely that in the wake of racially charged police protests in the United States, when he asked the leaders of each of the bank's twenty-five regions to hold listening events, of which he joined a handful. "It had nothing to do with banking. Shareholders didn't care if we did that," he shares, "but at the end of the day, it's so important to be heard, and there was a wonderful rush of gratefulness for just doing it."

Best Buy's Hubert Joly expands on the idea even further: "The CEO can't just lead from the brain. They need to lead with their heart, soul, guts, ears, eyes, and so forth." He continues, "These qualities paint a portrait of a CEO who is very different from the standard one of twenty years ago."

Today, more than ever, social purpose has a business purpose. The best company builders, however, have always known profits and purpose are inextricably linked. In keeping with Viktor Frankl's observations back in 1946, social purpose has far more impact beyond the higher profits it can bring. People who report they are "living their purpose" at work report levels of well-being that are five times higher than those who aren't, and are also four times more likely to be more engaged with the business. Beyond the workplace, research also shows that purpose-filled individuals live longer and healthier lives.[76]

The best CEOs capture the full impact that social purpose can deliver by first getting razor sharp on their company's societal reason for existing (their "why?"). They then embed their purpose into the core of how the business operates. Next, they leverage the company's strengths to address contemporary environmental, social, or governance (ESG) issues. Finally, the best CEOs use their platform to speak out and make a stand when situations demand it.

A clear sense of social purpose provides a strong foundation on which to build stakeholder relationships. Creating the right connections, however, requires that CEOs stay as attuned to their stakeholders' "why?" as their own.

CHAPTER 14

Stakeholder Interaction Practice

Get to the Essence

You never really understand a person until you consider things from his point of view.

—Harper Lee

A popular cartoon shows two people each pointing to a number on the ground. One person, standing on one side of the number, says the number is a 6. The one standing on the other side says it's a 9. Beneath the cartoon is the commentary, "Just because you are right, does not mean, I am wrong." This very simple illustration shows how different interpretations can be made of the same situation depending on one's perspective. The meme provides a powerful metaphor for the complexity of dealing with multiple stakeholders.

Doing so is the CEO's job more than anyone else's, and the stakes can be extremely high. As Majid Al Futtaim's Alain Bejjani states: "When you think about what gives you the license to be in business, it's the people you impact—be they individuals, communities, or societies. You can have the best strategy, technology, and balance sheet, but when something changes for those people—regardless of whether it's within your control or not—it can have a huge (direct or indirect) impact on your organization. There are many instances where something that seemed quite mundane at the outset turned into an issue to manage. Mishandling these relationships can cause irreparable reputation damage, which at best can end a career and at worst kill a business or drive it to change strategy."

For the reasons Bejjani lays out, management guru Peter Drucker once observed, "In any organization, regardless of its mission, the CEO is the link between the Inside, i.e., 'the organization,' and the Outside . . . Inside, there are only costs. Results are only on the Outside."[77] The "Outside" Drucker is referring to includes shareholders, creditors, investors, analysts, government regulatory agencies, government legislative bodies, customers, suppliers, distributors, local and national communities, the public at large (global community), the media, labor unions, industry trade groups, professional associations, advocacy groups, competitors, and the list could go on. Many of these stakeholders themselves are interlinked in a complex web of sometimes competing and other times interdependent relationships.

To get the most out of their relationships with their stakeholders, the best CEOs travel whenever, wherever, and do whatever is necessary to support the business. Peter Voser, the former CEO of the oil giant Royal Dutch Shell, faced a world in which international oil companies like his were becoming less dominant, and national oil companies were becoming more and more powerful. To keep Shell growing, Voser knew he'd have to build better relationships with the state-owned national oil companies as well as with the politicians who controlled them. The oil giant, for example, generated around 80 percent of Brunei's gross domestic product (GDP) and around 65 percent of Oman's. "Do you think the sultans of these two countries would talk to anybody other than the CEO?" says Voser. "No! We have a huge responsibility to them and absolutely need to deliver.

"I had strong conviction," continues Voser, "that I was the CEO but also the ambassador for Shell. I represented our 100,000 employees, our 350,000 people in retail sites, and our half a million workers who build projects for us—so almost a million people in all." He estimates that he spent half of his time on external stakeholder engagement, not including dealing with shareholders. That time was largely spent traveling, visiting country after country to explain and show how Shell shared a long-term interest in their prosperity. "If the president of Russia or China or the sultan of Oman wants to see you," he shares, "you can't say, 'I'll come in three weeks.' No, you're there tomorrow."

As with all of the CEOs we spoke to, Voser found the grueling task of stakeholder engagement to be fruitful: "The biggest pleasure of all was that I could open doors that nobody else could open," he says. Not every CEO experiences managing the external world in the same way the best do, however. Overall, less than 30 percent of CEOs feel they engage effectively with external stakeholders. Those that get it right share a number of commonalities in that they . . .

> . . . contain the time spent "Outside"
> . . . understand the other party's "why?"
> . . . gather as many good ideas as possible from the interactions
> . . . maintain a single narrative across all stakeholders

Contain the Time Spent "Outside"

When management guru Peter Drucker asserted the definition of the CEO as the link between the Inside and the Outside, he also emphasized the importance of prioritization. "To define a *meaningful* Outside of the organization is the CEO's first task," he wrote in a 2004 editorial in the *Wall Street Journal*. "The definition is anything but easy, let alone obvious." He went on to describe how no company can be a leader in every area of the Outside, and concluded that deciding which stakeholders to concentrate on is "a highly risky decision and one very hard to change or reverse. Only the CEO can make it. But also the CEO must make it."[78]

So how should CEOs prioritize? Most simply identify and rank their stakeholders using some criteria. The best, however, start one level higher. They place a firm, absolute boundary on how much time they will spend with the Outside. Intuit's Brad Smith explains, "Start with the container, whatever it is for you. Mine was twenty percent of my time was spent externally. Then realize that anyone who wants a part of the twenty percent has to prove why they're a better use of your time than something else that falls in that bucket. My assistant would color code everything and measure at the end of a month whether I was spending my time the right way. There needed to be a justification as to why I should take time away from our top shareholder to go speak with *Fortune* magazine, for example. They needed to give me a good reason why that trade-off made sense. Going over twenty percent wasn't an option."

Across all the excellent CEOs we spoke to, we found that an average of 30 percent of their time was spent with external stakeholders in one form or another, but with a high standard deviation. Ahold Delhaize's Dick Boer, for example, kept his external involvement to 10 percent of his time. Netflix's Reed Hastings, on the other hand, allocated a third of his time to government, public relations, and shareholders. Add to that the time he spent with customers, trying to understand focus group input or what shows are getting watched and why, and his total external commitment grew to be 50 percent of his schedule. That's a lot, though not as much as Shell's Peter Voser, as we showed earlier. It's important to note that such allocations typically change as a CEO's situation changes. "I focused on my colleagues and internal initiatives more early in my tenure," U.S. Bancorp's Richard Davis shares. "Once I had the right team in place that I trusted, the amount of time with external stakeholders went up."

Once they set the amount of time they want to spend with outside stakeholders, the best CEOs prioritize those meetings based on which interactions help the company live its purpose, deliver on its strategy, and manage short- and long-term risks. Nancy McKinstry at Wolters Kluwer puts the vast majority of her external facing time into customers. For Duke Energy's Lynn Good, it's important to be spending time with regulators and politicians. U.S. Bancorp's Davis chose to spend a significant amount of time "on community stuff." Lockheed Martin's Marillyn Hewson emphasized establishing international relationships. IDB's Lilach Asher-Topilsky invested heavily in building a relationship with the labor union. Equity Group's James Mwangi chose to sit on numerous UN and other advisory boards. And so on.

For any public company CEO, regardless of their company's purpose and strategy, the investment community is an important stakeholder. The best CEOs typically spend time with their company's fifteen to twenty-five most important investors (those who are most knowledgeable and engaged) and assign the rest to the CFO and their investor relations department. They also limit themselves to one or two conferences a year, but nothing more.

Initially as CEO, DSM's Feike Sijbesma went with his investor relations team to visit shareholders. Several, as he recalls, "Would especially ask me questions because they want to know what's happening in the short term, even the next quarter. They cared much less about the future of the company." Sijbesma suggested they sell their shares if that was their goal. His investor relations team questioned if that was the best strategy to deal with shareholders. "Absolutely," he said. "Especially because we're going to transform the company."

Sijbesma knew what he was doing. "We made a list of shareholders who would fit with us, and there were a lot that weren't holding our shares yet. The narrative often used was: 'You cannot determine who owns you; they determine who they will own.' I said, 'Yes, it's their money, I cannot decide for them. But let us seduce the investors that fit with our journey.' We spent a lot of time on that. Your shareholders aren't just a given. Work on it. And communicate even more with them, so you can bring them along your journey and create trust." Greg Case did the same at Aon. "About ten years ago we said, 'We're not particularly happy with our investors.' They were highly biased to the short term, so we started changing them." He shares: "We did the analysis, 'Who should own us based on our strategy?' We talked to the ones we had, we identified those we didn't, and we went after those."

Once there is clarity on how much time should be spent with outsiders and with whom, the best CEOs optimize their schedules to make every minute count. Westpac's Gail Kelly was well known in Australia for jamming as many stakeholders as possible into her quarterly visits to regions. She met with the community, her employees, her customers, the local government, and the media. "I was rigorous and relentless about it," she says. Marillyn Hewson of Lockheed Martin adds that while it's important to have a strict schedule, one has to be flexible: "Every September we look a year ahead and lay out what we'll do and when: investor calls, customer visits, airshows, conferences. If something new arises, I either can't do it or something else has to come off my plate. Of course, it's not so strict that things can't be adjusted, but you know where your priorities are for the year."

Understand Their "Why?"

We devoted the last chapter to the importance of grounding stakeholder engagement in a clear understanding of a company's "why?" In the same vein, the best CEOs go out of their way to go beyond the "what" and understand their stakeholders' "why?" Doing so enables more profound connections to be made, conflicts to be resolved, and, at minimum, a baseline of respect to be created from feeling heard and understood.

Reed Hastings reveals how he thinks about some of Netflix's stakeholders. "Take the press, for example. My general view on the press is they want to be truth tellers, but they're forced to be entertainers. If you can understand that conflict, you can help them be entertaining and also get some truth through. With politicians, the thing is keeping the majority of people in a society supportive. That's an enormously difficult challenge, and once you understand that you can forgive them when they do things that don't seem rational in your little world, because you have high respect for their unique skills in channeling the public mood. Those are both examples of trying to have real understanding of the other side."

Lockheed Martin's Marillyn Hewson's very public, high-stakes experience dealing with former US president Donald Trump further illustrates the point. In 2016, she was making her way to the Israeli Nevatim Air Force Base in the southern region of Israel. Her visit marked the delivery of the first two F-35 stealth fighters to the Israeli Air Force. Out of the blue her mobile phone buzzed with a tweet that then-president-elect Trump had just sent to more than sixteen million followers. "The F-35 program and cost is out of control. Billions of dollars can and will be saved on military (and other) purchases after January 20th [Trump's inauguration date]." Lockheed Martin's stock price started plummeting at a rate that would ultimately wipe out nearly $4 billion of its value in a single day. On Hewson's arriving at her destination, Israeli prime minister Benjamin Netanyahu promptly inquired as to whether his country would get a rebate on the planes that were being delivered if the new US president was going to get a better deal. There was no precedent for the situation or road map to follow.

Keeping her characteristically cool and calm demeanor, Hewson convened key members of her team to discuss how to move forward. They quickly outlined what information they could provide the president-elect and his team. They also made the F-35 program manager available to the media to field questions to expand the pool of understanding and provide the latest facts. A week later, Hewson was invited by Trump to his seafront estate in Florida, Mar-a-Lago. As she entered the room, she was met by a host of government officials and industry leaders. Hewson came prepared to help the president understand the program better. She also came with a promise: that she would personally ensure costs of the F-35 program would continue to be aggressively driven down. Coming out of the meeting, she felt they had had "a very good conversation." Later that day, however, another tweet came from the president-elect: "Based on tremendous cost and cost overruns of the Lockheed Martin F-35, I have asked Boeing to price out a comparable F-18 Super Hornet!" Lockheed Martin's stock immediately began to tumble again, on top of the damage it had already taken from his previous tweet.

Hewson relates what happened next: "I spent time with a couple of my trusted senior leaders to really think through what was going on, and it dawned on us that while we're the subject of the conversation, Trump's goal is to let the American people know, 'I'm going to focus on defense of the nation. I'm going to get a good deal. I'm going to spend your tax payer dollar wisely.' Understanding that, we thought, 'Let's engage in new ways that show we understand his needs. We also let the press know that we agree with the view that defense spending is important and it should be spent wisely.' " Hewson reinforced this message of responsible stewardship in her public enagements, in company press releases, and in one-on-one customer meetings.

A few months later, after an agreement on cost savings had been reached, headlines would proclaim, "Lockheed Martin's Hewson turns Trump from foe to friend." The president, now in office, also paid her the ultimate dealmaker's compliment in a White House meeting, saying, "She's tough!" Hewson reflects on her experience with the F-35: "It goes beyond just listening to what they say," she shares. "If you take time to understand why they're saying what they're saying, you can help shape their longer-term thinking."

Understanding stakeholders' "why?" doesn't have to involve guesswork—in most cases the question can and should be asked directly. When Matti Lievonen, the former CEO of Neste, decided to make the Finnish oil refiner more sustainable, it wasn't an easy journey. While the company wanted to achieve its goal of using more renewable feedstock to make its fuel—think: municipal waste, recycled lumber, and plastic—progress was slow. Then one day in October 2011 Lievonen was driving to the office for the company's quarterly earnings call when he looked up and saw Greenpeace banners hanging on the outside walls surrounding his headquarters. Activists were trying to block the main entrance and climb the walls. Lievonen's communications director was nervous, and his employees in shock. Greenpeace was protesting Neste's use of palm oil as a feedstock for refining. "We'd done hard and groundbreaking work to ensure sustainability in everything related to palm oil," says Lievonen, "but I knew we had to listen and address their concerns given the impact they could have on our operations and reputation."

The CEO invited them into the building for a discussion, which took place in front of around five hundred people in an auditorium. Lievonen committed to answering their questions and addressing their concerns, as long as they'd offer the same courtesy to him. "Transparency goes both ways," he says. "We didn't have all the answers for them in that very first meeting. But it started a dialogue that has made Neste a better company. Even though we didn't agree on everything, it was important to listen to a highly critical party." Seeing the transparency of the management team also changed the atmosphere within the company. Neste improved its research and sustainability efforts, and studied new raw materials. By the end of Lievonen's tenure, Neste had significantly expanded its portfolio of recycled raw materials, and became the world's largest producer of renewable diesel and jet fuel refined from waste and residues.

"I believe that criticism must be seen as an opportunity to change," he says. "It was important to put ourselves in the shoes of other stakeholders. Not only to win their trust, but also improve ourselves. We're better off for it today."

Harvest New Ideas

Most CEOs engage their stakeholders with a clear objective in mind, typically to make a decision, reach an agreement, or achieve an understanding. The best CEOs always have a further objective, which cuts across all of their stakeholder interactions: to harvest new ideas that can make the business better. At both Shire and Galderma, for example, it was often conversations with customers that led Flemming Ørnskov down the path of various mergers and acquisitions. "At least two or three deals we did at Shire got their inspiration from doctors I got to know who said to me, 'You should really think about this thing,' 'I'm involved in this product development,' or 'I've seen patients in this clinical trial.'"

At Aon, Greg Case picks up new product development ideas regularly from client conversations—risk products for cybersecurity and intellectual property theft being two examples. Case explains his philosophy: "You, of course, interact with clients to try and actually serve them, but you also interact with clients to understand how you want to change."

Inspiration can come from stakeholders other than customers. Suppliers, partners, and even politicians can spur powerful new thinking. Perhaps surprisingly, the best CEOs even turn the tables on investors and analysts who are looking for information from them. Ken Powell at General Mills recalls, "I spent a lot of time with our top shareholders. There were, of course, some who wanted a quick hit, but others who were very constructive and had a long history of really understanding the industry. I got a lot of energy from those conversations. And that helped refine our thinking or reinforce what we were already thinking about."

Dupont's Ed Breen does the same with activist investors. "I engage with the activists. If you listen, they often have good ideas. I agreed with eighty percent of what they wrote in their white papers, and what I didn't agree with was how to go about fixing the problem that they were worried about. Their view is, 'If Ed has a better way to fix it, good, go do it.' They just want it fixed. With that approach, I've found they often become your ally."

For Total's Patrick Pouyanné, special interest groups are often a source of inspiration. At a UN meeting on climate, for example, he heard a hundred company leaders talking about carbon neutrality. "There were no oil or gas bosses there," he recalls. "When I came out of that meeting I realized that there had to be a real story in that." Such interactions have influenced Pouyanné to spend billions on moving more aggressively into renewables in pursuit of Total's mission to be a global player in responsible energy.

Sometimes good ideas can flow from outside partnerships. When Nestlé and Disney formed a partnership to improve their communications strategy, former CEO Peter Brabeck-Letmathe spent some time in Los Angeles at the Disney studios. There he learned how Disney, as they began to conceive each animated film, was already thinking about how to make the most of that film over the next ten years. It would start by defining the characters and thinking about how to merchandise them later on. After the film appeared in theaters, it would go to DVD and so on, and the whole time they'd be using elements from the film to multiply the value over a ten-year period. In other words, Disney thought not just about creating a movie but a whole franchise.

When he returned to Nestlé, Brabeck-Letmathe wanted to do the same thing with its products. He asked his research people to create nutritional ingredients that he could brand. The first one was LC1, a bacterium that would be included in different products. Says Brabeck-Letmathe: "So instead of creating just one ingredient for one product, which has limited value, I was thinking about how to transform a nutritional ingredient into a brand, and how to exploit it over the next ten years. It doesn't matter where you are or what role you play—people always make things and do things in different ways, and you always can learn something and apply it in your own organization."

Maintain a Single Narrative

With so many stakeholders to interact with, the best CEOs know it's a fool's errand to try to manage different messaging for each. The best CEOs find it both productive and liberating to employ a single narrative when interacting with the Outside, not just on a company's social purpose (as we discussed in the last chapter), but in relation to all aspects of the business. Jacques Aschenbroich exemplifies the idea in how he manages Valeo's stakeholders: "What I present to the board of directors is exactly the same that I present to our shareholders, exactly the same that I present to leaders, exactly the same that I present to the unions," he shares. "I don't want to have a difference in terms of communication—it has to be the same."

IDB's Lilach Asher-Topilsky stresses the importance of being open, honest, and consistent, especially with the stock market. "You put forth your vision and then show how you continue the vision. When something happens, internally or externally, you continue to communicate in the same way and say to them, 'This is what we told you, this is what happened, and this is in line or not in line because of 1, 2, 3.' Don't overpromise. Be frank about the problems, not just the opportunities, and then you won't face a market that's saying, 'You overpromised. Let's drop the price.'"

Such candor—even if uncomfortable in the moment—is the only way to establish real trust and credibility. U.S. Bancorp's Richard Davis explains how he dealt with investors when he had some negative news: "I often said to them, 'Look, we're giving you the unvarnished truth here. This is what we're working on. You deserve the truth, and we deserve for you to believe us. So when we tell you that things are going amazingly well, you will remember us telling you when they weren't. Because we're going to be honest with you all the way through.'"

Aon's Greg Case learned early in his tenure the importance of having a clear and consistent story for the Outside. As he took the job at the professional services giant in 2005, he was told he had to present at an investor day that was scheduled to take place a month after he arrived. The company hadn't had one in many years. As Case recalls, "Had I been more seasoned, I would have said: 'That's wonderful. We're going to cancel that.' But I didn't know any better. So, I said, 'Okay, we'll get ready.' What are we going to say in a month about the future strategy of Aon that's meaningful and compelling? Nothing. If we had that answer in a month, we sure wouldn't be talking to investors about it. We'd be talking to our colleagues about it. We'd be laying the foundation to build something great. And *then* we'd deliver to investors. But I had no idea at the time. So we showed up in a month and it was a massive fire drill from hell." The lesson for Case was clear: "You've got to have a plan. Then you've got to make sure that everyone understands what you're trying to do."

Having a single narrative that cuts across all stakeholder groups creates a virtuous cycle that often enables CEOs to spend less time with stakeholders as they build a track record of consistency. Best Buy's Hubert Joly explains: "The key with any stakeholder is to get the 'say-do' ratio right: the ratio between what we said we were going to do and what we actually did. That's how you get credibility. And if you're doing what you are saying you'll do, they'll actually want to see less of you. They'll want you to be spending your time working on the business and delivering on your commitments."

Managing the Outside is an essential part of managing a business. "Relationships with our stakeholders—governments, dealers, suppliers, unions, and communities—aren't a nice-to-do," confirms GM's Mary Barra. "That's part of running the company well." As we've seen, engaging stakeholders requires an inordinate amount of work, which can consume a significant amount of a CEO's time. Make no mistake that it's hard work, too. Whereas a CEO has direct authority over employees, they have none over the many stakeholders who can influence the company's destiny. Further, stakeholders are scrutinizing companies more than ever, and activists are developing increasingly sophisticated tools to attack management.

That said, the best CEOs, as Esquel's Marjorie Yang puts it, "mitigate the common trap of spending too much time with external groups and not enough time with their own colleagues." They build a container that sets boundaries and optimizes time spent with stakeholders and make each interaction as productive as possible by understanding and connecting with the other party's "why?" In addition, the best CEOs approach every contact outside the company as an opportunity to harvest new ideas to take back to make their businesses better. Finally, excellent CEOs maintain a single narrative over time with all stakeholders—enhancing credibility and adding simplicity to managing an otherwise complex external landscape.

The value of strong relationships with stakeholders is always important, but when a crisis strikes, stakeholder relationships become make-or-break.

CHAPTER 15

Moments of Truth Practice
Stay Elevated

There's no harm in hoping for the best as long as you're prepared for the worst.

—Stephen King

In 2015, Wells Fargo's CEO John Stumpf received Morningstar's CEO of the Year title. Ten months after receiving the award he was handing in his resignation amid the company's sales practices scandal. Boeing's CEO Dennis Muilenburg was *Aviation Week's* 2018 person of the year. Eleven months later his board asked him to step down amid the company's 737 MAX debacle. BP's Tony Hayward resigned soon after the Deep Horizon oil spill. Uber's Travis Kalanick was asked by several board members to resign over concerns about the company's culture. Unfortunately, "from adulation to resignation" is a CEO narrative that plays out again and again.

The best way to manage a crisis is, of course, to prevent it in the first place. No matter how well a company is run, the question for even the best CEOs isn't "if" they'll have to lead through a crisis, it's "when." In the last decade, headlines that carried the word *crisis* alongside the names of the 100 largest companies on the *Forbes* The Global 2000 appeared 80 percent more often than they did in the previous decade.[79] This isn't surprising given the ever-increasing complexity of products and services driven by technology and global supply chains. Further amplifying matters, as we've discussed in the previous chapters, are, first, higher and higher stakeholder expectations, second, social media platforms like Twitter and Facebook that quickly and effectively amplify concerns, and, third, governments in many regions that have shown an increased willingness to intervene on behalf of their constituents.

A crisis can arise from anywhere. It may be sparked by the high-profile media coverage of a passenger sustaining injuries while being dragged from an overbooked plane, as then United Airlines CEO and later executive chairman Oscar Munoz experienced. Or by a widespread cyber-breach, as Richard Smith, the former CEO of the credit agency Equifax, confronted. Or by a costly safety issue, an ethical-conduct issue, a hostile takeover attempt—the possibilities are endless. Not all crises are company specific. Macroeconomic events, pandemics, international conflicts, natural disasters, social conflict, terrorist attacks, and countless other external factors can all create crisis conditions for CEOs.

In January of 2014, only a couple of weeks after Mary Barra took over as CEO of GM, the carmaker had to start recalling millions of vehicles due to faulty ignition switches, which were implicated in a number of fatal crashes. As she recounts: "When you have a crisis, it's not like you know the significance of it immediately. On the day you learn about some bad news, you don't initially think, 'Oh, my gosh, this is going to be a huge crisis,' but as the events surrounding the ignition switch began to unfold, we quickly realized the situation was serious." She sought advice from Warren Buffett, one of GM's shareholders, who told her that his mantra when he took over a troubled Salomon Brothers was: "'Get it right, get it fast, get it out, and get it over.'"

Barra assigned five people from her leadership team of fifteen who met every day to deal with the crisis. Often in the early stages of the crisis, the team had more questions than answers, so Barra kept sending them off to get the answers. Sometimes they met for two hours; sometimes it was twenty minutes, but Barra kept in close contact. In the meantime, she told the rest of the leadership team to run the business—to drive sales every day and keep vehicle programs on track.

Interestingly, she saw in the crisis an opportunity to accelerate needed culture change. "As we got into the crisis," says Barra, "we said, 'These are our values, and they're not just something we paste on a wall. We're going to live them through this difficult time.' With 'putting customers first' as one of the values, we said, 'We're going to be transparent. We're going to do everything possible to support the customer and everything possible to make sure something like this never happens again.'"

In the spring of that year Barra appeared before Congress and got a grilling. Under harsh questioning she sometimes had to confess that she simply didn't yet have answers, and wouldn't until the investigation was complete. Recalls the CEO: "I was highly criticized for that, but I'm so glad I didn't try to guess what exactly the root issues were, because I would have been wrong. That would have made it worse. Then I would have been hearing, 'Before, you said it was that, and now you say it's this.'" As Barra's team learned more and more, they would immediately share the information with the public, and they did whatever they could to help their customers. In the end GM recalled more than 2.6 million vehicles and resolved thousands of personal injury claims. GM entities paid $120 million in a class action settlement that primarily addressed the alleged economic harm suffered by car owners or lessees with recalled ignition switches.

Her handling of the crisis earned Barra recognition as "crisis manager of the year," by *Fortune* in 2014. As she reflects on what she learned, aside from continuing to be deeply sorry for the human tragedy, she says, "My big 'a-ha' in all of this is that sometimes as a leader you think you have a decision to make when you really don't, because there's only one right thing to do. Yes, you need to think it through, but you really don't have a choice. A lot of times, people will say, 'We've got this issue. It's going to have this kind of impact on our financials.' And I reply, 'What's the right thing to do? If it's going to be a hit to the financials, that's not great, but what's the right thing to do?'"

A crisis can end an otherwise great CEO's tenure, or it can be deftly used to propel the company to new levels of postcrisis performance. The swing factors between the two extremes are the extent to which a CEO . . .

. . . stress-tests the company regularly

. . . creates a command center when a crisis hits

... maintains a long-term perspective

... shows personal resilience

Stress-Test the Company Regularly

The best CEOs adhere to the old proverb: "An ounce of prevention is worth a pound of cure." Says Ecolab's Doug Baker: "The way you get prepared for a crisis is never on the day of the crisis. It's creating resilience before it ever happens." Esquel Group's Marjorie Yang provides a helpful analogy: "When you have a crisis it's like a sailboat going into a storm. You've got to prepare your boat before you head into the storm, and once you're underway you can't expect people will know what needs to be done at the last minute."

Virtually every company uses some form of forecasting methodology to predict the future. The better companies do such forecasting based on a "best," "middle," and "worst" case scenario. By contrasting the extremes, contingency plans can be made to mitigate downsides and maximize upsides. The best companies go one step further and also stress-test their company's ability to respond to a small number of "black swan" events: crises that are rare, severe, but often obvious in hindsight.

At Netflix, for example, Reed Hastings runs an exercise that poses this problem: "It's ten years out, and Netflix is a failed firm. Estimate the probabilities of the different causes." Let's say one cause is that a plane crash takes out Netflix's headquarters. The probability of that is 0.00001. Then Hastings and his team work through the rest of the list, making assessments of the respective probabilities. "It's surprisingly challenging," he says, "to assess what those scenarios are. Sometimes the discussion turns to what we can do about some of these risks. But many times, just defining what risks we face will prompt people to adjust behavior in smart ways that make us more resilient."

Stress-testing on multiple fronts can reveal patterns across various scenarios that CEOs and their teams can use to create crisis-management playbooks. As Intuit's Brad Smith puts it, "While each crisis is unique, if you step back and look at them, they share seventy to eighty percent of the same characteristics. The same playbooks work, but you have to tailor them to the specific situation."

A good crisis playbook lays out the leadership protocols, warroom configuration, action plans, and communications approaches for when a crisis hits. It will also define and measure the leading indicators of an escalating threat. As General Mills' Ken Powell puts it: "One secret about crisis management is recognizing when you have one. They're not always as apparent as the COVID-19 pandemic. Sometimes you really have to bang the drum because it may not be quite so apparent. A crisis can come from a very committed start-up that is about to beat you. You've got to be on the lookout for those companies who have a thousand rabid users. Let it grab your attention, and then react early, or you won't see the crisis coming."

Caterpillar's Jim Owens shares how responding to early warnings changed his company's trajectory: "In 2007–2008, everyone on my team was convinced we needed to double the capacity of our mining equipment. But I was spending time in New York and Washington, and I could see that although the optimism at Caterpillar was running high, we were cruising toward the waterfall. We chose not to increase production because we were worried about the global economy—meanwhile, the mining companies were telling us we weren't building enough to satisfy their demand. The next year they took less than half of what they had on order!"

For playbooks to stay relevant, CEOs should demand that managers "run the plays" in the form of periodic simulations so everyone knows what to do when a real crisis situation emerges. Owens describes how he had to push leaders to stress-test annually at Caterpillar. "I had all of the divisions tell me what they'd do to maintain profitability in their businesses if they were hit by the worst cyclical drop in the last twenty-five years," he says. "Everybody had to go through that exercise once a year. They all were beginning to think it was a stupid exercise after five years of record growth and profit. But in the sixth year, it turns out that was a pretty good exercise. In November of 2008 [during the global financial crisis], we said, 'Okay. Get your deep recession scenario out and implement it.'"

Stress-testing efforts also helped the Dangote Group navigate the COVID-19 crisis. "Prior to the pandemic, we strengthened and improved our business processes, governance, and organizational structure," says CEO Aliko Dangote. "During this exercise, for example, we instituted a robust risk management function to ensure preparedness for such times as these." Despite the challenges of the pandemic, Dangote was able to proactively monitor key dimensions of their operations and mitigate negative financial impacts. "Having a well-functioning business continuity framework helped ensure we kept our businesses running across the Group," Dangote says.

Even if a crisis doesn't arise, regular stress-testing can reveal opportunities to make a business more resilient. It can lead to divesting underperforming businesses, cutting excess costs, doubling down in high-growth geographies, enhancing the M&A plan, improving the effectiveness of the top team, and making needed investments in technologies. Ecolab's Doug Baker explains the importance of such actions: "There are always problems in business. And you have to get after the problems you can immediately see so that you have the capacity to manage what you can't foresee, but know is certain to come. A lot of resilience is just making sure you keep dealing with the stuff as it comes up. Don't let business challenges pile up."

Beyond business challenges, stress-testing also shines a light on the importance of managing Peter Drucker's "meaningful Outside" stakeholders that we discussed in the previous chapter. As Baker says, "You've got to build goodwill with stakeholders when you don't need it. Look at it as a currency you're saving up over time. I sat on the board of U.S. Bank. They built a ton of currency in the form of trust and credibility with regulators before the financial crisis. They did it by being transparent, not getting into subprime lending, and overall being a good citizen. This changed how they were perceived and it influenced how they were treated when the crisis came. If you've built goodwill, you're innocent until proven guilty, instead of the other way around."

In keeping with the aphorism "to fail to plan is to plan to fail," those CEOs who build resilience ahead of a crisis will find it far easier to deal with what comes. However, planning ahead isn't everything. As former heavyweight boxing champion Mike Tyson put it, "Everyone has a plan until they get punched in the mouth." We now turn our sights to a CEO's actions during the crisis, which if handled correctly, can dramatically shape both their own and their company's fortunes.

Create a Command Center

When a crisis hits, here's what CEOs should expect: There might have been serious damage to the community, customers, livelihoods, and/or the environment. Investors will be livid; the board and any relevant regulators will be looking to assign blame. Natural antagonists will start to take advantage of the company's misfortune—activists may mobilize, consumers might boycott, competitors will move to steal customers or employees, hackers may target your systems, and the media will likely dig up every past error the company has made. At the same time, the facts on the ground will be few and far between, and opinions and rumors will fly about the severity of the crisis and the company's level of complicity. Top team members might be implicated. Others might prove too inexperienced to be helpful or be simply temperamentally unsuited to a stressful situation.

In the middle of this chaos, too often companies only issue cryptic statements to the outside world as they wait for more facts and hope that things turn out to be not as bad as they seem. As the crisis builds, they often find themselves in a vicious cycle of reacting to the latest negative headlines. In Mary Barra's case at GM during the ignition switch recalls, for example, she says, "Certain members of our leadership team thought that if we put out a press release, it would go away. I had to say, 'This is not going away. We have to do much more. We can't stay silent or communicate only through a press release.' So we did a press conference against the advice of some."

As Barra did at GM, the best CEOs immediately activate a cross-functional "command center" team that is empowered to tackle both primary (interrelated legal, technical, operational, and financial challenges) and secondary (reactions by key stakeholders) threats. These teams are typically small and agile, with a full-time senior leader, very high levels of funding, and adequate decision-making authority to make and implement decisions within hours rather than days. Without such a team, organizations quickly fall into well-intended dysfunction: Managers end up taking actions in an uncoordinated fashion and with incomplete or inaccurate information, and central decision-making slows as dozens of sign-offs are required to move. In the worst case, turf wars and finger pointing emerge, resulting in gridlock.

A key role of the command center is to coordinate and enable good communications internally and externally. When the COVID-19 pandemic hit, Cincinnati Children's Michael Fisher dramatically ramped up communication with both his internal and external stakeholders. He had his crisis team create an online "frequently asked questions" page. He and his senior team created a series of videos from the executive team aimed at employees. Every Monday for an hour, the executive team communicated with eight hundred of the company's managers. "The focus was both us informing the managers on 'What we all need to know' and them informing us on 'Here are things you, Michael, and your leadership team ought to know,'" he shares. As Fisher saw it, it was an opportunity to "not only preserve trust with stakeholders, but strengthen it."

As Fisher's experience illustrates, having the right team dedicated to the crisis has many benefits. It provides the best possible understanding of the magnitude, scope, and facts behind the crisis. This information will help leaders guard against biases and provide a sober appraisal of how long resolving the crisis will take, and it will ensure that promises aren't made that down the road can further erode a company's (and a CEO's) credibility. The team will take actions to calm the extreme reactions of stakeholders, buying time for the threat to be better understood and addressed. For example, the team might propose an emergency financial package for business partners, goodwill payments to consumers, or a product recall. It will also urgently respond to regulators as necessary.

Perhaps the greatest benefit of having a command center in place is that the essential—and at times existential—work described above can be handled while allowing the CEO not to become all-consumed by the crisis.

Maintain a Long-Term Perspective

If you're the captain of a battleship and are hit by a torpedo, what do you do? The best send a portion of their crew to contain the hull breach but themselves stay on the bridge, increase speed to full, and deploy the rest of the crew to keep fighting the war. When a crisis hits a company, a similar ethos applies. Many crises directly affect one or two parts of an organization, and it's up to the CEO to keep everyone else focused on driving the business forward. CEOs need to provide a broad sense of calm and perspective so all employees can continue to do their best work. Even when the whole organization is affected, "What people need in a crisis is not just constant communication," American Express's Ken Chenault explains. "The CEO has to set the context, too—how are you defining expectations in the short, moderate, and long term?"

Maintaining a long-term perspective served Diageo well during the COVID-19 pandemic. As bars and pubs around the world were shutting down, Ivan Menezes and his team decided to buy back all the kegs of beer that were sitting idle and about to expire, no questions asked, at a cost of tens of millions of pounds sterling. "We had a drop in earnings those two quarters, but I didn't care where the financials were going to fall," says Menezes. "Taking that short-term pressure off the table was the best thing we did. It sent the message to our teams to support the brands, support the customers, do the right thing. And emerging from that period, we've gained share in the vast majority of our markets."

"When I reflect on crises in my career, there are three lessons for CEOs that come to mind," Ahold Delhaize's Dick Boer shares. "First, do not chair or lead your crisis team. Let them report out to you. This gives you the space and time to oversee all the elements of the business, not only the crisis. Second, show confidence in your organization—show that you're in control, that you know what you're doing, and that you'll take care of your people and your customers. Third, think of what's next even when the storm is still around you, because there'll be opportunities and other situations you have to manage as a consequence of the crisis that you might not have thought about."

Boer's insights reflect then-senator John F. Kennedy's observation: "When written in Chinese, the word *crisis* is composed of two characters. One represents danger and the other represents opportunity."[80] While the crisis team is minimizing the danger, the CEO also needs to be looking at the opportunity—as GM's Mary Barra did in using the crisis to accelerate the company's needed culture change. Adidas's Kasper Rørsted expands on the idea: "I know it's commonplace to say never waste a good crisis, but it's actually the best time to make radical change in a company. This is when you can be more dogmatic and say, 'We're not going to do this anymore.' Whether it's cutting unnecessary travel, leveraging digital channels, or anything else—it's the time to move two or three years ahead of where you would have been otherwise."

Beyond using a crisis to trigger change in the organization, the best CEOs sometimes use it as a reason to pursue a new direction for the business. Intuit's Brad Smith expands: "Be cognizant of what secular trends the crisis will accelerate. In the financial crisis the adoption of platforms, mobile devices, and globalization accelerated faster than anyone anticipated. The COVID-19 crisis will likely accelerate virtual collaboration, omnichannel commerce, and the need to have better financial literacy and money management. As a CEO, you need to ask yourself what just got faster that you'll have to quickly adapt and adopt." Smith also recognizes that some practices adopted during a crisis can be superior to previous approaches. "Keep a running list of the things that are now actually working better than they were before the crisis, review that list, and decide what will become part of your new operating model," he suggests. "During COVID-19, for example, Zoom became the great equalizer. Everyone had an equal voice. Perhaps we all don't have to work in the office."

By thinking long-term, the best CEOs help their organizations avoid short-term solutions that will be damaging in the long run. When hit by a recession, Eaton's Sandy Cutler told his executive team: "We don't want to fire people. When we grow again, we're going to need the skills of all these people, so we have to find a better concept." They made layoffs voluntary, as well as asking employees if they'd be willing to take some time off to save the jobs of other teammates. The entire senior leadership team gave up all their incentives and cut their base salaries as well.

"The response was just unbelievable to see," says Cutler. "The point we were trying to make to people is, 'We can all tuck our belt in here a little bit and take care of one another, but we're also going to have a better business in the future.' Those were tough decisions, because we got a lot of criticism from people. Wall Street wanted to see us provide numbers that showed we were laying off 30,000, 40,000 people. But we said, 'We're not doing that. We actually think that's old thinking. The new thinking is about preserving resources and making your expenses more variable.'" Cutler was clear with investors who criticized his decision. "Well, your choice is not to own us," he told them, "but you're going to make a big mistake. Because you will see us snap back faster than the people who laid off all those people."

The board is often one constituency CEOs overlook during a crisis—at their peril. As Duke Energy's Lynn Good explains: "When you're in a crisis, there may be media scrutiny and criticism of the company. You want your directors to understand the context of that media coverage and, of course, what you're doing to address the situation." And it's not just a one-way street; as we covered in previous chapters, the board can help the business. Good continues, "There have also been times when the board has designated a subcommittee to focus on a specific issue, drawing on specific skills of the board and allowing for more frequent, in-depth discussions. When you're in a crisis, you aren't waiting for the next scheduled board meeting, but you are flexible, adapting, and communicating—using all of the skills on your board."

After the initial frenzy of the crisis recedes, the best CEOs don't try to put it behind them unless they're convinced that their team has addressed the root causes. These are seldom technical; more often they involve people issues (culture, decision-rights, capabilities), processes (risk governance, performance management, standard setting), and systems and tools (maintenance procedures)—all of which are likely to take years to tackle. Further, the company's stakeholders will demand that the CEO hold accountable anyone who played a role in creating the crisis, that a large and lasting gesture to relevant stakeholders be made to make amends, and that, for years to come with respect to the issue, the CEO will be the face of the company to the media and lawmakers.

Show Personal Resilience

A crisis is a moment of truth not just for the institution, but also for its leader. When a debacle hits, the best CEOs know that their stakeholders' anger will likely center on them and in ways that affect their family and friends. They must prepare for one-sided reporting, parody on social media accounts, protestors showing up at their home, and their family being targeted online. The spotlight rarely fades away in a matter of days, weeks, or even months—it often last years.

In 2014, sportswear maker Adidas was hit by a confluence of events that caused its performance to nosedive. First, its golf business collapsed. At the time TaylorMade and Adidas Golf were under the same corporate umbrella and constituted the biggest golf company in the world (double the size of Callaway). Then the ruble tanked in Russia, the company's third-biggest market. Following the political situation in Ukraine, the European Union (EU) placed sanctions on Russia, which caused the industry to take a dive, wiping out $350 million of Adidas's profit within a month. Adidas issued a profit warning, and with it the share price fell. The negative sentiment that stormed in was directed personally at Herbert Hainer. "The investors nailed me," he acknowledges. "They said, 'The economy is booming, what's going on? He's too old now; he's running out of ideas—thirteen years as CEO is too much.'"

Hainer dug deep to maintain perspective. "That was one of my toughest times. I'm just a human being," he says. "I had to go for a walk for an hour after lunch to get some fresh air." As he walked, Hainer steadied himself. "First, I thought to myself, 'What are these guys talking about? Don't they realize what I've done here over the last thirteen years? Where is the acknowledgment of that? Why are they all complaining?' Second, I said, 'Ah, okay. They're all crazy. I'm fed up. If they don't like me anymore, then somebody else should do it.' In the final phase, I said to myself,

'Okay, stop it now. I will show the world, especially these critics, that I can do it again.'" Hainer then got back to work, reminding his people that they were incredibly talented (because they'd previously excelled) and assuring them that they'd weather the storm. Within twelve months, Adidas's share price doubled from $55 to nearly $110, putting the company back on a positive trajectory that has continued since.

Hainer was able to steel himself, having built personal resilience through the course of his tenure. When an athlete whom Adidas sponsored came under fire, so did Hainer. "I used to be asked, 'What are you doing? Do you punish these people? How can Adidas allow that?'" he reflects. "That was the most challenging thing at the beginning of my tenure—to recognize that I was on the front line with external stakeholders: financial investors, the media, and other general exposure." As he dealt with this CEO-only front-line role, Hainer gradually realized, "It doesn't matter how difficult times are, there is always a world after a crisis. Even if the situation looks bleak, believe in yourself and your people and maintain a positive attitude. Don't let yourself or the company be influenced too much by uncontrollable circumstances."

Andrew Wilson, the CEO of Electronic Arts, uses what he learned from practicing the martial art of Brazilian jiu-jitsu for sixteen years to stay resilient when crises hit. As he explains: "An important lesson from jiu-jitsu is that a small person—say, 150 pounds, close to my weight—fighting a 300-pound person will end up in a bad place at some point in time, no matter how good you are. Jiu-jitsu teaches you to find comfort in the uncomfortable. It teaches you that as long as you can breathe, you can continue. Even when I'm on the bottom, under a 300-pound person in the most difficult of situations, my job is to find that wriggle room that puts me in a position where I can breathe and plan my next move. And instead of fighting a losing battle, take the battle to where I'm strong."

In business, Wilson has found himself struggling many times with what feels like a three hundred–pound individual on top of him. "As we face the challenge of recruiting and retaining top talent, and launching high-quality products in a highly competitive industry, you're going to find yourself in uncomfortable positions. Our job is not to freak out. Our job is to find comfort and find

our breath and plan our next move. We always figure out how to
compete or work in an environment where we're strong. And to
the extent we're competing against others, we try to move them
out of their environment. We find our breath and get comfortable,
and then we work to get to a stronger position where we might
take positive and affirmative action."

Just three months into his tenure, a leading economic magazine
in Finland put Neste's Matti Lievonen in a group of the worst
CEOs in the country and suggested he should be fired. "The reality," he says, "is you can't be too negatively impacted by the lows,
or let the highs go to your head. There's a public element to the
role, and you have to stay grounded and just do the best you can
do. I used to let stress get the better of me but learned the hard
way due to health issues. I'm lucky to have a supportive family
that provides balance and acts as a sounding board. I celebrated
the successes with my team and organization but kept an eye on
our bigger purpose. And I recognized that there is life beyond the
CEO role." Years later, Neste was heralded for its transformational pivot from crude to biofuels, and the CEO won accolades
for value creation.

Lockheed Martin's Marillyn Hewson, reflecting on her ups and
downs in the role, shares, "There have been times when I received
criticisms that I don't think were deserved." To deal with such situations, she separated herself from the role. "I never took it personally," she says. "The comments may have been directed at me
because I was the personification of the company. They weren't
about me as an individual." American Express's Ken Chenault
points out that consistently returning to the "why?" of the organization is also a powerful way to stay centered. "Everything should
be grounded in what the firm stands for," he shares. "During
the financial crisis, for example, I had to reassert that American
Express is at its heart a service business. We needed to focus on
that and really understand what it meant to serve people."

Being resilient enough to depersonalize the role, respond to individual criticism in a thoughtful and measured manner, and stay
grounded in the company's values isn't easy. The best CEOs know
that the process is greatly aided by sleep, short breaks (as Hainer
role-modeled in going for a walk to gain perspective), nutrition,

exercise, and quality time with loved ones. Santander's Botín captures the idea in her motto of "*Estar bien para poder hacer más*," which translates to, "If you're feeling good, you can do many more things." We'll discuss further ways the best CEOs build their personal resilience ahead of crises when we focus on time and energy management practices in the next chapter.

In their book *Leadership on the Line*, authors Ron Heifetz and Marty Linsky advise leaders to periodically get off the dance floor and up on the balcony.[81] A crisis will by definition draw a CEO onto the dance floor so they can face reality, solve pressing problems, and push for operational change. The best CEOs also find ways to maintain a view from the balcony so they can see patterns, find hope on the horizon, and look for opportunities. They stress-test their company on a regular basis, and therefore enter a crisis as prepared as possible and build a full-time command center team to establish the facts, direct traffic, and problem-solve the issues at hand. While putting all this in place, these CEOs take a long-term view, have the resilience to withstand personal attacks, thoughtfully respond to criticism, and keep the company's "why?" in the forefront of decision-making.

●   ●   ●

We've now discussed how the best CEOs navigate the tricky and sometime treacherous role of engaging with their stakeholders. Among the many insights and examples, we learned about Shell's Peter Voser, who went to great lengths—including traveling to far parts of the world at a moment's notice—to engage with his most important stakeholders. We saw how Lockheed Martin's Marillyn Hewson successfully reacted to President-elect Trump's negative tweet about the F-35 program by understanding the "why?" behind his comments, and how Mary Barra skillfully navigated GM through its ignition crisis by being transparent with all parties involved.

Below is a summary of how the mindset of connecting on the "why?" with stakeholders—a mindset that research suggests materially affects up to a third of corporate earnings—translates into three main dimensions of stakeholder engagement: demonstrating social purpose, shaping strong relationships, and leading through moments of truth.

Connecting with Stakeholders: What separates the best from the rest

Mindset: Start with "Why?"	
Social purpose practice:	**Impact the Big Picture**
	▮ Clarify your societal "Why?"
	▮ Embed purpose into the core
	▮ Use strengths to make a difference
	▮ Make a stand when warranted
Stakeholder interaction practice:	**Get to the Essence**
	▮ Contain time spent "Outside"
	▮ Understand their "Why?"
	▮ Harvest new ideas
	▮ Maintain a single narrative
Moments of Truth practice:	**Stay Elevated**
	▮ Stress-test the company regularly
	▮ Create a command center
	▮ Maintain a long-term perspective
	▮ Show personal resilience

Even for readers who may not be CEOs, these lessons can be valuable for navigating the "Outside" of an organization or a project. Ask yourself: Am I fully cognizant of how what we're doing will have a big-picture impact on society? What are the tangible things I can point to that indicate we're making progress to that end? How are we using our strengths to give back to society? Are we speaking out on social issues that matter to us? Do we limit time spent engaging stakeholders to what is appropriate? Who are my most important stakeholders and what is the "why?" behind what they do? What new ideas have I harvested from stakeholder interactions? Am I telling a consistent story across stakeholders? Are we "stress-tested" against inevitable crises that will happen? Do I have a personal resilience plan in place that will enable me to keep perspective and have sound judgment during a crisis? Every leader can benefit from having good answers to such questions.

We've now discussed five CEO mindsets and practices that separate the best from the rest. We just spoke about maintaining personal resilience amid moments of truth, which moves us seamlessly to the topic of leading oneself—having a personal operating model that enables a CEO to keep all the plates spinning that need to be spun.

PERSONAL EFFECTIVENESS MINDSET

Do What Only You Can Do

There is nothing so useless as doing efficiently that which should not be done at all.

—Peter Drucker

The various CEO responsibilities we've discussed in this book often require a soul-crushing schedule. To meet this challenge, the best make sure they're both psychologically and physically fit—no easy task. As Majid Al Futtaim's Alain Bejjani puts it, "Leading yourself is the most difficult and the most daunting task. It requires the most courage."

Daunting is right—so much so that not every CEO we spoke to felt they could give advice on the topic. As one CEO said to us, "I felt like I was walking through land mines every day. I didn't thrive, I just didn't get blown up. It's a lot of work." Having said that, they also recognized that—more than with any of the other areas—managing personal effectiveness was under their control. As Mastercard's Ajay Banga pointed out, "If you, as the CEO, can't figure out what matters to you, and if you're not willing to make the time for it, then it's your problem. Nobody can help you." In fact, this topic was seen as so essential and difficult that many of the CEOs we spoke to suggested it should be the first chapter of any discussion about the job. We've left it to the end only because we felt it was important to first deeply understand the assortment of responsibilities placing demands on a CEO's energy. After all, almost 50 percent of chief executives say that the role is "not what I expected beforehand."[82]

The choices the best CEOs make to manage their personal well-being and effectiveness are precisely that—personal. There are, however, some commonalities. In the words of Galderma's Flemming Ørnskov: "People are successful operating in very different ways. But if I look at the CEOs I admire and know well, I think they all display discipline." Ørnskov's observation raises the question: Discipline around what? Many CEOs answer that question with: "My job is to do what needs to be done." That isn't how the best CEOs think, however. Rather, their mindset is: "My job is to do what only I can do." Caterpillar's Jim Owens explains that the key to personal effectiveness is: "Prioritizing the most critical issues that only the CEO can solve and delegating any remaining tasks."

The best CEOs "do what only they can do" in managing the three crucial dimensions of personal effectiveness: using time and energy, choosing a leadership model, and maintaining perspective.

CHAPTER 16

Time and Energy Practice
Manage a Series of Sprints

I must govern the clock, not be governed by it.
—Golda Meir

How heavy is a sixteen-ounce glass of water? On one hand, the answer is in the question. If you pick up the glass of water, you could probably guess the weight. But what if you held the glass of water in the air for an hour? Your arm would likely be aching, and it'd feel a lot heavier than sixteen ounces. And what if you held it in the air for a day? At that point we'd probably have to call an ambulance. The message: Even though the weight of a glass of water doesn't change, how heavy it is depends on how long it's been held.

This metaphor applies to performance in most human endeavors. The key to bodybuilding, for example, is to oscillate between energy expenditure and recovery. In tennis, research shows that in between points the best competitors use precise recovery rituals that dramatically lower their heart rates by as much as 15 to 20 percent. Jack Nicklaus, one of the greatest golfers in history, wrote in *Golf Digest*, "I've developed a regimen that allows me to move from peaks of concentration into valleys of relaxation and back again as necessary."[83] When he was urged to spend longer stretches of time on his masterpiece *The Last Supper*, Leonardo da Vinci immodestly responded, "The greatest geniuses accomplish more when they work less."

The best CEOs similarly recognize that this dynamic also applies to them. As Intuit's Brad Smith shares, "My executive coach often said, 'No one has ever lived to outwork the job. It will always be bigger than you. No matter how much you think you got here by hard work, you are not going to outwork it.' " Cincinnati Children's Michael Fisher confirms, "Had I not taken care of myself and been consistent about it, there's no way I could have made it ten years in this role." Adidas's Kasper Rørsted shares, "I think your return becomes dilutive the more time you spend. As a CEO, it's easy to start diving into matters that are none of your business. However, if you create time constraints for yourself, you figure out what's more important."

In practice, what Rørsted's philosophy translates into is a clear and disciplined operating model. He leaves the office most days at 6:00 p.m. He ensures he has time to run and exercise to keep in shape and is an enthusiastic skier. On weekends he's resolute about spending his time with his wife and four children. "It's not that I don't like my colleagues," he says, "but I don't want to meet for a barbeque with one versus the other." Not only does this allow him to remain objective as the boss, but he also sees it as a matter of fairness: "I think it's inappropriate if I treat somebody differently than the others in the team—it creates a two-tier society." He also says no to social opportunities that may come with the role unless they have a clear business reason. "If I were invited to the Oscars, I wouldn't go," he shares. "I'm just not interested."

To make sure his time is spent only on his priorities, he plans everything at least three months ahead and with enough flexibility built in to respond to urgent matters as they arise. He clears his emails by the end of every day to keep issues from building up. He also ruthlessly prioritizes where he gets involved in the workplace. If leaders are doing well and have a good plan, he sees no need to spend time with them that could be better allocated elsewhere. "If the people do their job, I'm not really interested in interfering in their job," he says.

The model Rørsted follows has worked well for him. During his eight years at the helm of Henkel, he tripled the company's stock price. And while his story at Adidas is still being written, in his first three years he doubled its shareholders' return and earned a place on *Fortune's* Businessperson of the Year list.

Rørsted's approach certainly isn't for everyone, but as we looked across how all of the best CEOs control their time and energy we found a number of commonalities. By and large, they . . .

. . . keep a "tight but loose" schedule
. . . care enough to compartmentalize
. . . infuse energy into their routine
. . . tailor their support staff to their needs

Keep a "Tight but Loose" Schedule

It comes as no surprise to find that the best CEOs are extremely structured about how they use their time. As Mastercard's Ajay Banga relays, "Time is your single most valuable resource, and it's finite. The first two years were really hard. I've stumbled my way through time management, to be completely honest. I started badly, because I was trying to do everything—communicating, getting to know people, leading change, finding the people I could build new relationships with, and getting them to carry my message." He continues, explaining what life is like when things aren't well in control: "I was traveling as well. It was hard to sleep. I'd come back to my hotel room in Asia at 11:00 at night and I'd have one hundred emails from the US waiting to be answered. And I'd promised my team that I'd respond to every email and every phone call within 24 hours."

Banga needed to get control of his calendar to strike the right balance of focus on different business priority areas, and to carve out some thinking time between meetings, especially when traveling. To do so, he adopted a color-coding system in his calendar. The time he spent for travel, with clients, regulators, internal, and so on were each assigned a different color. "If I wasn't spending time in the right places in any of these areas, a quick look at the calendar would make that abundantly clear," he shares. "One of my chief of staff's primary jobs," says Banga, "was to make sure that the balance of meetings was correct."

To keep on top of a busy schedule and the demands of the job, some CEOs turn to an old-fashioned technique: making a list. "Even now I handwrite quarterly objectives for myself," says

Ecolab's Doug Baker. "What do I need to get done? It could be as simple as starting the search for a leader. My objectives come out of the annual company objectives. It's basically what needs to get done to make the strategy happen. That's how I hold myself accountable." Baker codes his list of objectives. One star means he's working on it. A circle means it's getting there. And a cross-out means it's done. "No doubt it's rudimentary, but when a lot of objectives aren't started, I tell myself that I've got to get three things done before I head out the door."

Check Point Software's Gil Shwed sorts his to-do list into three categories. First are areas that need minor tweaks or improvement. Next are those that are bigger issues to solve that still require a lot of work. The last category comprises the big bold moves meant to get the business moving in the right direction. Explains Shwed: "If you're finding every day that everything you're doing is in the first category—trivial stuff—then either everything is wonderful, or you're probably not needed or not adding enough value to the system."

Notwithstanding all the structure CEOs put into their schedules, they're just as disciplined about building in flexibility. Says Lockheed Martin's Marillyn Hewson, "I tracked my time every month to make sure I was doing what was necessary to meet my goals. At the same time, you have to realize the job of a CEO is different every day. Stuff just drops in. If you don't have a framework, you're going to constantly be dealing with the crisis of the moment or with things that aren't that necessary, and you can't delegate because you don't have a good rhythm. However, if you get a message, 'We want you at the White House next week,' you've got to be agile enough to move things around."

Some of the best CEOs build blocks of open time into their schedules. Majid Al Futtaim's Alain Bejjani sets a stretch target for how much time is *not* booked: "My aspiration is actually to be free seventy percent of the time, so I can think, reflect, and have the capacity to deal with important things as they come up. This is a struggle, but I haven't lost hope!" He continues, "If I can become redundant, as in, the vast majority of things can be done the way I expect without my being in the room, I will have succeeded as a CEO. It's a sign that we've developed the strength, brains, and muscles that are needed for the organization to thrive."

With all the demands on a CEO's time, any effective system requires learning when and how to say "no." Galderma's Flemming Ørnskov explains his philosophy: "It's very important for me that not every single hour of the day needs to belong to the company. I don't think I become a good CEO in that way. Get balance in your life and stay in shape, because the CEO job is mentally and physically tiring and time-consuming." To get this balance, he says, "The thing I had to learn was to say no. When someone calls me and says, 'I want you to be the keynote speaker,' or, 'Don't you want to do this off-site?,' or 'Let's do a dinner,' saying no feels uncomfortable initially, because people mean it in a friendly way. But to say no politely is important. After that, the key thing is how do I make the hours I've said 'yes' to be as productive as possible."

Westpac's Gail Kelly shares a final tip on how to manage time-consuming outside events. "When I had to do a corporate dinner," she shares, "I'd make sure I walked the tables or the room, but then when it was the right time to go I'd go." Her team played a role with this, too. They'd move her on to the next group to speed things up or help her make a low-key exit. "Tomorrow would be another busy day, and I knew I needed to manage my energy," says Kelly. "I had the discipline to get in my car and drive home."

Time management is essential, but also relatively mechanical. Managing one's mental and emotional state is vital to using the time effectively, and it starts with the ability to compartmentalize.

Care Enough to Compartmentalize

In psychology, the concept of "being in the moment" is vital to high performance. At its core, it means that one isn't preoccupied with thoughts of the past, future, or other events in ways that would detract from being the best one can be. More simply, as Galderma's Flemming Ørnskov puts it, "When you're there, you're there in body and mind." With so much on a CEO's plate, one of the most challenging aspects of the job from an emotional perspective is to move from meeting to meeting without letting what happened in one spill over and sabotage the next.

U.S. Bancorp's Richard Davis further explains this idea, "Compartmentalization is essential. If you bring every burden to every meeting, if you let the day start to pile up on you, if you're known to be tougher and more irritable at the end of the day than the beginning of the day, then you don't know how to compartmentalize. You just have to take everything as it is and isolate, manage it; isolate, manage it. And I think, at the end of the day, the best CEOs will find themselves able to do that, while not forgetting anything, but simply not adding to the burden. People start seeing that you're disciplined and focused."

Being fully in the moment applies as well to home life. Doing so is vital given the impact the job can have on family. As Aon's Greg Case says, "The role affects your family more than you think it will because so much is public. Sometimes the things that will be said about you won't be overly positive." General Mills' Ken Powell relates his experience: "I can tell you our daughters were not thrilled at all. They hated it," he shares. "You're in the newspaper, they're publishing your salary or talking about when you screw things up. It can be hard on kids. That part is unpleasant, and you need to talk it over with your partner if you have one. In my case, my wife and I agreed, 'Okay, this is just part of the plusses and minuses.'"

Caterpillar's Jim Owens talks about his daily ritual to keep a degree of separation between public and private life: "I compartmentalized my life and time. Specifically, I could walk out the door of the office with a full briefcase, put it on the backseat of my car, and never think about work again that day. By the time I got home, I had shifted gears to my family." Mastercard's Ajay Banga applied a similar approach, New York City style: "I'd walk home after work. The reason for walking back wasn't the exercise, it was to detox from work and just leave my work behind, so when I walked into my house, I was done."

While at home, there are also methods to keep non-urgent work at bay. Dupont's Ed Breen works from home most weekends because "it's a good time to decompress and think about the bigger things," but he also takes steps to not let it completely take over his family life. "My main trick that I almost hate to admit, but my whole team knows it so I can't hide it, is I don't get my email on my cell phone. My team knows if something is urgent, they can pick up the phone and call me. That way if I'm out to dinner Saturday night, I'm not constantly looking at my phone to see what's come across it."

The best CEOs also proactively protect vacation time. Mastercard's Banga shares his approach: "When I go on vacation, all the people who work for me know that you'll get two bursts of emails from me each day," he says. "One is at about 7:30 in the morning, because nobody in the family is interested in me at that time. The other is at about 4:00, because everybody has had a couple of glasses of wine, and they're hanging around near the pool, so they won't miss me. My wife locks the device in the safe with a code that she sets, so I have to get her to open the thing and give it to me!"

When it came to vacation time at Shell, Peter Voser found that members of his executive team would each take their leave at different times. The idea was that they could more effectively cover for each other. One year they decided to all go on leave at the same time and delegate down instead of sideways. "You know what?" Voser shares, "My email dropped like a stone, and for the others as well. This was the best move because when we empowered people they actually managed. If there wasn't a crisis, normally they didn't phone."

Compartmentalizing also applies to tuning out external criticisms from the press or from Wall Street. When Cadence's Lip-Bu Tan was initially named CEO, social media buzzed with assertions that he wasn't the right person for the role. Because Tan was a successful venture capitalist, the speculation was that he'd flip the company and disappear. Others questioned what he really knew about the company's core chip design software business. "I was more than a little discouraged," he shares. "My youngest boy was sitting in my office listening to the some of the comments as I read them aloud. Then he gave me some very good advice: 'Dad, do your job; don't keep looking at those comments.' That turned out to be the best advice for me. I never look at any comments about me anymore."

Infuse Energy into Your Routine

Leading researchers in the field of energy management have long asserted that managing energy levels is as important as managing time, and can have a bigger payoff. As Best Buy's Hubert Joly points out, "In physics, we learned that energy is finite. It's not true in human dynamics. Energy is something you create out of nothing."

The best CEOs are aware of what generates and what depletes their energy, and work hard to avoid energy troughs—long periods of activity after which they're worn down and frustrated. Intuit's Brad Smith describes how he keeps his energy levels up: "The first thing you have to assess is what are your natural peaks and valleys, and what is your recovery time. I'm a morning person. My morning meetings are awesome. My late afternoon meetings aren't when you really want to get me. So I'd schedule the most strategic, important meetings early in the day."

"Everybody does it in different ways," says Galderma's Flemming Ørnskov. "If you start getting signs and symptoms that things are getting too burdensome, then you need to take a break, because of the damage you can do to yourself and your reputation if you're overly tired or overreact." Westpac's Gail Kelly made sure that she had what she called "white space" between meetings in her schedule. "I needed to be the best I could be and bring my whole self to every single engagement. So, we'd build in 10 or 15 minutes between things to create that mental space," she says. Kelly also made a point to get out of the office at a reasonable time on weekdays. "It didn't mean I stopped work, but I'd leave," she shares. "I'd try to have dinner with the family, get some breathing space, go for a walk, and just regroup."

Some CEOs gain energy by interacting with employees. Herbert Hainer explains that for him, "Interacting with employees gave me a big boost. I'd visit the canteen where all 5,000 people ate, choose a table, and join the conversation: 'Hey, in which department do you work? What do you do? How do you feel?' " Allianz's Oliver Bäte also draws energy from interactions with his people but is mindful that not all are the same—some generate, others reflect, and still others absorb energy. "I'm trying to find energy givers, which is where I want to spend my time."

Beyond managing their energy during the workday, excellent CEOs also find ways to recharge their batteries outside of work. As Steve Tappin reported in his study of *The Secrets of CEOs*, "the major emotions a CEO has are frustration, disappointment, irritation, and overwhelm." When these emotions persist over time, the result is burnout. Just as in the sporting world, the key to breaking this chain is to ensure that high-intensity periods are intermixed with periods of "recovery"—characterized by low-intensity, positive activity that feels restorative.

Lockheed Martin's Marillyn Hewson explains how she recovers: "You need to have some fundamentals—eat right, sleep, and exercise. You're what somebody termed years ago a 'corporate athlete,' so in that sense you've got to take care of yourself. You've got to have time with your family. And part of my business rhythm was making sure I've got my vacations outlined well in advance, and honored those vacations with family. You have to make time to refresh." Similarly, Santander's Ana Botín meticulously organizes her agenda, prioritizes sleep, and plays the piano. "I have a Fitbit, and I measure what I eat, how much I sleep, how much exercise I do," she says. "Some of my friends say I'm a bit boring. I don't think I'm boring, just very disciplined."

Excellent CEOs also know that recovery time is important for others as well. Intuit's Brad Smith shares an example: "Sometimes people would send me a fifteen-page PowerPoint deck to read over the weekend. I'd send them a note, 'I'll let you know how it looks on Monday.' All I was trying to do was to carve out space for people and their families to be able to recharge their batteries. Putting those boundaries in place helped me be a role model for a better work/life balance."

Atlas Copco's Ronnie Leten adds that if some *want* to work, that's okay, too. "As CEO, you need to be creative and encourage an atmosphere in which everyone can be at their best and have balance in their lives, but everyone is different. Some people enjoy taking time to recharge on the weekends. Some people like to play soccer. Others like to watch films. But some people may like to work, and that's okay, too. They find relaxation in that and can perhaps avoid family stress. I embraced these differences and tried to meet people where they were so that the organization was positioned for success."

While these energy-generating practices are relatively clear, applying them is easier said than done. "I didn't know whether I'd be successful and so I went one hundred percent, totally all in," LEGO's Jørgen Vig Knudstorp confesses. "My health suffered quite badly the first five years. I went to a checkup and the doctor said, 'You have the fitness of a 65-year-old.' I was, at the time, approaching 40. I then started becoming a bit more sensible."

Microsoft's Satya Nadella describes how he's framed his experience: "The senior jobs are 24/7, and I do sometimes feel that work-life balance is tough," he shares. "I've tried to reframe it for my own sake as harmony, rather than balance, because once you start saying 'balance' then I start feeling bad because it's not balanced. I don't look at it as my work intruding on my life. After all is said and done, I want to look back and say, 'God, I spent my time *well*—the people I learned from, the people I've formed real connection with both inside and outside of Microsoft.' "

Tailor Your Support to You

To get to the kind of outcome Nadella describes, it's crucial for the CEO to have a strong office staff. The best CEO's personal team always includes a talented, dedicated administrative assistant, if not two, who manages the calendar and logistics for travel and events. The assistant explicitly helps the CEO manage their time by making sure it's focused on priorities and they look after the boss's energy by building needed recovery time into the schedule.

This kind of support is typically not new to executives entering the CEO role. Some of the degrees of freedom they have, however, are. "One of the wonderful things about being CEO is you control the corporate calendar," explains GE's Larry Culp. "I was always maniacal about managing it." Culp is so maniacal that he's been known to call the athletic director at his children's school to get the sports schedule well before it's published. When his daughter was pitching softballs against a rival school, "there was one loud father in the stands," he says.

What is also often new is that many CEOs add a chief of staff (COS) to help manage the complexity of the job. Many CEOs start out thinking they don't need a COS, but then change their minds once they feel the weight of the job. Intuit's Brad Smith shares his journey: "I entered the job having an administrative assistant and no chief of staff," he says. "I eventually decided to adopt a chief of staff and it was a game-changer. It gave me the ability to scale my leadership more exponentially than I would have ever imagined. That person is a change agent who can help you drive transformation and ensure your agenda is getting applied and executed in a way that makes sense."

Sometimes a CEO inherits an overstaffed office and has to trim it down. When Mastercard's Ajay Banga entered the role, the office of the CEO consisted of eleven people, plus three secretaries. He narrowed his office to one COS and two assistants. Banga describes his COS's job description simply as, "making sure I don't screw up." To deliver on that mandate, the person has to have access to his email, calendar, and anything else needed to be effective. "I share everything with my chief of staff," Banga says. "There's no gap between us. If I'm traveling, I expect them to travel with me as often as they can. They're in the meetings with me, to remind me about things I should be worrying about. They help me join dots and make me a better CEO." Banga continues, "The best chiefs of staffs can get in your head. They can complete your sentences. They have your back. They can see things coming that you haven't because, most often, you're so preoccupied that you forget things. I know I wouldn't have been the person I was without the folks I've had as my chiefs of staff over the last ten or eleven years."

Banga also changes his chief of staff every eighteen months to two years. He chooses someone for the slot who has high potential, wants to have a new career path, and can benefit from the learning and mentoring opportunity. "I aim to give back as much as I get," he says. There's an added benefit to this rotate-in-new-blood approach. When a CEO uses a COS as an extension of themselves the way Banga does, there's a possibility of the role becoming too powerful. Cycling in new talent in the role mitigates that risk.

Many of the CEOs we spoke to similarly rotated up-and-coming talent through the COS position. Others, however, made the position more permanent. At Cincinnati Children's, for example, Michael Fisher has a long-term COS he empowers to do everything from preparing strategic presentations to helping drive organizational change. "My chief of staff is a versatile partner by my side who has strong intellect, high integrity, good judgment, and doesn't need to be in the limelight," he shares. "She helps me juggle all the balls and advance work thoughtfully between meetings, and she has unique access to me. In a one-hour visit, I can deal with eight different topics and know those things will keep moving forward without having to schedule eight different meetings. She also coordinates our biggest transformation endeavors, serves as the liaison to the board of trustees, does the preparation for day-to-day meetings with the performance leadership team, all while leading our marketing and communications department."

Aon's Greg Case adds another role for a COS: "She's also a safety valve when people become a little disgruntled about the decisions we're making. They can go to her and then she'll filter their concerns and bring them to me." Duke Energy's Lynn Good adds two more: "My chief of staff handles a lot of my community work, ensuring I'm well supported for my role on industry and community boards," she says. "She also works closely with me on staff meeting agendas, to ensure the right topics are coming at the right time to the senior table. Coming out of 2020, with the significant impact of social unrest on our country, she's also taking the lead on our diversity, equity, and inclusion agenda, working closely with the head of Human Resources. Her work with me ensures DE&I has the right focus and attention at the top of the company." For some CEOs, "office" support may even transcend the boundary between work and home. In Marjorie Yang's case at Esquel, "As a woman chairman and CEO, I also need some support outside the office. I have people who help manage my whole life. I run two households and have a 95-year-old mother. I have a personal assistant who helps me with that."

A CEO shouldn't manage their role as a continuous sprint or, like holding a glass of water in the air for a day, they'll likely end up in an ambulance. At the same time, a marathon isn't really an apt analogy either, as there's little room for slow and steady in the highest echelons of the business world. Interval training—alternating short, high-intensity bursts of activity with periods of rest and recovery in between—fits the bill. It allows for more work to be done in a shorter period of time as part of a sustainable pattern.

The best CEOs do this by keeping a "tight but loose" schedule—one that is highly structured but flexible enough to deal with unplanned issues. They compartmentalize, making the conscious choice to be in the moment with those they're with whether at work or at home. They infuse energy into their routine, avoiding energy troughs and ensuring enough recovery time is built into their schedules so they won't burn out. Finally, they tailor their personal support structure to their needs and preferences, which allows them to maximize their impact on the company.

We've discussed what CEOs do to manage their time and energy. The best put the same discipline into showing up as mindful leaders day-in and day-out.

CHAPTER 17

Leadership Model Practice

Live Your "To-Be" List

Doing is never enough if you neglect being.
—Eckhart Tolle

Among the hundreds of people waiting to visit with Mahatma Gandhi were a mother and her young son. When it was their turn, the woman asked Gandhi to speak with her son about eating sugar. Gandhi asked her to come back in two weeks and said he would talk to the boy then. She wondered why he didn't just speak to her son when he was already there, but she complied with his request. In two weeks they returned, and after waiting for a couple of hours, she was able to approach Gandhi once again. Hearing her repeated request, Gandhi immediately spoke with the boy, who agreed to begin working to eliminate sweets. After thanking Gandhi for his wise and compassionate words, the mother asked him why he wanted them to return instead of offering his advice the first time. Gandhi replied, "Upon your visit two weeks ago I, too, was eating sugar." He explained that he couldn't speak of or teach her son to not eat sugar if he himself hadn't taken that journey.[84]

This story, and many like it, are reflective of why Gandhi, the man who led India's nonviolent independence movement against British rule, is revered the world over as one of history's greatest statesmen, alongside such figures as the Dalai Lama, Golda Meir, Margaret Thatcher, Martin Luther King Jr., Nelson Mandela, Simón Bolívar, and Winston Churchill. American nineteenth-century abolitionist and theologian James Freeman Clarke captured the essence of what separates this group from their public leader peers when he said: "The difference between a politician and a statesman is that a politician thinks about the next election while the statesman thinks about the next generation."

What's fascinating about Clarke's juxtaposition for our purposes is that if one looks at what a statesman and a politician do, it's strikingly similar: communicating, persuading, networking, and so forth. It's "who they are" that makes a difference. A statesman doesn't govern by opinion polls. He or she stands on a platform of what they believe to be fundamental truths. They adhere to a set of core values. Their goal is not to get ahead in politics, but to serve a greater purpose.

The best CEOs are keenly aware of the difference between doing and being, and the tremendous potential of getting both right. Cincinnati Children's Michael Fisher clarifies the distinction: "I've always had a decent amount of discipline around writing down 'to-dos.' I want to make sure I do A, B, and C today. I print out my daily calendar, I have it with me all day, and I make notes as I go. But I also purposefully give thought to and am really *intentional* about how I want to show up every day. So I've added a 'to-be' list to my repertoire. Today, for example, I might want to be generous and genuine. I hope I'm that way every day. But today I want to make sure it stays top of mind. If I have a couple of important meetings with some key people from my senior team, I want to make sure it's not just a necessary, tactical interaction but one where I'm generous in my appreciation for them. On a different day, a part of my job might be to be collaborative and catalytic. So I pick out two qualities, two kinds of ways to be, every morning as part of my normal routine."

Introspection regarding one's being is sometimes prompted by comments from others. "When I was offered the CEO role," shares Intuit's Brad Smith, "I asked my predecessor, Steve, if the decision was unanimous. He said, 'Yes, it's unanimous you're the right person. It's also unanimous that we all have an open question. Can you be tough? You're Southern, self-effacing, and we're about to go through some difficult stuff here. Are you going to be able to overcome your kindness?'" Smith took the feedback to heart and reached out to his father. "He said, 'Don't mistake kindness for weakness.' He gave me the example of the children's TV show

Mister Rogers. The first week Fred Rogers was on air, his topics included death, divorce, and bigotry. People were pouring Clorox into Holiday Inn pools because African Americans had gone swimming. So Mister Rogers put his feet in a backyard wading pool and invited Officer Clemmons, who was a Black man, to join him. Although Mister Rogers was soft and gentle, he managed to make his point," Smith shares.

The story his father told him was all Smith needed to know about being the kind of CEO he wanted to be. "That mindset taught me how to show empathy, while also making a tough decision," he says. "Maya Angelou's poem reflects what I was trying to achieve. It says: 'I've learned that people will forget what you said, people will forget what you did, but people will never forget how you made them feel.'" Smith was able to live by his convictions; when he retired, the company put his name on the building, and underneath was engraved a phrase he always used, "Work hard, be kind, take pride."

The best CEOs, like Fisher and Smith, have a number of things in common when it comes to how to "be" at work. They . . .

   . . . act in a way that is consistent with their strengths and values
   . . . adapt their leadership to what the company needs
   . . . embrace and act on feedback in the spirit of continuously growing as a leader
   . . . provide hope for the future in all situations, no matter how dire

Show Consistency of Character

Consistency of character means following the same principles in all circumstances. Consider the role of being a parent. When children observe their parents compromising their principles—"Junior, even though we ask you to tell the truth, it's okay to say you're younger than you really are to get a discount at the movie theater"—they learn to do the same. Kids also learn to predict a parent's inconsistency and figure out how to get around the rules. By waiting until a parent is busy or tired, they can slip things by. Leadership is similar in that all eyes on are on the person in the most senior role. Best Buy's Hubert Joly, whose book is titled *The Heart of Business: Leadership Principles for the Next Era of Capitalism,* describes the dynamic at play: "It's important to lead not just with your head but also your soul and your heart. When CEOs act consistently in these ways, their principles get translated to the organization, not top down but organically."

Staying true to one's values can in the short term feel like a losing proposition, but in the long term the best CEOs find it always pays off. Jørgen Vig Knudstorp explains how this played out for him at LEGO. "I'm not a pleaser. I'm not walking into a room and thinking about, 'How do I make sure everybody likes me?'" he shares. "We all have our own crucibles and life stories. And somehow that has made me risk-taking and willing to do courageous things that might make other people say, 'How did you stand up in that group and just say that?'" When he was thirty-five years old and had been an executive at the company for only three years, Knudstorp felt obligated to write a memo to the LEGO board explaining his view that the company was in trouble. "It basically said that although the company had an accounting profit over most of the prior fifteen years, it hadn't produced a positive economic profit for a single day. Somehow everyone's happy, but we're losing money.

"It was a shocker to the board," recalls Knudstorp. "I remember being kicked out of the board meeting and I called my wife and said, 'This has been amazing, but now I'm going back to academia.'" The next day, however, the chairman called Knudstorp, indicating he'd read the memo three times and that he wanted to have a serious conversation. Less than a year later the board announced that Knudstorp would be the next CEO of LEGO. He won the top job because of his consistent character, which also helped him lead a successful turnaround. "It's a danger for a CEO to seek to fit in," he observes. "The wonderful LEGO company I came into was a little bit of a boy's club. People did not challenge each other, and they were very, very similar to one another. There was not a lot of diversity. I think when I was made CEO, a lot of the existing management ranks thought, 'Whoa, that's a pretty weird choice.'" Knudstorp's call it like it is, no matter how uncomfortable approach quickly changed the culture, enabling the transformation. "As I have been successful I have gained even more confidence in just being myself," he confirms.

The lesson isn't that all CEOs should be as blunt as Knudstorp, but all should know what their convictions are and stay true to them, even if costly or difficult. Mitchell Elegbe, the founder and CEO of Interswitch, a pan-African fintech and one of the continent's few unicorns (defined as a start-up worth at least $1 billion), describes the tough decisions he's had to make to stay consistent to his character. "The first powerful lesson I learned was the difference between victory and winning. When you go to war, lose all your soldiers but win the battle, and you come back home the only survivor—that is winning, okay? But when you go to war, and you win the battle, and all the soldiers come back home—that is victory. So most times when I'm faced with situations, I ask myself, 'Do I want victory or do I want to win?' I've come to the conclusion that victory is a better form of winning than just winning itself."

In practice, when Elegbe makes a decision, he looks at the impact it will have on his colleagues, their families, his shareholders, and society. If he's not happy with the picture he sees, he doesn't get involved. This is especially true, he says, when it comes to corruption. "There are many times we are faced with situations whereby somebody in government wants something done and so forth," says Elegbe, "and I just walk away because I recognize that this is not going to be victory. We may win this deal, but deep down we know who we are, and would not enjoy the proceeds that come with it."

Telstra's David Thodey found that consistency of character was essential in trying to pull off a deep cultural transformation. In his campaign to make his Australian telecom more customer-centric, he asked his employees to do whatever it took to please the customer, no matter the cost—within certain limits. But some weren't getting the message. One day his head of field engineering walked in and said that because of the heavy rains in the north, many of their copper lines were experiencing faults, and that to make that quarter's budget he was going to wait until the next quarter to fix them. It would have been easy for Thodey to nod in approval and make his numbers, but instead he said to the engineer, "Well, hang on, is that what our priorities are?" The CEO then explained to him the impact the faulty lines were having on Telstra's northern customers. But the engineer replied that it would cost $40 million to fix it. Thodey simply said: "Do it." It was by staying consistent to what he believed, even when it was hard, that Thodey turned Telstra into the most trusted company in Australia.

Adapt to What the Company Needs

Being consistent doesn't mean that CEOs should be inflexible. Without betraying their core values the best are willing and able to modify how they lead if the circumstances demand it. The notion of "situational leadership" was introduced almost fifty years ago by Dr. Paul Hersey, author of *The Situational Leader,* and Kenneth Blanchard, author of *The One Minute Manager.* The thesis is that if leaders are able to adapt their style to the situation—while maintaining their authenticity—they'll be able to achieve superior results.[85] LEGO's Jørgen Vig Knudstorp sums it up: "It's important to figure out what kind of CEO the company needs."

But doesn't situational leadership fly in the face of being authentic? No. DSM's Feike Sijbesma had an experience decades ago, a vivid memory, that helped him square the circle. "In the beginning of my career I thought, 'Hey, to be authentic is very good,'" he reveals. Then, one time in a session with his whole team and a consultant where everyone was prompted to give feedback to each other, Sijbesma got fed up with some remarks addressed to him. "Listen, that's just the way I am. It's authentic," he admonished the team. Some of the team members indicated that was fair enough. The consultant, however, looked at Sijbesma and said, "Feike, this is your authenticity? Okay, but tell me, why do we sometimes need to suffer from that?" Sijbesma was silent. The message was: You need to be authentic, but with better leadership skills. "It was not the most pleasant experience, but it was so true. It really had an impact on me and helped my career," Sijbesma reflects.

Westpac's Gail Kelly shares how she initially resisted changing her style, but ultimately decided it was the right thing to do for the company: "I found that my language with our investors wasn't resonating because I spoke the customer's language. I wasn't doing enough to speak the language of banking, making myself sound like a technical banker like my peers. The feedback I'd get from investors was 'She's obviously strong on the soft stuff, but it's good she's got a CFO who knows the numbers.' It used to drive me mad."

Kelly's chairman strongly advised her to change her language and her messaging, but she initially resisted. "I said, 'No, I'm going to be me.'" She continues, "And then I realized, 'Actually, hang on, I'd better listen to this.' So I changed. I didn't shift what I focused on. But I shifted my language with investors and started to include a lot of numbers in my answers. I took on the questions that I might otherwise have left to the chief financial officer or chief risk officer to answer. And the message is, do listen. There may be some things you need to change as you go along in your tenure."

At Intuit, Brad Smith initially adopted an approach of praising in public and coaching in private. The approach worked for a period of time, but he soon realized that a change in his leadership model was long overdue. "In year six of my eleven-year journey," he explains, "one of my 360 feedbacks came back with, 'Brad is lowering the standards in the company because he's being too kind in reviews and isn't willing to call anybody out. He has this philosophy of praise in public and coach in private. But it's robbing the rest of us of knowing where his standard of quality really is.'"

Smith wasn't about to change his beliefs, but the company needed him to be different, so he changed his approach. "I started to coach business performance in public and personal performance in private," he reveals. "I challenged myself to be kind to the person but tough on the issue, and everyone in the company knew it. I told people, 'Keep me true to this if you don't think I'm being concrete enough about whether the work is good enough. But I also want you to know that I'm not embarrassing people. I want to treat you with dignity and respect.'"

Lockheed Martin's Marillyn Hewson shares how sometimes the answer lies less in adapting one's actions and more in giving the reasons why you behave the way you do. "I'm an intense person, but my style is intimidating to some as I ask a lot of questions. I've learned that situational leadership is important, but I'm not going to stop asking a lot of questions. It's important, though, to explain to people why I do what I do, and why it's a product of who I am."

Being who the company needs you to be while staying true to your convictions doesn't happen without feedback, as we've seen. The best CEOs don't leave it to chance that they'll get the input they need.

Seek to Continuously Grow

Given the level of scrutiny directed at CEOs, one might think that they're swamped with continuous feedback. This couldn't be further from the truth. As we've discussed, the CEO role is peerless. While the board oversees the CEO, no one closely observes their daily behavior. As a result, CEOs generally receive very little direct coaching and are increasingly isolated from constructive criticism. "When you get the top job, people always put their best face on when they come to see you," says DBS's Piyush Gupta. "People are scared to give you bad news." Intuit's Smith confirms: "As a CEO, you often don't realize how much of the input you get is filtered by the job you have. It's no secret that we all get ten inches taller and our jokes get funnier the day we assume the role."

When Smith would give a speech in a town hall meeting he'd always make it a point to ask a few employees, "How did I do?" Inevitably they'd say, "Oh, you were great." The consistency of the feedback prompted him to sit down with his chairman and confess that he wasn't sure if he was getting the truth. "You're not," was the simple and seasoned response. Smith shares the advice that followed: "He suggested that next time I get off the stage I ask them, 'What could I have done to make it better? What could I have done differently?'" In other words: Avoid asking general and broad questions; rather, ask the question you want the answer to. "That's how you're going to get real feedback," he says.

Ahold Delhaize's Dick Boer reinforces the importance of asking the right questions to get the right feedback. "One of the big lessons I learned was to keep asking for constructive criticism," he says. "Real feedback. You have to train your people to provide that. I had to challenge them. Whenever we had a long meeting I'd always end with, 'Do you have something for me? Tell me. And not what I want to hear, but what you think we should do better.'"

Many CEOs also work with a coach to help them gather and act on feedback. Best Buy's Hubert Joly explains, "Years ago, if somebody had told me, 'Scott is working with a coach,' I would have wondered, 'Uh-oh, what's wrong with Scott? Is he in trouble? Is the firm going to fire him?' Now I realize an executive coach can help successful leaders get better. One hundred percent of the world's top one hundred tennis players have a coach, and one hundred percent of NFL teams have a coach—in fact, a coaching staff. So why on earth should CEOs and management teams not have a coach? What we need isn't just an intervention, but an ongoing process to support continuous improvement."

Lockheed Martin's Marillyn Hewson used a coach to help gather objective feedback from her team. "By definition you don't see your blind spots, so you need mechanisms to tell you the impact you're having on the organization that you don't even know about," she says. "I'd use an external coach who would help me take the temperature of my leadership team by asking them some questions. As a result, I would modify my style. I'd talk about it with the team and say, 'You told me this, and this is what I'm going do, and check me on it, but this is how I'm going to change.'"

Continuous learning also happens by reaching down into the organization for feedback. Reed Hastings reveals that at Netflix, "I run a question by my top fifty people: 'If you were CEO, what would be different at Netflix?' They write a couple of sentences or paragraphs that's put on a shared spreadsheet document." Intuit's Brad Smith goes even deeper in the organization: "I had two meetings a week with people many levels down in the organization, and with eight to ten people in each group. Sometimes it was with employees one to three years out of college. Other times it was engineers only, or people in customer care. To all, I posed three questions: 'What's getting better than it was six months ago? What's not making enough progress or going in the wrong direction? And what's something you're afraid no one is telling me, that you believe I need to know?' It was incredible, because you skip levels and go right to the front lines of the area you're trying to learn about. You cut everybody else out and eliminate the filter."

Inspiration for new and better ways to "be" can also come from outside the company. ICICI's KV Kamath, who believes that curiosity is the foundation of good leadership, says, "I have to reinvent and recharge myself every year. I say loud and clear that nobody should have any shame in saying, 'I don't know.' " To keep up with the world, Kamath would spend a few days each year with the noted management professor C. K. Prahalad, who, according to Kamath, "put the fear of God in me and taught me to think." He also learned from businesses other than his own. Being a Formula 1 racing fan taught him two lessons. He explains: "First, how is it possible to change all four tires on a car in less than three seconds? If you can understand the processes and the learning that goes into that, you can become much more capable. Formula 1 also teaches you to consider how to drive at the limit but not over it—the coordination required, the mind and eye, the nervous system. It led me to ask how we can use that in business. Maybe we have to touch the brakes well before the moment we lose control."

Dupont's Ed Breen says he tells up-and-coming CEOs to join one or two groups where they can get together off the record with other CEOs and talk through key topics. "You learn a lot from hearing what people are seeing in their markets, and it's on a level that goes deeper than what you read in the *Wall Street Journal*," says Breen. "I still meet with groups like this now. I always walk away with six or seven new ideas." Total's Patrick Pouyanné looks for meetings that give him a better understanding of what's happening globally, which often lead to tangible impact. "Seeing others, feeling the change, and talking to them has to make you think. Then you set up networks and you spend time on the issues." In Pouyanné's case, one of those networks included a meeting with industry leaders in India, which led in early 2021 to Total's taking a 20 percent stake in India's Adani Green Energy, the world's largest solar developer.

Continuous learning takes courage. "We have this image of the CEO as the superstar," Best Buy's Hubert Joly explains. "The notion of vulnerability in a leader is a recent notion. We have to accept our imperfections. If we expect perfection of ourselves and of people around us, it's very dangerous. We're going to become angry. It's okay to want zero defects in a process. But wanting a zero-defect process is different from expecting zero defects in a person."

As Joly points out, there'll always be challenges, but it's how CEOs show up in the face of such challenges that matters.

Always Give Hope

In Richard Boyatzis, Frances Johnson, and Anne McKee's book *Becoming a Resonant Leader* the authors discuss how neurological and psychological research has shown that the leader's mood is quite literally contagious, spreading quickly throughout a company. When issues arise, if the CEO is angry, fearful, or uncertain, those feelings will permeate through the company. On the flip side, if CEOs look for opportunity, have hope, and show resolve, the organization will follow suit.[86]

Duke Energy's Lynn Good shares that same sentiment as a kind of epiphany. "It's always showtime," she declares. "I think one of the things that I probably didn't appreciate fully before is, even in dark moments, I have to express optimism internally and externally because the team isn't going to believe we can get through it if I don't." Esquel's Marjorie Yang reinforces the importance of showing up with a positive attitude. "My job is to drive away fear and frustration," she says. "Fear is the worst enemy of any business. If I come into the office with a positive spirit, it uplifts everyone else. As a leader, my job is to maintain confidence in the future and radiate that confidence."

Taking such a stance doesn't mean ignoring the facts of one's current reality. "My leadership mantra, which I think about literally every day," says American Express's Ken Chenault, "is that the role of a leader is to define reality and give hope. I paraphrased it from Napoleon, but I always add the caveat that I don't want to wind up like Napoleon! It's the simplest definition of leadership. Defining reality is very challenging. It requires a level of transparency and courage to articulate what is the truth, what are the facts. But that isn't enough. What are the tactics? What are the strategies? What are the reasons why people should be hopeful? That focus on defining reality and giving hope is something that I've used to guide me as a leader."

As Chenault alludes to, giving hope can't be artificial—it's the role of the CEO to find a genuine reason to believe, otherwise employees pick up on the incongruence between being and doing. "I always see the glass half-full—I'm an optimist by nature. It doesn't matter how difficult the situation is because there is always a solution," Adidas's Herbert Hainer shares. "Let's talk about the solution, not the problem. When you have this mindset, it spills over to other people. Also, when you're artificially motivated, people realize that. If you falsely claim, 'Hey, I am so motivated,' and then appear lethargic, your words are meaningless."

JPMC's Jamie Dimon talks about how he confronted reality while providing hope in his early days as CEO of Bank One. While talking with his team, he was brutally honest: "You guys talk about morale. You have done so many things in the name of morale. But everyone in the company knows we're political, bureaucratic, and losing. Morale's going to stay very low until we're a good company." At the same time Dimon gave hope by bringing them the right people to fix the problems, and letting them know, "From now on, we're here because we're going to become the best."

Andrew Wilson at Electronic Arts believes that organizations today look to their CEOs not just for professional guidance but also for personal, spiritual, and philosophical support. Sometimes it just takes showing a bit of humanity to inspire the troops. During the COVID-19 pandemic when people had to work remotely and Wilson was hosting a Zoom meeting with seven thousand employees, Wilson's five-year-old son walked in the room and wanted him to make a paper airplane. Wilson paused the call and made him a paper airplane. "At the time," he recalls, "I just did it because that's what I'd do as a father. It took thirty seconds, and it was all good. Afterward, people reached out and said, 'Thank you. You just gave us permission to be parents. You just gave us permission to spend the time.'

"These moments," says Wilson, "are ones when you do things naturally that empower or inspire your organization. When I speak to friends of mine who are great CEOs, the things I hear about aren't how big the company is, how high the share price is, how much money they make, or how important they are to global GDP. What I hear is how they make their people feel. That's the legacy of a great CEO."

• • •

Best-selling American writer Kurt Vonnegut famously coined the phrase, "I am a human being, not a human doing." Indeed, when most people take a quiet moment to reflect on what leaders they're most inspired by, the answer rarely seems based on leaders' specific acts of "doing" but rather, the nature of their "being." This is why the best CEOs strive for continual clarity as to who they want and need to be in the role.

The starting point is to connect with one's convictions and to stay authentic to a set of core beliefs regardless of the circumstance. At the same time, the best are willing to adapt their leadership style to suit what the company needs from them, as long as it doesn't violate their core beliefs. To make such a shift, they proactively seek feedback since they're unlikely to receive honest and constructive advice otherwise. All the while, they ensure employees have hope for the future.

We've now discussed how CEOs approach the *doing* and *being* aspects of personal effectiveness. We'll conclude our discussion by stepping back and seeing how the best CEOs keep their role in perspective.

CHAPTER 18

Perspective Practice
Stay Humble

A large chair does not make a king.
—Sudanese proverb

Legend has it that American president George Washington was riding one day with a group of friends near his home when, in the process of leaping over a wall, one horse knocked a number of stones off it. Washington said to his friends, "We had better replace them." The others responded, "Oh, let the farmer do it." That didn't sit right with Washington. When the riding party was over, he went back the way they came. He found the wall and dismounted and carefully replaced each of the stones. As one of his riding companions rode by and saw what he was doing, they called out to Washington, "You're too big to do that." He responded only with, "On the contrary, I am the right size."[87]

We rarely read in the news about acts born out of humility. Sports stars, entertainers, and politicians fight for the spotlight, and the media give it to them. The word *humility* can evoke different impressions. *Merriam-Webster's Collegiate Dictionary* defines humility as freedom from pride or arrogance. Note that it doesn't say anything about lack of confidence or competence. As British writer and lay theologian C. S. Lewis once wrote, "True humility is not thinking less of yourself, it's thinking of yourself less." By that definition, even though the word *humility* doesn't come to mind when people think of the leaders of the world's mega-corporations, it should. Despite the lofty heights to which their careers have taken them, those CEOs we spoke to came across as down-to-earth and genuinely wanting to be of service to their colleagues and the institutions they represent.

Majid Al Futtaim's Alain Bejjani shares a theme common to this group: "It's easy as CEO to feel you're the best thing that happened to the company, and that most of what you do is fantastic and visionary. In reality, that's not the case. It's important to never lose yourself in these thoughts of grandeur, but to always put things in proper perspective. At the end of the day, you're the chief executive 'officer'—the 'officer' in your title denotes that you're an employee, who just happens to be sitting in that chair. That privilege is something you have to earn on a daily basis."

IDB's Lilach Asher-Topilsky used a daily ritual to help her stay humble. "Every morning, when I went to my office, I entered the room, looked at my chair, and reminded myself that people were going to walk in and talk to the chair. I sit in this chair now, but I have to remember that I have to be humble. I have to remember that everyone is the same. I sit in this chair, and it makes me powerful, but tomorrow I'm not going to be in this chair."

Microsoft's Satya Nadella displays humility by ascribing a meaningful portion of his success to his predecessor. "My dad, a civil servant in India, always used to talk about institution builders as those people whose successors do better than they did themselves," he says. "I love that definition. I feel that if the next CEO of Microsoft can be even more successful than I am, then maybe I've done my job right. If the next CEO of Microsoft crashes and burns, that may result in a different verdict. That's why I think too much credit is given to me and not enough to Steve [Ballmer, Nadella's predecessor] for what he set in motion. I don't think I would have been able to achieve what I've achieved if not for his work, including our transition to cloud computing."

The best CEOs keep their job and themselves in perspective by . . .

    . . . never making it about themselves
    . . . embracing servant leadership
    . . . creating a diverse "kitchen cabinet"
    . . . displaying genuine gratitude for the opportunity to sit in the chair

Don't Make It About You

When we asked Aon's Greg Case about his personal operating model, his instinctive response was, "Give me a break, this is not about me. At the end of the day it's about your clients and colleagues. My job is to take care of them. It's my privilege to carry their bags." Itaú Unibanco's Roberto Setúbal expands on this idea: "All CEOs need to ask themselves, 'What do you want to be remembered for—as a great person or a person who made the company great?' If you want to make the company great, then you must think about the company first, yourself second. It's human nature to want to be recognized, so it's not easy to put the institution ahead of yourself. But when you can do so and have a good support system, mindset, and dedication, you can do great things."

Mastercard's Ajay Banga memorably reinforces the point with an analogy. "The fact is, when you're gone, nobody will remember you," he says. "That's actually good. You want them to not remember you. You want the company to be successful where it's headed. You do not own the business unless you created the company and were Steve Jobs or Bill Gates, and then they *should* remember you. Guys like us, we're just stewards of the system in a ship sailing through the sea. You have to make sure that the boat doesn't sink while you're there and that it picks up a couple of extra sails and some new engine technology. You make the boat work better. But you don't brand the boat with your name and call it the Ajay Banga boat."

The people one interacts with outside of work can make a difference in keeping oneself humble. "I think staying grounded made me a better CEO," Ecolab's Doug Baker says. "And you have to have ways to do it. Early in my CEO career, my kids were key. It's hard not to stay grounded when you have three teenagers at home. Once the kids were gone, friends were even more important. Find people and places where you're valued as a neighbor and a friend, and position power doesn't matter but rather, who you are."

As Ecolab's Baker just mentioned, family time can play an important role. U.S. Bancorp's Richard Davis recalls, "My kids used to say, 'I'm sure people laugh at your jokes at work because they have to, but you're honestly not as funny as you think you are.' When you leave the job, you're reminded of that immediately, because people don't laugh at your jokes anymore and they don't call anymore." Cadence's Lip-Bu Tan adds his experience: "My wife keeps me grounded. Sometimes you get carried away being a CEO. Success can get to your head. Every morning she reminds me to bless the people I work with. She tells me, 'It's not your work; you're just doing your part. Give the glory to God.' That keeps me grounded."

For the Dangote Group's CEO, spiritual grounding is important. "I can say that my mainstay comes from my faith and belief in God. Over the years, that has kept me constantly finding ways to improve humanity." Although Aliko Dangote is the wealthiest person in Africa, this ethos helps him keep his eye on the bigger picture. "Our vision of transforming Africa's economy keeps me grounded," he says. "I'm always driven by the need to improve the continent's narrative. My joy is to see in how many ways we can improve lives across the continent."

Make no mistake, maintaining an attitude of "it's not about me" while holding one of the most powerful positions in world— one that brings with it an element of celebrity—isn't easy. This may explain why the best CEOs go one step further and embrace a servant leadership mindset.

Embrace Servant Leadership

In *Journey to the East*, published in 1932, Nobel Prize–winning German-Swiss novelist Hermann Hesse tells the story of a character named Leo who, while on a pilgrimage, joins the members of a sect called "The League." Leo is portrayed as a simple servant, just like all the others. The journey is fun and enlightening until one day Leo disappears, and everything changes as the group plummets into dissention and bickering, only to come to the realization later that Leo was far more than a servant—he was actually the president of The League.[88]

Hesse's character, Leo, is cited by Robert K. Greenleaf as inspiration for the idea of "servant leadership" in his 1970 essay "The

Servant as Leader." In Greenleaf's formulation, servant leaders find success and power in the growth, support, and empowerment of others.[89] While cynics may dismiss that notion as idealistic jargon, we've found that the best CEOs strongly adhere to it. As American Express's Ken Chenault shared, "I strongly believe that leadership is a privilege. And if you want to lead, you have to be committed to serve."

Lockheed Martin's Marillyn Hewson exemplifies the mindset when she says, "Lying awake at night, thinking about making decisions that affect the people we have to send into harm's way, our troops, and their families—that's always been real for me. It's one thing to have fiduciary responsibility. If you buy stock in Lockheed Martin, I'm concerned that you don't lose money. But the 100,000 employees whose families rely on Lockheed Martin, that's all always real to me. I come from very humble beginnings, so I know what a good job means to a family."

Before Reed Hastings founded Netflix, he experienced the power of servant leadership. "I was a twenty-eight-year-old engineer working around the clock, loving it," he relates. Hastings would arrive early, around four o'clock in the morning, and over the course of a week coffee cups would stack up around his work area. "Every week," he says, "the janitor would clean them all and set them out for me." One day when he arrived as usual at four o'clock in the morning, he found his CEO in the bathroom, washing my coffee cups. "Of course, it turned out that all that year, it wasn't the janitor after all," he reveals. "The CEO had been washing the coffee cups. When I asked him why, he said, 'You do so much for us, and this is the one thing I can do for you.' The fact that he was doing it humbly and not getting credit for it made his personal example so compelling that I admired him. I would follow him to the ends of the earth."

Hastings's experience sheds light on the paradox of servant leadership—a leader serves because they are the leader, meanwhile they are the leader because they serve. U.S. Bancorp's Richard Davis explains further. "I don't think enough CEOs understand," he says, "that practicing humility is not only good behavior, but it will win you more followers than any strategy or tactic or mandate you'll ever, ever have." In keeping with this idea, Davis would go out of his way to avoid putting on airs. When he visited branches, he wouldn't have handlers. He'd walk straight to the teller line and meet every teller. Only then would he walk around and meet management. "I'm not sitting in the ivory tower having one of my emissaries go out and talk to the rank and file," he emphasizes.

Assa Abloy's Johan Molin embraces a similar ethic. One of the first things he did when he took the top role was go to England, where the company had a number of operational problems, and work side by side with employees on the production line to understand the situation. "I had no idea what a sash lock was, but I know now," he reports. At Best Buy, Hubert Joly showed that servant leadership was real by letting his officers know, "If you believe you're serving yourself or your boss or me as CEO, it's okay. I don't have a problem with that. Except you cannot work here." He says, "But if you're serving people on the front line and you're making a difference for them, then we're good."

Another way for a CEO to engage in servant leadership is to think of the organization as an inverted pyramid with the customers and frontline workers on the top of the chart and the leader on the bottom. At Home Depot that view of things was first adopted by founders Bernie Marcus and Arthur Blank. But what did it actually mean in practice? "That idea," says Frank Blake of Home Depot, "got me out of my office. I always loved the phrase that something cascades down. And as soon as you think of an inverted pyramid, you realize, 'Nothing I say is going to cascade down to anyone. No one cares what I have to say.' So I'm going to spend my time pushing a message up through a series of layers of people who are inclined not to care. That being the case, I need to understand what they *do* care about, how do I mesh what I care about with what they care about, and how do I move that up through the organization? That meant I needed to listen, and I needed to listen intently."

Create a Diverse "Kitchen Cabinet"

One group we haven't yet touched on that can help keep a CEO grounded and humble is a kitchen cabinet. The term comes from US president Andrew Jackson who convened a small group of informal advisors in the White House kitchen. These people gave him discreet advice beyond what his formal cabinet members provided. Jackson's wise use of this shadow group helped him become recognized as one of America's great practical politicians. Similarly, a CEO's kitchen cabinet provides him or her with discreet and confidential feedback and advice beyond what can be obtained from formal coaches or forums.

The best CEOs build a kitchen cabinet that is typically composed of highly capable thinkers and listeners—able to ask thoughtful questions and share wise and diverse views. They also must be able to keep confidences so that sensitive topics related to personal leadership, colleagues, employees, customers, investors, and other stakeholders can be openly discussed. Further, they should be as objective as possible, with the CEO's and the company's best interests in mind, not their own. Itaú Unibanco's Roberto Setúbal adds an important characteristic: "It's important to have people close to you who aren't afraid of you." Mastercard's Ajay Banga puts a premium on having diverse perspectives. "I wanted the views of people who didn't look like me, walk like me, go to the same schools, have the same experiences, or the same backgrounds," he explains.

So why does a CEO benefit from such a group? Duke Energy's Lynn Good explains. "As a CEO, where do you go when you need to talk to somebody?" she says. "It is a real issue, because I can't always share every issue with my senior leadership team, as good as they may be." Good used a banker as confidant on certain issues. She also reached out to other CEOs, depending on the situation, though she notes, "They're busy people and so I use them sparingly." She also has a consultant whom she calls, "when I just need to talk to somebody. He plays the role of critic and encourager, depending on the situation, and frequently serves as a sounding board."

Adobe's Shantanu Narayen included in his kitchen cabinet some other CEOs who started out around the same time he did, including John Donahoe of eBay, Brad Smith of Intuit, and Enrique Salem of Symantec. "This self-help group is so important to me," he says. "You have your board, but you also need a group of people that you can call on for anything. The ability to call a CEO out only exists with two sets of people. Your family will tell you what's what every single morning—and that's the best thing that can happen. But these people in my self-help group also have that ability, because they've seen me through my entire journey, and they've been on it, too. When you're not acting on something or when you're being timid, they can speak bluntly to you. You certainly don't ever put them in a position where you're sharing confidential material, but you can ask them things that others don't have the experience to answer." This group helped Narayen live the philosophy he learned from his parents of constantly evolving as a leader. "What I'm good at changed over time," he says. "I always talk about how in a company you need both the flag planters and the road builders. When I first took over as CEO, I was a road builder. I was an engineer, I liked detail. I was good at connecting the dots, but probably not aspirational enough."

Diageo's Ivan Menezes similarly describes the importance of having CEOs from other companies in his kitchen cabinet: "As you get into the job, it is incredibly lonely at first. I found it very helpful to have a set of peers to talk to, outside of your board and shareholders and management team. Building and maintaining a trusted group would be immensely valuable for any new CEO."

Adidas's Kasper Rørsted shares how a member of his kitchen cabinet helped him get perspective: "I have a small circle of people I bounce ideas off," he says. "For example, at one point, I was getting criticized almost every day in the media. One Saturday morning, I called one of my informal advisors to discuss the situation with him. He said, 'You're taking it too seriously. Nobody will care about the papers tomorrow, so stop whining. Spend some time with your wife and have a good bottle of wine.' He wasn't very empathetic, but it did make me think, 'Okay, I'm getting hung up with something that maybe I shouldn't.' It helped me put certain situations in context."

LEGO's Jørgen Vig Knudstorp used to meet with one of his advisors for tea every quarter. When he first took the CEO role, the advisor asked him two questions: "What went wrong?" and "Why does the company exist?" "My first answer to why we exist," Knudstorp recalls, "was a long story about children and dreams. On what went wrong, I spoke about the US dollar declining, partners letting us down, and other external factors. My advisor said 'Drink your tea, come back next quarter. We're not done.' "

Every quarter Knudstorp returned with a refined answer. It wasn't until two years into the role that he gave his advisor a satisfactory answer. "I was sitting in his garden drinking tea again, and he said, 'So tell me what went wrong.' " Knudstorp recalls that he answered, "Well, it's really poor management." And on the question of why the company existed, Knudstorp replied, "To offer systematic problem-solving and creativity that's super relevant in the 21st century." At that point the advisor said, "I think we're done now. You can go home."

Knudstorp sums up: "He wanted me to take responsibility and own the problem and have my own vision of why the company should exist and how the brand is relevant."

As the examples above show, CEOs rarely bring together their kitchen cabinets as a group; instead, they typically call them individually. That's not always the case, however. Some other excellent CEOs, like Cadence's Lip-Bu Tan, have their kitchen cabinet meet together on a regular basis. He started what he calls the Accountability Group. It's a small group of trusted friends from different disciplines. They meet every month at one of their houses, on a Saturday from ten to noon. They discuss what they've learned from the books they're reading and the implications to their business and their lives. They share some of their personal challenges, either from the workplace or family. Everything is confidential. "One of the main reasons I set up the Accountability Group," says Tan, "is that I want to finish strong in my job. A lot of temptations can derail you. You have to stay focused on things that really matter, and also on things that benefit not only yourself but others—things that have an impact on the community, the society."

Feel Gratitude

Gratitude is another word that most wouldn't quickly equate with CEOs, but when it comes to the best, they should. "We're very lucky," JPMC's Jamie Dimon says. "We should all acknowledge that. Most of the almost seven billion people on this planet would gladly trade places with us. So those of us here today are very lucky—and that gives us deep responsibility and obligations." Aon's Greg Case adds: "Let's don't kid ourselves. We could all think we're geniuses, but we're really very lucky to be in the role. You have to take where you are with a grain of salt and be grateful for it."

When GE's Larry Culp stepped down from the CEO role at Danaher, he knew what he missed immediately. "I liken it to the flow I remember in high school when I was on the basketball team," he shares. "We ran fast, took care of each other, and we were successful. That's what we had going at Danaher for a long time and what's coming together at GE. Running fast with incredible people working at this level—I just find it to be great fun and rewarding in a whole host of ways."

Lockheed Martin's Marillyn Hewson shares her perspective. "How fortunate to come from nothing to the place of privilege," she reflects. "My dad died when I was nine, and my mom had five kids. We really struggled. I worked my way through school, worked nights. I value all of that, because it made me who I am. But I look back and think, how could you come from those circumstances and end up being the CEO of the largest defense contractor in the world? Doing some of the most incredible, innovative work with 100,000 incredibly smart people who are giving their best every day? It's just amazing. I never forget that."

Boston Scientific's Mike Mahoney's gratefulness stems from his ability to plant seeds that will give shade long after he's stepped down from the role. "I'll probably be retired when I see some of the innovation we're working on come to light," he says, "but we have developments in human trials now that are really fascinating. It's easy to cut the long-term, riskier bets to make the short-term numbers. But to create long-term differentiated value, you have to be comfortable taking risk and be committed to keeping the innovation engine going. I'm very proud of how we stick to it, and our commitment to advancing science for life. I just got an email this morning from a patient who has severe Parkinson's disease and his tremors prevent him from living a normal life. We recently launched a new brain stimulation device that has remarkably changed this patient's life. His tremors are now under control, he's able to live a normal life, and he's even able to play the drums again. Those kinds of stories motivate us to do more."

General Mills' Ken Powell recounts a particularly magical moment. "There are just incredibly privileged experiences you have when you're the CEO. The most memorable for me was when I was at a high-level industry meeting where support for Haiti after the earthquake was discussed. After it was over, President Obama, who is a very personable guy, said to me, 'Hey look, I want to thank you for your leadership on this, we've got to help these people.' I mentioned to him that my daughter, who worked for a nonprofit humanitarian agency, was on her way there to help build refugee camps, and he said, 'You tell her that the president is proud of her . . .'" At that point Powell's voice trailed off and a tear of joy emerged at the memory of sharing the president's message with his daughter.

Gratitude for the role isn't just a "feel good" emotion. Psychology tells us it also relates to improved health and increased ability to deal with adversity, and it increases one's ability to build strong relationships. In turn, a virtuous circle is created: CEOs who feel gratitude tend to perform better, and in having a positive impact, their gratitude only increases.

There's no question that great CEOs are productive, successful, and confident. It would be easy to assume they're therefore cocky, arrogant, and easy to dislike. This couldn't be further from the truth. The best CEOs proactively take steps during their tenure to maintain a humble perspective. They realize that in the scheme of one's lifetime, the time spent in the role will very likely be relatively small, and that holds for even the most successful and longest tenured. They're also aware that humility isn't a box to be ticked: It'd be easy to be proud of showing humility. The goal isn't to succeed at being humble so much as to surrender to it.

To accomplish that surrender, the best CEOs never make it about themselves. They take concrete steps to stay grounded in their role as a servant leader. They create a diverse kitchen cabinet to ensure they're getting the truth and not getting caught up in themselves. Finally, they display a deep and genuine sense of gratitude for the opportunity to lead at the very highest levels and are keenly aware of the obligations that come with such a position.

● ● ●

We've now discussed how the best CEOs manage their personal effectiveness, which is essential for keeping all of the different plates spinning. Though everyone's personal management model is unique to them, the best CEOs apply a "do what only I can do" mindset to the three dimensions they can control: using time and energy, choosing a leadership model, and maintaining perspective.

Managing Personal Effectiveness: What separates the best from the rest

Mindset: Do What Only You Can Do

Time and energy practice:	**Manage a Series of Sprints**
	Keep a "tight but loose" schedule
	Care enough to compartmentalize
	Infuse energy into your routine
	Tailor your support to you

Leadership model practice:	**Live Your "To Be" List**
	Show consistency of character
	Adapt to what the company needs
	Seek to continuously grow
	Always give hope

Perspective practice:	**Stay Humble**
	Don't make it about you
	Embrace servant leadership
	Create a diverse "kitchen cabinet"
	Feel gratitude

These lessons from the best CEOs in managing personal effectiveness are applicable to any leader. What are your priorities and is your time allocated appropriately to them? Do you fill your schedule so full that unexpected events throw you into a panic? Are you able to be fully present in every interaction, or are you preoccupied with the past or future? How have you structured recovery time into your routine? What gives you energy and are you making enough time for those things? What mechanisms help you manage your time and energy? What qualities of character as a leader do you embody? How do you get feedback on who you are as a leader and what do you do with it? Do you generate energy for others by defining reality and giving hope? Do you have a small group of advisors who are a candid sounding board? At the end of the day, is it all about you or are you driven by the humble pursuit of a greater good?

We've now covered the mindsets and practices that separate the best from the rest. However, understanding the key parts of an engine (e.g., the crankshaft, connecting rod, camshaft, valves, cylinder, and piston) doesn't explain how an air-fuel mix ignites to create a power stroke that generates the force required for movement. The question remains: How do they all fit together?

Conclusion

Your big picture will never be a masterpiece if you ignore the tiny brush strokes.

—Andy Andrews

Who's the greatest athlete of the twenty-first century? Among many contenders we'd put on our list: Argentinian footballer Lionel Messi, Swedish golfer Annika Sörenstam, Jamaican sprinter Usain Bolt, German Formula 1 racer Michael Schumacher, Brazilian mixed martial artist Amanda Nunes, and five Americans—gymnast Simone Biles, tennis player Serena Williams, swimmer Michael Phelps, quarterback Tom Brady, and basketball player LeBron James.

Many more superstars could be listed. More interesting, however, is that the person who perhaps has the strongest case for being this century's greatest athlete would make few, if any, people's lists. When American decathlete Ashton Eaton retired in 2017, he held the world record in this grueling two-day event. In a decathlon, participants compete in ten disparate disciplines including the 1,500-meter run, the pole vault, and the javelin throw. When Jim Thorpe won the decathlon at the Stockholm Olympics in 1912, King Gustav V of Sweden told him, "Sir, you are the world's greatest athlete."[90]

Eaton didn't just set the record once. During the course of his career he set five heptathlon and decathlon records, became the third person in history to win back-to-back Olympic gold medals in the event, and won four back-to-back world championships. To compile that sort of record, Eaton wasn't just competent in each

289

event. He had to be among the best on the planet at several of them. In 2012, when Eaton broke the decathlon world record at the US Olympic trials, his long jump of 8.23 meters was the fourteenth best in the world that year. His 10.21-second 100-meter sprint made him one of the one hundred fastest men in the world.

What does that have to do with CEO excellence? Simple: We believe the role has more in common with being a decathlete than mastering any one skill. The best CEOs aren't necessarily the world's number one at direction setting, aligning the organization, mobilizing leaders, engaging the board, connecting with stakeholders, or managing personal effectiveness, but they're world-class at integrating all of these responsibilities simultaneously.

KBC's Johan Thijs confirms the notion: "I'm good at a lot of stuff and perhaps I can do one or two things very well, but I'm not necessarily the best at it all. But that's not important. For a CEO, what's important is that you can balance everything together. You're not supposed to manage just one dimension within the framework." Assa Abloy's Johan Molin reinforces this idea. "As CEO, you need to realize that you're only one person and you're not the best person because you're such a generalist," he says. "You're not trying to be the smartest of the smart, but you can give good advice, facilitate, and encourage people to work."

Although a number of CEOs we interviewed have a degree of celebrity status (Jamie Dimon, Satya Nadella, Reed Hastings, et al.), the decathlete analogy explains why many of the corporate athletes who qualify as being the best in the world are little known outside of business circles. They work hard and quietly behind the scenes to manage the key responsibilities of a CEO by applying the mindsets and practices we've discussed. Pulling off this balancing act is extremely difficult, and it's why we've done a deep dive into every aspect of the role. We live in an era in which much of the management advice on social media is characterized by sophomoric recipes and quick rules of thumb. Large, global companies are simply too complex for a short list of simple precepts to constitute the recipe for CEO success. In the end, we've done our best to abide by Einstein's edict that everything should be made as simple as possible, but no simpler.

Now that we've looked at all aspects of the role, let's explore the extent to which instructive patterns and archetypes have emerged from our research.

Patterns and Archetypes

In the Hindu epic the *Ramayana*, the sage Vishwamitra helps the godly avatar Rama by giving him divine weapons and knowledge. In Greek mythology, Athena gave the hero Perseus a mirror shield to slay the Gorgon Medusa. When Cinderella was in trouble, a fairy godmother whisked her off to the ball. These stories, written millennia apart and in different corners of the world, have in common the hero's receiving aid from the supernatural. This is an "archetype": the recurrence of a similar pattern throughout various, seemingly unrelated cases.

In our research, once we defined the role of the CEO and determined the mindsets and practices that differentiate the best from the rest, we conducted a number of quantitative and qualitative analyses to determine if there were any archetypes that cut across the CEO's various responsibilities. Are there patterns related to how CEOs prioritize their time and energy? Are there archetypes related to how the best shift their focus? To what extent does the business environment—for example, a turnaround situation (as 55 percent of our CEOs faced) or the company trying to move from good to great or great to greater still (faced by 45 percent)— dictate which responsibility to focus on? We hoped some practical guidance would emerge, but no such similarities were found. No matter the situation, our CEOs made vastly different choices as to where to focus and when.

At DSM, where Feike Sijbesma initially faced a turnaround situation and ultimately transformed the company from chemicals to life sciences, his focus in his early days was weighted toward the external. "I spent twenty-five percent of my time on the investors' world in the beginning when I needed them to take the journey," he says. "About forty percent of my time was with the market and customers, because I had to get a sense of how they look at the world and what they find important." Though faced with a similar turnaround situation, Henrik Poulsen did the opposite as he shifted Ørsted from an oil and gas to a clean energy company. "I could have spent all my time traveling the world to visit people who wanted to hear about the transformation," he says, "but we didn't take our eyes off building a culture that could execute our strategy."

On the "good to great" front, Mastercard's Ajay Banga started with a deep internal focus, spending most of his time setting the direction and aligning the organization. His goal was to take the company along with him on the journey. "The idea of devoting more time to something outside of Mastercard was very hard," he shares. As those efforts became established, he shifted more of his efforts to external matters, further increased the time he spent with the board, and paid more attention to managing his personal effectiveness. Brad Smith at Intuit, on the other hand, stuck to a 40/30/20/10 split largely from day one: 40 percent of time driving business performance, 30 percent coaching, 20 percent with outsiders, and 10 percent on personal growth and learning.

We did, however, find some common themes when it came to how these CEOs stepped into and out of the job.

Starting and Finishing Strong

When it came to transitioning into the CEO chair, all emphasized the benefits of investing time in a listening tour. Intuit's Brad Smith asked the same three questions of board members, investors, fellow CEOs, and employees: "What are the greatest opportunities we haven't yet capitalized on? What are the greatest threats that could end this storied franchise if not addressed? What's the one thing I could do to screw it up?" In the job's honeymoon period it's important to conduct listening tours because, as Lockheed Martin's Marillyn Hewson explains, "People will tell you things because you're the newbie that they're not going to tell you two or three years from now." The best shared a wealth of advice about how to get the most out of listening tours, including hosting sessions alone (people talk more), listening more than talking, not making promises, visiting places you've never been, and being sure to include customers and ex-employees.

Another common theme was for new CEOs to do their own diagnosis of the situation. When we asked three-time CEO Ed Breen to share his success factors for ramping up, he revealed, "As a CEO, when you go into a company, even if you've been in the company and you get promoted to CEO, you need to take a good, clean look at everything: return metrics, cash conversion—all the key metrics. Then you can see where you sit vis-à-vis a really good company that has a business model like yours, and you can ask, 'Well, why aren't we there? If they can be there, why can't *we* be there?' There's always a way to get there." Galderma's Flemming Ørnskov, also a three-time CEO, draws an analogy from his background as a physician. "The first step is what a doctor will call anamnesis, studying case history," he says. "I try to get the story, the content, understand the history. Then I look at the facts—the symptoms and the signs—and I generate a hypothesis as to the diagnosis. Once I've homed in on one or two things, then I ask, 'What is the treatment?'" Diageo's Ivan Menezes emphasizes the need to be clinical in one's assessment. "Get to grips with reality and be brutally honest," he advises. "Get a dispassionate view of the market, the competition, your positioning, and the culture. Be really objective about all of it."

Once a diagnostic is completed, a third theme is to convey the new direction with elegant simplicity. Virtually every CEO we spoke to could describe their strategy in an elevator ride. They also often had a "one pager" that told the whole story crisply. DBS's Piyush Gupta describes, "We put together a one-page visual we call the DBS House—on it is everything: our vision, strategy, values, targets, et cetera. It allowed us to all talk the same language about what we wanted to do and, more important, what we did not want to do." Diageo's Menezes carries around one piece of paper called the "Diageo Performance Ambition" that has the company's purpose and vision at the top, and then lays out the company's six strategic pillars—written in simple English with no jargon. Menezes describes why it's so useful: "Whether you're on a bottling line in Kenya or doing sales in Vietnam, you can find yourself on the page and know where you could make a difference. It's very helpful in depicting the clarity of the strategy, and the change that is needed." At Greg Case's Aon, the equivalent one pager was called the "Aon United strategic blueprint." For Michael Fisher at Cincinnati Children's, it was one page outlining the hospital's overall vision and laying out its "4C's" strategies and success measures in the areas of Care, Community, Cure, and Culture.

When it comes to stepping out of the role, many spoke of not staying too long. "I'm mindful that even the best CEOs can outlive their sell-by date, and I recently put this concept to the test," says TIAA's Roger Ferguson. "The big risk for CEOs is missing how much the world has changed—I thought about how everything I see now doesn't conform to some idea I had five years ago or ten years ago. I looked in the mirror and asked, 'Am I the best person for the next leg of the journey?' and in my case, I felt that it was time for me to pass the baton to another leader after twelve years of leading TIAA."

Herbert Hainer chose to leave Adidas when the digital world started to kick in and he realized the company needed someone who understood that arena better than he did. Similarly, after the Ahold Delhaize merger Dick Boer felt that, in his sixties, this was the time to execute a handover, since, after the integration, the company needed to stabilize and build onto the new foundation a layer of operational excellence. Regarding his departure from Shire after the acquisition by Takeda, Flemming Ørnskov simply states, "It was obvious to me that I wasn't the best to lead the integration, that there'd be others who would do it better. It didn't play to my strengths." Sony's Kazuo Hirai felt that while he was the right person for the transformation phase of the company, he was less suited for the more stable phase that followed.

Medtronic's Bill George suggests the following litmus test questions be asked regularly: Do you still find fulfillment and joy? Are you still learning and feeling challenged? Are there new personal circumstances that you should be taking into account (e.g., family or personal health issues)? Are there unique opportunities outside that won't come around again? How is succession shaping up? Are there company-specific milestones (e.g., integration of a major acquisition, the launch of an important new product, the completion of a long-running project) that make transitioning out more or less natural? Is the industry changing so dramatically that the company would benefit from a new perspective? Are you staying primarily because you can't imagine what comes next?[91]

When it does come time to go, the best CEOs orchestrate a seamless transition. Caterpillar's Jim Owens describes what great succession planning looks like: "At any large company, shame on them if they don't have at least three strong candidates to take over the top job when you leave. The board should be able to evaluate them, so I gave these individuals more autonomy toward the end, and let them give more strategy presentations to the board. I also had each candidate present to the investor community on the strategy for their units." Other elements of a seamless transition include not leaving unpleasant decisions to one's successor, giving them plenty of time to do a listening tour and get their thoughts together on strategy before taking the chair, and thinking about "what's next?" for your own career. "In the end, the hardest part of the CEO role is leaving," Owens adds. "You really need to get out of the way and let your successor critique what you did and talk about what needs to go way better."

Before Intuit's Brad Smith stepped down as CEO, he suggested that he and his successor, Sasan Goodarzi, talk to Steve Young, the American football player who succeeded an iconic quarterback, Joe Montana. "He talked to us about how for part of his first year he tried to be Joe Montana," Smith recounts. "He grew his hair out like Joe and began to dress like Joe. He even tried to change his throwing mechanics like Joe. And he had the worst half year ever. Eventually, Steve stopped trying to be like Joe and had a great career. Steve looked right at Sasan and said, 'You need to be the best Sasan Goodarzi in the world.' He looked at me and said, 'And you have to *let him* be the best Sasan Goodarzi in the world.'"

Prioritizing across Responsibilities

Without any clear archetypes or patterns, how does a CEO know which plates to spin, how fast, and when? As we mentioned in the introduction, the answer lies in the interplay between the business situation and the CEO's unique capabilities and preferences. These aren't independent variables, however. As the business situation changes, and the CEO responds, their capabilities increase and their approach changes. The dynamics are similar to riding a bike. The external terrain combines with internal factors like the rider's coordination and balance. The more the person rides, the more they're able to tackle more diverse and challenging terrain, and their preferences regarding where to ride change accordingly.

This dynamism is at the heart of why most CEOs believe that the only way to learn the role is to be in the role. Medtronic's Bill George explains, "No one is prepared to become CEO no matter how much they think they are. You have to grow into the job. The world evolves around you, and meanwhile you grow as a human being as you take over. You think you know how to run a business, but that's really more the COO [chief operating officer] role." Cincinnati Children's Michael Fisher draws an analogy: "Preparing for the CEO role is like being an assistant coach on a professional sports team—you think you know the head coach role, but you really don't."

All this is to say that there's no generic answer for how to prioritize. The advice in this book will help a CEO perform the biking equivalent of "gearing up" (donning helmet, riding clothes, reflectors, etc.), finding the right seat height, and pumping the tires. They'll know how to pedal, break, and work the gears. Signaling safely in traffic won't be a problem. And so on. The knowledge this book offers will get a leader riding faster and better than otherwise, but at the end of the day it's only by getting on the bike and riding that one learns exactly what to do and when.

Once pedaling has begun, the best CEOs keep taking on ever more challenging terrain, upgrading their equipment, and striving to become the best riders they can be. Over time, many become known for a signature strength, the same way great riders typically excel in a specialty area (road racing, BMX, downhill, cross-country, etc.). Jamie Dimon's ability to drive execution both at Bank One and at JPMC is the stuff of legend. Brad Smith's ability to inspire leaders through culture at Intuit is well recognized. Ørsted's Henrik Poulsen's strategic foresight is envied by many. Ed Breen's ability to reshape business portfolios across numerous companies led the *Wall Street Journal* to nickname him "the breakup expert."

To help leaders on their journey, we've created a set of prioritization and assessment tools to ensure they're being the best they can be in the areas that matter most. These tools can be found in appendix 1. We acknowledge that such an approach is quite mechanistic. We'd liken it to classical physics—the sophisticated reality of the quantum realm and relativity aren't accounted for—yet Newton's equations do a pretty good job of explaining our day-to-day reality.

The Future of the Role

In the beginning of this book, we extolled the virtues of being an exceptional futurist. Yet we've based all that we've shared here on the mindsets and practices of the best CEOs over the past twenty years. Some readers might wonder if the saying, "It's hard to drive looking in the rearview mirror" applies here. It's a good question, and one we've thought a lot about. Will the responsibilities of the CEO role that we've discussed be as relevant for the next twenty years as for the last twenty? Will the mindsets and practices that differentiate the best from the rest produce the winners of the future in the same way they have the past?

We believe so. After all, at its core the business of business is unchanging. As German philosopher Friedrich Nietzsche once wrote, "To fix prices, adjust values, invent equivalents, to exchange things—all of this has to such an extent preoccupied the first and earliest thoughts of humankind, that it may be said to constitute thinking itself."[92] The same can be said for leading large organizations. The *Officials of Chou,* written at the behest of one of China's most revered ministers in 1100 BCE, for example, prescribes many of the same practices that predominate in modern business: clarifying decision-rights, establishing clear operating procedures, monitoring performance, maintaining productive relationships between leaders and employees, creating a culture of respect for one another, and leading by setting a good example.[93]

Sailing provides a good analogy of the dynamic at play. Visual depictions of the first sailing boats date back as far as 5500 BCE. These boats, used on the Nile River, were simple, square-rigged reed ships with a single square sheet of papyrus attached to a mast.

Since then, great innovations have taken place: steering oars and rudders, the keel, marine engines, GPS navigation, and so on. At the same time, the fundamentals of sailing have remained the same: sail trim (getting the sail in the most efficient position), centerboard position (correcting sideways drift), boat balance (not letting it tip), boat trim (keeping the boat level), and course made good (adjusting for tide and leeway to get most directly from A to B).

In exploring the CEO role and the mindsets and practices that separate the best from the rest, we've purposely focused on what's *true* versus what's *new*. No matter that recent history has been a series of trends and counter-trends—globalization, the internet, social media, consumer activism, digital transformation, social unrest, pandemics, economic crises, new generations entering the workforce, etc.—direction still needs to be set, organizations aligned, leaders mobilized, boards engaged with, stakeholders connected to, and personal effectiveness managed. We're confident that approaching these responsibilities with a mindset of being bold, treating the soft stuff as the hard stuff, solving for the team's psychology, helping directors help the business, starting with "why?" and doing what only they can do will continue to stand CEOs in good stead navigating whatever seas lie ahead.

Even though the role and the mindsets for success don't change, one's priorities and tactics do. The breakup of legacy, bloated organizations in the 1970s as they started to face global competition elevated the importance of the shareholder. The advent of cable TV news in the 1980s brought CEOs into the limelight, requiring them to focus more on their external image. The technology revolution at the turn of the century ushered in a shift from physical to digital and intellectual assets, driving increased attention to the people side of leadership. It also brought with it personal productivity enhancers such as the then virtually ubiquitous BlackBerry, which simultaneously saved time and drained energy by creating the expectation that one had to be "on" 24/7. After the 2008 financial crisis, boards were mandated to play a more hands-on role, which shifted the CEO's role in corporate governance.

This brings us to our final observation regarding great CEOs: They have a good filter for what in their environment is signal and what is noise. This aptitude will be even more crucial in the future amid what will undoubtedly be an ever more raging torrent of trends, ideas, and information. As we write, for example, the best CEOs are coping with digital transformation, employees' health and well-being, diversity and inclusion, climate change, the future of work, the challenge of reskilling, the potential rise of cryptocurrencies, a growing split between China and the United States, and the strengthening of stakeholder capitalism. Also, while they understand why "agility" and "purpose" are the buzzwords of the day, they avoid treating them as the panaceas they're often peddled as.

Looking ahead, these issues—and many more we can't even imagine—will keep consuming the attention of our leaders. Whatever the future brings, we believe, however, that the best CEOs of the future will be even more . . .

> . . . *Ethically accountable:* The real-time transparency and activism that social media brings will hold CEOs to higher standards of personal and company conduct, diversity and inclusion, philanthropy, leadership principles, and corporate culture.
>
> . . . *Diverse:* CEOs who reflect greater diversity in gender, race, ethnicity, and class will finally put a nail in the coffin of the outmoded "CEO as the hero" image and will adopt best practices such as servant leadership, continuous growth, and humility.
>
> . . . *Resilient:* Escalating demands on a CEO's time and energy combined with increasing public scrutiny will make the role increasingly frustrating and exhausting. Having a thick skin and an effective personal operating model will no longer be table-stakes to thrive but to survive.
>
> . . . *Impactful:* As CEOs are called on to serve as societal leaders, using their voice to advocate for policies that benefit many stakeholders, the impact they can have in the role will increase, making the job both more fulfilling and challenging.

As the role becomes more expansive, some might suggest that the job will become too big for one person to fill. Others may counter that the escalation of artificial intelligence (AI) will make many aspects of the role obsolete (the management equivalent of placing airline pilots in planes that can be flown remotely). We believe that the more machines drive the technical side of leadership, the more competitive advantages will accrue to leaders who are skilled at raising aspirations, inspiring, and unleashing creativity and collaboration.

We started our search for CEO excellence by narrowing down the pool of twenty-first-century CEOs to the very best. We now realize that the screens we used were nothing more than a proxy for how well a leader helps others achieve things that they never imagined they'd be able to do. That's something every leader can aspire to, and we hope that this book has increased your ability to do so in whatever leadership position you may hold.

Acknowledgments

Although there are three of us whose names are on the cover, beyond those we interviewed who are the heroes of our story (see appendix 2 for more on them), there were countless heroes working behind the scenes without whom this book wouldn't have become a reality. To start with, there are those who helped us conduct the needed analytics, sort through the more than 1,500 pages of interview transcripts, and find and digest the extensive external information that was needed. The head of our research team was Anand Lakshmanan, without whom we never would have been able to travel so far, so fast, and with so much fun. Anand was joined by Annie Arditi, Michelle Call, Aungar Chatterjee, Justin Hardy, Pex Jose Parra, James Psomas, Elisa Simon, and Jonathan Turton. The interviews themselves only happened because of the magic touch of Jodi Elkins, who coordinated the process. Overseeing the entire project in addition to managing McKinsey & Company's global CEO Excellence service line through which we consult to CEOs directly is Monica Murarka. She not only helped us assemble and guide the aforementioned team, but as a certified executive coach was also an exceptional thought partner to us as we created the content.

We always knew our content would be dense if we were going to truly do the CEO role justice and that finding a way to convey it in an interesting, readable manner would be challenging. This is where our collaboration with *Fortune* journalist and *Bezonomics* author Brian Dumaine came into play. Brian helped ensure that we were getting the best balance possible between content and storytelling. Together, we were all expertly guided by our editor at Scribner, Rick Horgan, who provided invaluable feedback and guidance throughout the process. Speaking of which, the entire

Scribner team was hands-down the most world-class we've ever worked with in the publishing world. Thank you also to Lynn Johnston for helping shape our early thinking and connecting us with Scribner, and to Raju Narisetti, the leader of McKinsey's Global Publishing group, for encouraging and enabling us to work with Lynn at the outset of our journey.

We also had numerous sponsors and sparring partners in McKinsey & Company, including our senior partner colleagues and the leaders of the firm's strategy and corporate finance practice: Chris Bradley, Martin Hirt, and Sven Smit, collectively the authors of *Strategy Beyond the Hockey Stick: People, Probabilities, and Big Moves to Beat the Odds*. They, in addition to Michael Birshan and Kurt Strovink, who are also leading thinkers and practitioners in the field of CEO counseling, gave us inspiration, ideas, and a substantial research base on which to build. Partners affiliated with the firm's CEO Excellence Service Line have also collectively been instrumental to this work: Eleanor Bensley, Blair Epstein, and Sander Smits. We also thank our many partner colleagues, who are too many to mention by name, for opening up their relationships with the CEOs we interviewed—without their being trusted counselors to these incredible leaders, we wouldn't have had the same access.

Most important, we want to thank our families for putting up with the years of "nights and weekends" work that went into writing this book. We all have full-time client service roles at McKinsey & Company that didn't let up during the process, and without our families' support and forgiveness for the seemingly unending time away from the home front, this project wouldn't have been tenable. Thomas Czegledy, Fiona Keller, and Mary Malhotra were unconditionally supportive and cheerleaders for the effort.

Lastly, we thank you, our readers, for your interest in this book. We want to continue to improve ourselves and have greater impact with each successive work, and, in this spirit, we welcome any feedback you're willing to share. You can reach us at carolyn .dewar@mckinsey.com, scott.keller@mckinsey.com, and vikram .malhotra@mckinsey.com.

Appendix 1

CEO Excellence Assessment and Prioritization Tools

As leaders of McKinsey & Company's CEO Excellence practice, we're often called upon to help CEOs transition into the role, take stock of how they're doing during their tenure, and determine when and how they should transition out of the role. In the course of that work, we've developed a series of tools to prompt reflection on CEO priorities and effectiveness. In this appendix we've included three exercises that CEOs tell us are extremely helpful.

The first involves looking at the CEO's six main responsibilities and, with respect to each, assessing the degree of change that you aspire to lead. Typically, that call is based on the potential you see in each area, along with any guidance or guardrails that may be coming from the board or from external stakeholders. The second exercise prompts reflection regarding how you're approaching the three sub-elements in all of the responsibility areas. The final exercise draws on the results of the first two, pinpointing high-leverage improvement areas and converting the insights into action.

Many CEOs find these exercises are most valuable when they're not only self-assessing against them, but, also, prompting others to provide their views (e.g., team members and board members). Any themes that emerge or differences in perception can then be debriefed with your "kitchen cabinet" (as discussed in chapter 18) to identify actions that will lead to even more success.

Worksheet 1 – My CEO mandate

What is the degree of change you aspire to lead?

Set the direction	Vision Strategy Resource allocation	①—②—③—④—⑤ Evolve being careful not to break any glass		Lead a massive transformation
Align the organization	Culture Org design Talent	①—②—③—④—⑤ Fine-tune what we have		Overhaul virtually all areas
Mobilize through leaders	Composition Teamwork Operating rhythm	①—②—③—④—⑤ Right people are working well together		Big changes in people & dynamics
Engage the Board	Relationships Capabilities Meetings	①—②—③—④—⑤ Board is effective, my engagement is strong		Board lacks skills & is challenging to work with
Connect with stakeholders	Social purpose Interactions Moments of truth	①—②—③—④—⑤ Relationships with key stakeholders are strong		Complete reset required with many stakeholders
Manage personal effectiveness	Time & energy Leadership model Perspective	①—②—③—④—⑤ My current working norms are sufficient		I need to adopt a new operating model

Worksheet 2 – How am I leading today? (1/6)

Which of the following statements best describes how you are currently leading the company? Make your assessment on each of the practices that appear in **bold** font in the first column. Related mindsets appear in *italics* for reference.

	Challenged	Able	Excellent
SET THE DIRECTION	*Let a thousand flowers bloom*	*Evolve the core*	*Be bold*
Vision	I avoid top-down vision in favor of **empowering businesses to have their own**	I motivate employees with a **vision to beat the competition** in our industry	I **reframe the game** to both significantly raise aspirations and reset what it means to win
Strategy	We aggregate and pursue hundreds if not **thousands of bottom-up initiatives**	Our corporate strategy is the sum of **business unit strategies plus synergies** across them	We **make big moves early and often** that are driven at the enterprise level
Resource allocation	We largely stay the course, evolving our budgets and resource allocation **gradually over time**	We **shift our resources annually** in a way that balances keeping harmony with pursuing opportunity	I consistently **act like an outsider** to ensure we frequently reallocate resources, even when it's hard

Worksheet 2 – How am I leading today? (2/6)

Which of the following statements best describes how you are currently leading the company? Make your assessment on each of the practices that appear in **bold** font in the first column. Related mindsets appear in *italics* for reference.

	Challenged	Able	Excellent
ALIGN THE ORGANIZATION	*Leave the "soft stuff" to others*	*Tend to the "soft stuff" on a best efforts basis*	*Treat the "soft stuff" as the hard stuff*
Culture	We have a set of values and a leadership model for which our **HR function is the guardian**	I ensure my **CEO messaging reinforces the culture** we desire and take relevant actions (guided by HR)	I **find the one thing** that matters most and personally own it/ensure we take a well-coordinated approach
Organizational design	We **reorganize ourselves regularly** (e.g. every 1–2 years) to address pain points	We **make necessary tradeoffs** between getting the benefits of global scale and local responsiveness	We **solve for "stagility"** by organizing around a stable, accountable core & being agile where needed
Talent	We rely on the same **short-list of talented leaders** to fulfill big roles and lead big initiatives	I personally encourage / **elevate our strong performers** and ensure concrete action is taken on low performers	I **(don't) put people first;** instead I ensure the highest value-creating roles have the best fit talent

Worksheet 2 – How am I leading today? (3/6)

Which of the following statements best describes how you are currently leading the company? Make your assessment on each of the practices that appear in **bold** font in the first column. Related mindsets appear in *italics* for reference.

	Challenged	Able	Excellent
MOBILIZE THROUGH LEADERS	*Handle the team diplomatically*	*Coordinate the team to execute*	*Solve for the team's psychology*
Team composition	I play **the hand I've been dealt** (making changes isn't worth the disruption)	I focus on ensuring everyone on the team is highly **competent and trustworthy** in their role	**I create an ecosystem** with a complementary set of skills (1+1=3) and attitudes to lead change together
Teamwork	The team is collegial when together and **operates largely in silos** outside the room	The team has **effective working norms** and engages in healthy debate	We **make the team the star** by continually improving our effectiveness in combining data, dialogue, & speed
Operating rhythm	Although everyone feels too much time is spent in meetings, all are willing to **go with the flow**	The corporate meeting **calendar is clear and coherent** and meetings are well organized	Our meeting timing, content, & protocols enable us to **get into a groove** as we set strategy and execute

Worksheet 2 – How am I leading today? (4/6)

Which of the following statements best describes how you are currently leading the company? Make your assessment on each of the practices that appear in **bold** font in the first column. Related mindsets appear in *italics* for reference.

	Challenged	Able	Excellent
ENGAGE THE BOARD	*Stay at arm's length*	*Support the board's fiduciary duties*	*Help directors help the business*
Relationships	I **provide requested information** and am available to board members as needed	I **proactively nurture a good relationship** with each board member	I **build a foundation of trust** with the board through radical transparency & interest in their views
Capabilities	I **leave it to the chair/lead Director** when it comes to matters of board composition	I **provide input on nominations** of new members and ensure the group is educated on the business	I'm able to **tap the wisdom of elders** having shaped membership & engaged and educated members
Meetings	I let the **board dictate the agenda** for board meetings and tailor my role accordingly	I help ensure board meetings are characterized by **efficiency and effectiveness**	I **focus on the future** with the board (beyond fiduciary topics) & start by sharing what's on my mind

Worksheet 2 – How am I leading today? (5/6)

Which of the following statements best describes how you are currently leading the company? Make your assessment on each of the practices that appear in **bold** font in the first column. Related mindsets appear in *italics* for reference.

	Challenged	Able	Excellent
CONNECT WITH STAKEHOLDERS	*Stay focused on the business*	*Tactically triage and target stakeholders*	*Always start with "Why?"*
Social purpose	I see social purpose as a trend but my real **focus is on creating shareholder value**	I ensure we have a compelling **Corporate Social Responsibility story** backed with facts	We **impact the big picture** by defining our societal "why?" and embedding it into the core of our business
Interaction	**I minimize external interactions** because my job is to first and foremost to run the business	**I proactively prioritize** which stakeholders I meet & have a clear objective in every interaction with them	I **get to the essence** of where our stakeholder needs intersect with our own and optimize accordingly
Moments of truth	Given how unpredictable crises are, we'll **improvise** to deal with any as they arise	We mobilize quickly to respond in crisis situations based on **clear protocols**	We **stay elevated** by building resilience ahead of crises, detecting them early, and finding opportunities in them

Worksheet 2 – How am I leading today? (6/6)

Which of the following statements best describes how you are currently leading the company? Make your assessment on each of the practices that appear in **bold** font in the first column. Related mindsets appear in *italics* for reference.

	Challenged	Able	Excellent
MANAGE PERSONAL EFFECTIVENESS	*Be "on" all the time*	*Stay organized and efficient*	*Do what only I can do*
Time and energy	My schedule is built around **what others ask of me** – I'm here to serve	I am disciplined about spending **time on priority areas** for the company, enabled by a good assistant	I manage my time and energy as **a series of sprints** enabled by office support tailored to my needs
Leadership model	I am being **who the company needs me to be** – anything else would be irresponsible	I simply try to **be who I am** – anything else would be inauthentic	**I live my "to be" list** – true to my convictions and values while adjusting my behaviors to what's needed
Perspective	Everything rests on me – my mood is up or down **based on external factors**	I have an important role in the company's success, but also **recognize much is out of my control**	I **stay humble** recognizing my privileged position to help others succeed & continually improve my ability to do so

Worksheet 3 – Prioritizing improvement areas and related actions

Reflect on your answers to worksheets 1 & 2 in answering the questions below

In any of the six responsibility areas where the magnitude of change you are driving is high (from worksheet 1), are there **any practice areas you should be aspiring for excellence in** that you aren't already (from worksheet 2)?

Are there any of the 18 practice **areas that you are "challenged" in that you should improve** (from worksheet 2)?

In those responsibility areas where the magnitude of change you are driving is low (from worksheet 1), are there **any practice areas you are potentially overdoing** (where "able" on worksheet 2 is enough)?

What does your mind and your gut tell you are the **top three areas in which you can/should improve** to have even more impact as the CEO?

What are your **concrete next steps** to validate these takeaways, set improvement actions in motion, and hold yourself accountable for progress?

Appendix 2

CEO Biographies

In writing this book we've gone deep into what makes a CEO excellent. In the end, we've emerged with a far greater appreciation for the role and a genuine respect and admiration for those who do it well. We're extremely grateful to the many exceptional leaders who acted as our tour guides along the way—all of whom have stories so full of human drama, high-stakes decision-making, battles won and lost, lessons learned, and wisdom gained that an entire book could be dedicated to each (for some that's already the case!). A brief biography for each participant is located below. Please note that for those who have been CEOs of multiple companies, we highlight their time as CEO of the company that put them on our target list, as outlined in the methodology described in our introductory chapter. Also note that revenue and employees for their respective companies are as of fiscal year 2019—and market capitalization as of 2019 year-end—so as to minimize any distortions created by the global COVID-19 pandemic.

Jacques Aschenbroich

Valeo

Revenue: $22B, Market cap: $8B

Employees: 115k in 33 countries

Career highlights

Valeo: Chair (2016–present), CEO (2009–present)

French Prime Minister's office (1987–1988)

On the boards of Veolia and BNP Paribas

CEO impact

Turned Valeo from a French "department store" for automotive parts into a global technology company focusing on, among other things, electric vehicle and self-driving technology. Tripled EBITDA and increased market cap more than tenfold largely through organic growth

Fast facts

Appeared six times in *HBR*'s Top 100 CEOs (three of them in the top ten)

Appointed a French Knight of the Legion of Honor and Knight of the National Order of Merit

●   ◆   ●

Lilach Asher-Topilsky

Israel Discount Bank

Revenue: $3B, Market cap: $5B

Employees: 9k in 2 countries

Career highlights

Israel Discount Bank: CEO (2014–2019)

Fimi Opportunity Funds: Senior Partner (2019–present)

Chair of G1, Kamada, and Rimoni Plast

On the boards of Amiad and Tel Aviv University

CEO impact

Changed the trajectory of Israel's third-largest bank, raising net income threefold, slashing its cost/income ratio by almost 20 percent, and reestablishing a productive relationship with the unions

Fast facts

Received the *Jerusalem Post* award for leaving her mark on the banking sector, 2019

Became youngest CEO of an Israeli bank

●   ◆   ●

Doug Baker Jr.

Ecolab

Revenue: $15B, Market cap: $56B

Employees: 50k in 100 countries

Career highlights

Ecolab: Chair (2006–present), CEO (2004–2020)

On the boards of the Mayo Clinic, Target, and the College of the Holy Cross

CEO impact

Converted this industrial cleaning products company into a global mission-driven organization committed to protecting people and vital resources. Made more than 100 acquisitions and grew market cap sevenfold.

Fast facts

Appeared five times in *HBR*'s Top 100 CEOs

Named in *Barron's* World's Best CEOs, 2020

Winner of Columbia Business School's Deming Cup for Operational Excellence, 2018

Ecolab is one of only seven companies to be named on Ethisphere's list of the World's Most Ethical Companies for fourteen consecutive years

● ● ●

Ajay Banga

Mastercard

Revenue: $17B, Market cap: $298B

Employees: 19k in 66 countries

Career highlights

Mastercard: Executive chair (2021–present), President and CEO (2010–2020)

Chair of the International Chamber of Commerce; on the boards of Dow and Weill Cornell Medicine

CEO impact

Dramatically expanded the US-based global payments company by redefining its market and building a culture of transparency and accountability. Tripled revenue and increased market cap thirteenfold.

Fast facts

Appeared six times in *HBR*'s Top 100 CEOs (once in top ten)

Ranked four times in the top ten in *Fortune*'s Businessperson of the Year list

Awarded the Padma Shri by the president of India

Served on US president Barack Obama's Committee for Trade Policy and Negotiations, and Commission on Enhancing National Cybersecurity

● ● ●

Mary Barra

General Motors

Revenue: $137B, Market cap: $52B

Employees: 164k in 23 countries

Career highlights

General Motors: Chair (2016–present), CEO (2014–present)

On the boards of The Walt Disney Company, Duke University, the Detroit Economic Club, and The Business Roundtable (including chair of the Education and Workforce Committee, and the Special Board Committee on Racial Equity and Justice)

Member of the Stanford Graduate School of Business Advisory Council, OneTen, and The Business Council

Chair and founding member of GM's Inclusion Advisory Board

CEO impact

Pushed an aggressive and innovative vision for GM by exiting unprofitable markets and launching a new strategy focused on the future of mobility and the electric and autonomous vehicle markets, almost tripling earnings per share along the way.

Fast facts

Named in the *TIME* 100 list of the world's most influential people, 2014

Ranked in the top seven of *Forbes*'s Most Powerful Women every year since 2014

Appeared four times in *Barron's* World's Best CEOs

Appeared three times in *Fortune*'s 50 World's Greatest Leaders (twice in top ten)

Received the Yale Chief Executive Leadership Institute's Legend in Leadership Award, 2018

●   ●   ●

Oliver Bäte

Allianz

Revenue: $126B, Market cap: $102B

Employees: 147k in over 70 countries

Career highlights

Allianz: CEO (2015–present)

On the board of the Institute of International Finance and the Geneva Association; member of International Advisory Panel to the Monetary Authority of Singapore, the Pan-European Insurance Forum, and the European Financial Services Roundtable

CEO impact

Turned this German firm into one of the largest and most digitally advanced insurance companies in the world, all while championing climate-change initiatives. Improved expense ratios to outperform the industry while increasing customer loyalty and delivering 6 percent excess shareholder return relative to the sector.

Fast facts

Appeared in *HBR*'s Top 100 CEOs, 2019

●   ●   ●

Alain Bejjani

Majid Al Futtaim

Revenue: $10B, Market cap: N/A

Employees: 43k employees in 16 countries

Career highlights

Majid Al Futtaim: CEO (2015–present)

Member of World Economic Forum (WEF) International Business Council and Atlantic Council International Advisory Board

Co-chair, WEF Middle East and North Africa Stewardship Board/Regional Action Group

Co-chair, WEF Sustainable Development Impact Summit

Co-chair, WEF MENA Summit

CEO impact

Redefined Majid Al Futtaim's long-term strategic direction to be a leading shopping mall, communities, retail, and leisure pioneer across the Middle East, Africa, and Central Asia, with a stellar international reputation. Led a company-wide transformation to set the organization on a different trajectory of performance and health, growing revenue by roughly 40 percent, EBITDA by 30 percent, and operating cashflow by 50 percent, while building a culture of customer-centricity and talentism. Championed a mindset of stakeholder capitalism that has seen Majid Al Futtaim become the first company in the Middle East to commit to a net-positive sustainability strategy.

Fast facts

Named as one of Top CEOs by *Forbes Middle East*

Named as one of Top 50 International CEOs Heading Local Companies by *Forbes Middle East*

Named as one of 50 Most Influential Expats (UAE) by *Forbes Middle East*

●   ●   ●

Frank Blake

Home Depot

Revenue: $110B, Market cap: $238B

Employees: 416k in 3 countries

Career highlights

Home Depot: Chair (2007–2015), CEO (2007–2014)

Georgia Tech, Scheller College of Business, distinguished executive fellow (2016–present)

Chair of Delta Air Lines; on the boards of Macy's, Procter & Gamble, and the Georgia Historical Society

CEO impact

Reinvigorated the US retailer's stores and service culture, boosting staff morale significantly and improving same-store sales, while offloading non-core operations. Increased operating margins by more than 300 basis points and market cap by almost 60 percent.

Fast facts

Received a Lifetime Achievement award in Leadership Character from the Turknett Leadership Group and the Robert K. Greenleaf Center for Servant Leadership

Named a Georgia Trustee by the Georgia Historical Society and the Office of the Governor of Georgia, 2019

⬢ ⬢ ⬢

Dick Boer

Ahold Delhaize

Revenue: $74B, Market cap: $27B

Employees: 353k in 11 countries

Career highlights

Ahold Delhaize: President & CEO (2011–2018), CEO Albert Heijn (2000–2011)

On the boards of Nestlé, Royal Dutch Shell, and SHV Holdings

CEO impact

His strategy of "reshaping retail" in the first phase of his tenure helped deliver the third highest economic profit in the sector, behind Walmart and Costco. Oversaw merger with Delhaize in 2016 to double the Dutch company's employees and create the second-largest supermarket retailer in the world.

Fast facts

Won the 2017 Holland on the Hill Heineken award for substantial contribution to US–Dutch economic relationships

● ● ◆

Ana Botín

Grupo Santander

Revenue: $56B, Market cap: $70B

Employees: 188k in 10 countries

Career highlights

Grupo Santander: Executive chair (2014–present), Santander UK: CEO (2010–2014), Banesto: Executive chair (2002–2010)

Chair of Empieza por Educar Foundation, Spanish subsidiary of NGO Teach for All; on the boards of Coca-Cola and the MIT Task Force on the Work of the Future

CEO impact

Delivered profitable growth for this Spanish global banking group, despite falling interest rates, and improved net operating income by 15 percent, while driving a relentless focus on customers and creating a "simple, personal, fair" employee culture.

Fast facts

Named in *Fortune*'s 50 World's Greatest Leaders, 2018

Named in *Fortune*'s Businessperson of the Year list, 2018

Appointed an Honorary Dame Commander of the British Empire

Santander listed in *Fortune*'s World's 25 Best Workplaces, 2020

◆ ● ◆

Peter Brabeck-Letmathe

Nestlé

Revenue: $96B, Market cap: $313B

Employees: 291k in 83 countries

Career highlights

Nestlé: Chair Emeritus (2017–present), Chair (2005–2017), CEO (1997–2008)

Formula 1 Group: Chair (2012–2016)

Chair of Biologique Recherche; vice-chair of the World Economic Forum

CEO impact

Grew the already sizeable Swiss food company by focusing on cost cutting, innovation, and speed of decision-making, while also acquiring the pet food company Ralston Purina. Refreshed at least 20 percent of products every year, shifting the company's focus to nutrition, health, and wellness, while almost tripling market cap.

Fast facts

Awarded the Austrian Cross of Honor for service to the Republic of Austria

Awarded the Mexican Order of the Aztec Eagle

Received the Schumpeter Society's Schumpeter Prize for innovative achievements in the field of economy, politics, and economics

● ● ●

Ed Breen

Tyco International

Revenue: $10B, Market cap: $14B

Employees: 70k in 50 countries

Career highlights

DuPont: CEO (2015–2019 & 2020–present)

Tyco International: Chair & CEO (2002–2012)

General Instrument: CEO (1997–2000)

On the boards of IFF and Comcast and the advisory board of New Mountain Capital

CEO impact

Stabilized scandal-plagued Tyco from the brink of bankruptcy by bringing a new level of integrity and accountability. Streamlined the business and eventually split up the industrial conglomerate into six focused entities, while boosting share price sevenfold.

Fast facts

Received the American Chemical Society's Leadership Award for Historic Corporate Reinvention, 2018

Named one of the 100 Most Influential People in Business Ethics by Ethisphere, 2009

● ● ●

Greg Case

Aon

Revenue: $11B, Market cap: $49B

Employees: 50k in 96 countries

Career highlights

Aon: CEO (2005–present)

On the boards of Discover, Ann & Robert H. Lurie Children's Hospital, Field Museum of Natural History, CEOs Against Cancer, and St. John's University School of Risk Management

CEO impact

Reorganized the global risk mitigator's portfolio through a series of bold M&A deals and divestitures, while undertaking a major cultural and operational transformation that has helped the Irish-domiciled firm double EBITDA and increase market cap sevenfold over his tenure.

Fast facts

Has received multiple awards for his role as an ally and advocate for inclusion and diversity

Appeared five times in *HBR*'s Top 100 CEOs

Received the Committee for Economic Development's Owen B. Butler Education Excellence Award, 2018

● ● ●

Marc Casper

Thermo Fisher Scientific

Revenue: $26B, Market cap: $130B

Employees: 75k in 50 countries

Career highlights

Thermo Fisher Scientific: Chair (2020–present), President & CEO (2009–present)

Kendro Laboratory Products: CEO (2000–2001)

On the boards of U.S. Bancorp, the US-China Business Council, Brigham and Women's Hospital, and Wesleyan University

CEO impact

Oversaw the US-based life sciences tools and diagnostics company's agile response to the COVID-19 pandemic, made possible by Casper ruthlessly prioritizing what's important for his top team to create value. Tripled EBITDA and increased market cap more than sevenfold.

Fast facts

Named on *Forbes*'s list of America's Most Innovative Leaders, 2019

Appeared twice in *HBR*'s Top 100 CEOs

● ● ●

Ken Chenault

American Express

Revenue: $44B, Market cap: $102B

Employees: 64k in 40 countries

Career highlights

American Express: Chair & CEO (2001–2018)

Chair, General Catalyst Partners; on the boards of Airbnb, Berkshire Hathaway, NCAA, the Harvard Corporation, and the Smithsonian National Museum of African American History & Culture

CEO impact

Expanded American Express's core business beyond T&E spending to serve the needs of its members across spending categories. Under his leadership, the company introduced and built one of the world's largest customer loyalty programs—Membership Rewards—and earned global recognition as a leader in customer service, while doubling revenue and growing net income more than fivefold. American Express remains one of the largest and most prominent credit card companies in the world.

Fast facts

Named in *Barron's* World's Best CEOs list multiple times

Honored by HistoryMakers in 2018, celebrating his extraordinary life and career

Listed as one of 50 "living pioneers" in the African American community by Ebony

Named as one of the World's 50 Greatest Leaders by *Fortune* in its inaugural list in 2014

● ◆ ●

Toby Cosgrove

Cleveland Clinic

Revenue: $11B, Market cap: N/A

Employees: 68k in 4 countries

Career highlights

Cleveland Clinic: CEO (2004–2017)

United States Air Force: surgeon (awarded the Bronze Star for his service in the Vietnam War)

CEO impact

Reorganized the nonprofit academic medical center by putting the patient first (a radical approach at the time), which improved both patient satisfaction but also medical outcomes, while also expanding geographically to boost revenues. Doubled revenue and lifted the institution from last to first in patient experience rankings for hospitals with more than 1,000 beds.

Fast facts

Elected to the Institute of Medicine, 2013

Received the Woodrow Wilson Center Award for Public Service

Named in Modern Healthcare's 50 Most Influential Clinical Executives every year from 2010–2017

● ● ●

Larry Culp

Danaher

Revenue: $18B, Market cap: $111B

Employees: 60k in 60 countries

Career highlights

General Electric: Chair and CEO (2018–present)

Danaher: CEO (2001–2014)

On the boards of Washington College and Wake Forest University

CEO impact

Scaled the concept of lean management to all aspects of the business at Danaher, improving efficiencies through a high-performance culture while freeing up capital to acquire high-growth businesses. Increased both revenue and market cap fivefold.

Fast facts

Appeared in *HBR*'s Top 100 CEOs, 2014

Named in *Barron's* Top CEOs of 2020

● ● ●

Sandy Cutler

Eaton Corporation

Revenue: $21B, Market cap: $39B

Employees: 101k doing business in 175 countries

Career highlights

Eaton: Chair & CEO (2000–2016)

Lead director of DuPont and KeyCorp

CEO impact

Diversified the US auto-parts maker into a power management company to stimulate growth, while promoting a culture of innovation, impact, and integrity. Grew revenue fivefold and market cap almost sevenfold.

Fast facts

Appeared twice in *HBR*'s Top 100 CEOs

After retirement, opened a high-end French-American restaurant with his wife and son

● ● ●

Aliko Dangote

Dangote Group	
Revenue: $4B, Market cap: n/a	
Employees: 30k in 17 countries	
Career highlights	

Dangote Group: Founder and CEO (1977–present), Dangote Foundation: Chairman (1994–present)

On the boards of the Corporate Council on Africa, the Clinton Health Access Initiative, and the ONE campaign

CEO impact

Grew the company from a small commodities trading firm to West Africa's largest conglomerate with key businesses in cement and sugar. Building Nigeria's biggest oil refinery and petrochemical complex in a move to increase group revenue sixfold and secure more economic independence for the country.

Fast facts

Appointed a Nigerian Grand Commander of the Order of the Niger

Named in the *TIME* 100 list of the most influential people in the world, 2014

Named in *Fortune*'s 50 World's Greatest Leaders, 2019

Listed in CNBC's First 25 list of the 25 people who had the most profound impact on business from 1989–2014

Named *Forbes Asia*'s Person of the Year, 2014

Received numerous other African business awards

● ● ●

Richard Davis

U.S. Bancorp	
Revenue: $23B, Market cap: $93B	
Employees: 70k in the United States	
Career highlights	

Make-A-Wish Foundation: President & CEO (2019–present)

U.S. Bancorp: Chair & CEO (2006–2017)

On the boards of Dow, Mastercard, and Mayo Clinic

CEO impact

Put customers and employees at the heart of a bold ten-year vision to expand the US bank's operations, while actively serving the local community. Grew net income by 30 percent and stock price by more than 60 percent.

Fast facts

Granted the US president's Lifetime Achievement Award, 2015

Named Banker of the Year by *American Banker*, 2010

•   •   •

Jamie Dimon

JPMorgan Chase

Revenue: $116B, Market cap: $437B

Employees: 257k in 60 countries

Career highlights

JPMorgan Chase: Chair & CEO (2006–present), President (2004–2018)

Bank One: Chair & CEO (2000–2004)

Citigroup: President (1995–1998)

On the boards of Harvard Business School, NYU School of Medicine, and Catalyst

CEO impact

Built resilience into America's largest bank ahead of the 2008 financial crisis, enabling it to withstand the shock, and helped shore up the nation's banking system, while becoming a leading voice in the business world known for his transparency. The only surviving major bank CEO from the financial crisis, he has more than tripled JPMC's market cap, making it the most valuable bank in the world.

Fast facts

Voted *Fortune*'s Most Admired Fortune 500 CEO, 2019 & 2020

Named four times in the *TIME* 100 list of the world's most influential people

Appeared three times in *HBR*'s Top 100 CEOs

Appeared in *Barron's* World's Best CEOs every year since 2009

•   •   •

Mitchell Elegbe

Interswitch

Revenue: ~$1B, Market cap: $1B valuation

Employees: 1k in 5 countries

Career highlights

Interswitch: Founder & CEO (2002–present)

On the board of Endeavor Nigeria

A Bishop Desmond Tutu fellow of the African Leadership Institute

CEO impact

Grew the Nigerian payment-processing company from an idea to one of Africa's rare fintech unicorns by expanding into twenty-three countries, and moving into personal and business finance.

Fast facts

Named in The Africa Report's Top 50 Disruptors, 2020

Named in the CEO Today Africa Awards list, 2018

Named West Africa Business Leader of the Year by CNBC's All African Business Leader awards, 2012

Received an Ernst & Young Emerging Entrepreneur of the Year (West Africa) award, 2012

● ● ●

Roger Ferguson

TIAA

Revenue: $41B, Market cap: N/A

Employees: 15k in 24 countries

Career highlights

TIAA: President & CEO (2008–2021)

Federal Reserve Board (1999–2006)

On the boards of Alphabet, Corning, General Mills, and IFF; member of the Group of 30, the Smithsonian Board of Regents, the New York State Insurance Advisory Board; fellow of the American Academy of Arts & Science

CEO impact

Saw the risk in the US financial-services group's business model where returns depended primarily on the investment portfolio, and created a new, less capital-intensive business, while reinforcing TIAA's core strengths. Led company through great financial crisis and its aftermath, as well as through the global COVID-19 pandemic, tripling assets under management and administration to $1.4T.

Fast facts

Served as economic advisor to President Obama (2008–2011)

As the only federal governor in Washington D.C. on 9/11, led the Fed's initial response to the terrorist attacks

Awarded the Harvard Graduate School of Arts & Sciences Centennial Medal, 2019

● ● ●

Michael Fisher

Cincinnati Children's Hospital Medical Center
Revenue: $3B, Market cap: N/A
Employees: 16k in the United States
Career highlights
Cincinnati Children's Hospital Medical Center: President & CEO (2010–present)
Cincinnati Chamber of Commerce: CEO (2001–2005)
Premier Manufacturing Support Services: CEO
Chair of the Children's Hospital's Solutions for Patient Safety

CEO impact

Significantly upgraded the Cincinnati Children's Hospital's capabilities as a premier academic medical research center, while improving access and experience for patients and families, and substantially increasing partnerships to address social determinants of health. Roughly tripled endowment growth, doubled revenue, and doubled patient care capacity.

Fast facts

Named in *Modern Healthcare*'s 100 Most Influential People in Healthcare, 2017

Cincinnati Children's ranked in the top three for ten consecutive years in *US News and World Report*'s Best Children's Hospital list

● ● ●

Bill George

Medtronic
Revenue: $29B, Market cap: $152B
Employees: 105k in 52 countries
Career highlights
Medtronic: Chair (1996–2002), CEO (1991–2001)
Harvard Business School: Senior fellow (2004–present)
Author of bestselling book, *True North: Discover Your Authentic Leadership* (2007)

CEO impact

Diversified the US medical device company's portfolio through a bold M&A strategy that grew company revenue fivefold and increased market cap more than twelvefold. Measured success by how many seconds it took until someone was helped by a Medtronic product, which decreased from 100 to seven seconds by the end of his tenure.

Fast facts

Received the Bower Award for Business Leadership from the Franklin Institute, 2014

Named one of The 25 Most Influential Business People of the Last 20 Years by PBS & Wharton School of Business, 2002

Received the Arthur W. Page Center's Larry Foster Award for Integrity in Public Communication, 2018

● ● ●

Lynn Good

Duke Energy

Revenue: $25B, Market cap: $67B

Employees: 28k in the United States

Career highlights

Duke Energy: Chair, President & CEO (2013–present)

On the boards of Boeing, Edison Electric Institute, and Business Roundtable

CEO impact

Intensified Duke Energy's focus on serving customers and communities. Completed transformation of company's business portfolio. Delivered 10 percent excess shareholder return relative to the sector, while leading the way to a cleaner energy future. Since 2005, the company has reduced carbon dioxide emissions by 39 percent and plans to achieve net-zero emissions by 2050.

Fast facts

Appeared for eight consecutive years (2013–2020) on *Fortune*'s Most Powerful Women in Business list

Appeared five times in *Forbes*'s The World's 100 Most Powerful Women

● ● ●

Piyush Gupta

DBS

Revenue: $11B, Market cap: $48B

Employees: 28k in 18 markets

Career highlights

DBS: CEO (2009–present)

Vice-chair of the International Institute of Finance; member of Singapore's Advisory Council on the Ethical Use of AI and Data, McKinsey Advisory Council, Bretton-Woods Committee–Advisory

Council, and the World Business Council for Sustainable Development Executive Committee; on the boards of Enterprise Singapore, Singapore's National Research Foundation, and the Singapore's Council for Board Diversity

CEO impact

Turned around the Singapore bank, now the largest bank in southeast Asia, by reinvigorating employees and redefining it as a technology company that delivers financial services. Doubled revenue and improved return on equity by almost 500 basis points.

Fast facts

Awarded the Public Service Star by the president of Singapore, 2020

Appeared in *HBR*'s Top 100 CEOs, 2019

DBS ranked tenth in *HBR*'s Top 20 Business Transformations of the Last Decade, 2019

Named World's Best Bank 2018, 2019, 2020 by *Global Finance*, *Euromoney*, and *The Banker*

● ● ●

Herbert Hainer

Adidas		
Revenue: $27B, Market cap: $64B		
Employees: 53k in 9 countries		
Career highlights		
Adidas: Chair & CEO (2001–2016)		
FC Bayern München: President (2019–present)		
On the boards of Accenture and Allianz		

CEO impact

Boosted the international footprint of the German sportswear company by investing in brands and R&D, while pushing the organization to deliver on the mission of being the best sports brand. Tripled revenue and increased market cap tenfold.

Fast facts

Appeared three times in *HBR*'s Top 100 CEOs (once in the top 5)

Received the Order of Merit of the Federal Republic of Germany

● ● ●

Reed Hastings

Netflix

Revenue: $20B, Market cap: $142B

Employees: 9k in 17 countries

Career highlights

Netflix: Co-CEO (2020–present), Cofounder & CEO (1997–2020)

Pure Software: Founder & CEO (1991–1997)

California State Board of Education: President (2000–2005)

On the boards of several educational organizations including KIPP and Pahara

CEO impact

Turned the American DVD-by-mail service into a global 200-million-subscriber streaming-media business by seeing an opportunity where others saw a challenge. Instilled a corporate culture famous for radical transparency, feedback, and creativity.

Fast facts

Ranked three times on *Fortune*'s Businessperson of the Year list

Named twice in the *TIME* 100 list of the most influential people in the world

Appeared three times in *HBR*'s Top 100 CEOs

Appeared nine times in *Barron's* World's Best CEOs

Awarded the Henry Crown Leadership Award by the Aspen Institute, 2014

Netflix ranked first in *HBR*'s Top 20 Business Transformations of the Last Decade, 2019

● ● ●

Marillyn Hewson

Lockheed Martin

Revenue: $60B, Market cap: $110B

Employees: 110k in 19 countries

Career highlights

Lockheed Martin: Chair (2014–2021), President & CEO (2013–2020)

On the boards of Chevron and Johnson & Johnson

Chaired or served on several nonprofit boards, industry organizations, and government advisory groups

CEO impact

Maintained a focus on the US defense contractor's mission to strengthen security and advance technology, while navigating tricky political waters and overcoming the challenge of being a woman in a male-dominated industry. Doubled EBITDA and more than tripled market cap.

Fast facts

Named to the *TIME* 100 list of the world's most influential people, 2019

Named 2018 CEO of the Year by *Chief Executive* magazine

Named in *Barron's* World's Best CEOs, 2019

Appeared four times in *HBR*'s Top 100 CEOs

Named in the top ten in *Fortune*'s Businessperson of the Year list, 2017

Named *Fortune*'s Most Powerful Woman in Business, 2018 and 2019 (and ranked in the top four 2013–2019)

Ranked twice in the top ten in *Forbes*'s Most Powerful Women in the World list

● ● ●

Kazuo Hirai

Sony
Revenue: $77B, Market cap: $87B
Employees: 112k in more than 70 countries and regions
Career highlights
Sony: Chair (2018–2019), President, and CEO (2012–2018)

CEO impact

Bucked Japanese corporate culture traditions with his style while turning around the media and consumer electronics giant by dramatically simplifying its portfolio. Increased operating margins by more than 900 basis points and restored the company to profitability after consecutive years of losses prior to his tenure.

Fast facts

Received a Lifetime Achievement Award at the 66th Annual Technology & Engineering Emmy Awards in 2015

● ● ●

Hubert Joly

Best Buy
Revenue: $44B, Market cap: $23B
Employees: 125k in 3 countries
Career highlights
Best Buy: Chair (2015–2020), CEO (2012–2019)
Carlson Inc: CEO (2008–2012)
Harvard Business School: senior lecturer (2020–present)

CEO impact

Moved the US consumer electronics and appliance retailer from potential bankruptcy into a profitable company centered on customer experience and a strong employee culture. Achieved five consecutive years of same-store sales growth and a quadrupling of the stock price.

Fast facts

Made a Knight in the French Legion of Honor

Appeared in *HBR*'s Top 100 CEOs, 2018

Named in *Barron's* World's Best CEOs, 2018

Named four times in Glassdoor's Top 100 CEOs in the United States (once in the top ten)

●   ●   ●

KV Kamath

ICICI Bank

Revenue: $14B, Market cap: $49B

Employees: 85k in 17 countries

Career highlights

ICICI Bank: Chair (2009–2015), CEO (1996–2009)

New Development Bank: President (2015–2020)

CEO impact

Turned a small Indian wholesale lender into the largest private bank in the country through a combination of foresight, investment in technology, revolutionary talent management, and a desire to learn constantly. Delivered 33 percentage points of excess shareholder return relative to the sector while growing revenue more than twentyfold.

Fast facts

Awarded the Padma Bhushan, 2008

Named CEO of the year by the World HRD Congress, 2007

Named *Forbes Asia*'s Businessman of the Year, 2007

●   ●   ●

Gail Kelly

Westpac

Revenue: $14B, Market cap: $61B

Employees: 33k in 7 countries

Career highlights

Westpac Banking Corporation: CEO (2008–2015)

St.George Bank: CEO (2002–2007)

On the board of Singtel

CEO impact

Made the Australian bank one of the world's most admired companies, while more than doubling market cap and skillfully steering it through the financial crisis through a relentless focus on customers. Championed diversity and inclusion, achieving goal of 40 percent women in the top 4,000 leadership roles.

Fast facts

First female CEO of a major Australian bank

Appeared in *Forbes*'s Most Powerful Women in the World list for seven consecutive years (2008–2014)

Ranked twice in the top twenty in the *Financial Times*'s Top 50 Women in World Business

● ● ●

Jørgen Vig Knudstorp | **LEGO**

Revenue: $6B, Market cap: N/A

Employees: 19k in 37 countries

Career highlights

The LEGO Group: President & CEO (2004–2016), Member of the board (2016–present)

LEGO Brand Group: Executive chair (2016–present)

On the boards of IMD School of Management and Starbucks

CEO impact

Turned the Danish family-owned firm into the world's most profitable toymaker, growing revenue fivefold and EBITDA sixteenfold. Centralized leadership, divested non-core assets, streamlined creativity, and embraced LEGO's adult consumers to reinvigorate the loss-making company.

Fast facts

Awarded an AACSB Influential Leader Honoree, 2015

Received the Committee for Economic Development's Global Leadership Award, 2015

● ● ●

Ronnie Leten

Atlas Copco

Revenue: $11B, Market cap: $47B

Employees: 39k in 71 countries

Career highlights

Atlas Copco: President & CEO (2009–2017)

Epiroc: Chair (2017–present)

Ericsson: Chair (2018–present)

Piab: Chair (2019–present)

On the board of SKF

CEO impact

Introduced a highly disciplined approach to capital allocation and made the Swedish industrial manufacturer more responsive to customer needs. Tripled EBITDA and grew market cap more than fourfold.

Fast facts

Appeared twice in *HBR*'s Top 100 CEOs

Named Belgium Manager of the Year in 2013 by *Trends* business magazine

● ● ●

Maurice Lévy

Publicis

Revenue: $12B, Market cap: $11B

Employees: 77k in 110 countries

Career highlights

Publicis: Chair (2017–present), CEO (1987–2017)

Pasteur-Weizmann: President (2015–present)

On the board of Iris Capital Management

CEO impact

Turned a small French advertising company into an international marketing and communications giant by marrying a global outlook and a rich understanding of digitization with a local cultural nuance. Fueled by bold acquisitions, he grew revenue more than fortyfold and market cap one-hundredfold.

Fast facts

Appeared twice in *HBR*'s Top 100 CEOs

Appointed a French Commander of the Legion of Honor and a Grand Officer of the National Order of Merit

Received the International Leadership Award from the Anti-Defamation League, 2008

● ● ●

Matti Lievonen

Neste

Revenue: $16B, Market cap: $27B

Employees: 4k in 14 countries

Career highlights

Oiltanking: CEO (2019–present)

Neste: CEO (2008–2018)

Fortum: Chair (2018–2021)

On the board of Solvay

CEO impact

Realized that the Finnish energy company's future lay in renewables, and over ten years led a widespread cultural and portfolio transformation that made Neste the world's top producer of bio-diesel and jet fuel. Quadrupled EBITDA and grew market cap almost sevenfold.

Fast facts

Neste was ranked on Corporate Knights' Global 100 list of the world's most sustainable companies every year Lievonen was CEO, peaking at number two in 2018

● ● ●

Mike Mahoney

Boston Scientific

Revenue: $11B, Market cap: $63B

Employees: 36k in 15 countries

Career highlights

Boston Scientific: Chair & CEO (2012–present)

J&J: Group chair (2008–2012)

On the boards of Baxter International and the Boys & Girls Club of Boston; chair of the Boston College CEO Club and the American Heart Association CEO Roundtable

CEO impact

Identified problems with the US medical device manufacturer's culture and business portfolio and quickly brought in new leaders and redefined the growth strategy. Grew market cap almost ninefold, and oversaw a culture shift that resulted in the company winning accolades as one of the best employee workplaces.

Fast facts

Named on *Forbes*'s America's Most Innovative Leaders list, 2019

Boston Scientific consistently scores highly in multiple rankings for its commitment to diversity

● ● ●

Nancy McKinstry

Wolters Kluwer

Revenue: $5B, Market cap: $20B

Employees: 19k in more than 40 countries

Career highlights

Wolters Kluwer: Chair & CEO (2003–present)

CCH Legal Information Services: CEO (1996–1999)

On the boards of Abbott, Accenture, and Russell Reynolds Associates; member of the European Round Table of Industrialists, and of the Board of Overseers of Columbia Business School

CEO impact

Carried out an overhaul of this US/Dutch professional information and software company, embracing a digital transformation focused on portfolio changes, while increasing innovation and growing profitability. Increased share of digital products and services to 90 percent, while doubling EBITDA and quadrupling market cap.

Fast facts

Appeared twice in *HBR*'s Top 100 CEOs

Named nine times in the top ten of *Fortune*'s Global Power 50 International (Most Powerful Women)

Ranked three times in the top twenty of the *Financial Times*'s Top 50 Women in World Business

Appeared twice in *Forbes*'s Top 100 Most Powerful Women in the World

● ● ●

Ivan Menezes

Diageo

Revenue: $16B, Market cap: $99B

Employees: 28k in 80 countries

Career highlights

Diageo: CEO (2013–present)

On the board of Tapestry

Advisory board member for Kellogg School of Management

Vice-chair, Scotch Whisky Association

Member of International Alliance for Responsible Drinking, CEO Group

CEO impact

Transformed the UK-based spirits company through consistent and rigorous strategy execution focused on premium brands and innovation, while building an inclusive culture and winning accolades for social responsibility. Almost doubled stock price since taking over.

No crops

Fast facts

Named Top Senior Executive in 2021 *EMpower-Yahoo! Finance* Ethnic Minority Role Model List

Appeared in *HBR*'s Top 100 CEOs, 2019

Received Men as Change Agents Award from Women's Business Council in 2018

Diageo named Britain's Most Admired Company by *Management Today* in 2018

● ● ●

Johan Molin

Assa Abloy

Revenue: $10B, Market cap: $26B

Employees: 49k in 70 countries

Career highlights

Assa Abloy: President & CEO (2005–2018)

Nilfisk-Advance: CEO (2001–2005)

Sandvik: Chair (2015–present)

CEO impact

Acquired more than 200 companies in his time as CEO of the global lock-maker, recognized early on the need to embrace digital technologies in a historically mechanical industry, and pushed heavily into emerging markets. Tripled revenue and grew market cap more than fourfold.

Fast facts

Appeared three times in *HBR*'s Top 100 CEOs

● ● ●

James Mwangi

Equity Group

Revenue: ~$1B, Market cap: $2B

Employees: 8k in 6 countries

Career highlights

Equity Group: CEO (2005–present), Equity Group Foundation, founder and executive chair (2008–present)

Meru University College of Science and Technology, chancellor

Kenya Vision 2030, chair (2007–2019)

Advisory board member of IFC and Yale University

CEO impact

Grew the Kenyan bank into the largest in East Africa (in terms of customers and market cap) by creating a clear vision that championed prosperity for communities. Grew revenue fortyfold and net income more than thirtyfold.

Fast facts

Received three Kenyan Presidential Awards

Named *Forbes Africa*'s Person of the Year, 2012

Named Ernst & Young's World Entrepreneur of the Year, 2012

Received the Oslo Business for Peace Award, 2020

Holds 5 honorary doctorate degrees in recognition of contribution to society

● ● ●

Satya Nadella

Microsoft

Revenue: $126B, Market cap: $1.2T

Employees: 144k doing business in over 190 countries

Career highlights

Microsoft: Chairman and CEO (2021–present), CEO (2014–2021)

On the boards of Fred Hutchinson Cancer Research Center, Starbucks, and the University of Chicago; chair of The Business Council

CEO impact

Quickly steered Microsoft to areas of profitable growth when it was struggling to stay relevant, in part by fostering a corporate culture that called for a "learn-it- all" not "know-it-all" mindset. Almost doubled EBITDA and grew market cap fourfold to make Microsoft the second most valuable public company in the world.

Fast facts

Named *Financial Times* Person of the Year, 2019

Named *Fortune*'s Businessperson of the Year, 2019

Appeared in the *TIME* 100 list of the world's most influential people, 2018

Appeared twice in *HBR*'s Top 100 CEOs, (once in top 10)

Appeared four times in *Barron's* World's Best CEOs

● ● ●

Shantanu Narayen

Adobe

Revenue: $11B, Market cap: $159B

Employees: 23k in 26 countries

Career highlights

Adobe: Chair (2017–present), CEO (2007–present)

Vice-chair of the US-India Strategic Partnership Forum (2018–present)

President Obama's Management Advisory Board, member (2011–2017)

On the board of Pfizer

CEO impact

Pioneered cloud-based subscription services, transforming the company's business model from packaged products to Software as a Service, with revenues growing more than threefold and market cap more than sixfold.

Fast facts

Awarded the Padma Shri by the President of India

Named three times on *Fortune*'s Businessperson of the Year list (once in top 10)

Appeared four times in *Barron's* The World's Best CEOs

Named Economic Times Global Indian of the Year, 2018

● ⬢ ●

Rodney O'Neal

Delphi Automotive (renamed as Aptiv in 2017)

Revenue: $14B, Market cap: $24B

Employees: 141k in 44 countries

Career highlights

Delphi: President & CEO (2007–2015)

On the boards of Delphi, Sprint Nextel, Michigan Manufacturers Association, Inroads, and Focus: HOPE

Member of Executive Leadership Council

Member of Automotive Hall of Fame (75th class)

CEO impact

Rescued the US automotive parts and technology company from bankruptcy by successfully proceeding through Chapter 11, refocusing its product portfolio based on industry-shaping trends ("safe, green, connected"), and diversifying its customer base, while instilling an execution culture, eventually turning Delphi into a leading global auto supplier. Restored the company to profitability, from loss-making to more than $2B in EBITDA.

Fast facts

Named Industry Leader of the Year by the Automotive Hall of Fame, 2015

Received a Distinguished Service Citation by the Automotive Hall of Fame, 2010

●　　●　　◐

Flemming Ørnskov	Shire
	Revenue: $16B, Market cap: $55B
	Employees: 23k in 60 countries
	Career highlights
	Galderma: CEO (2019–present)
	Shire: CEO (2013–2019)
	Waters Corporation: Chair (2017–present)

CEO impact

More than tripled both revenue and market cap, and expanded into twenty-five new countries in just six years—all built on a vision to make pharma company Shire the world's leading rare-disease company.

Fast facts

Named in Fierce Pharma's 25 Most Influential People in Biopharma, 2015

Qualified as a medical doctor from the University of Copenhagen

●　　●　　●

Jim Owens	Caterpillar
	Revenue: $54B, Market cap: $82B
	Employees: 102k in 27 countries
	Career highlights
	Caterpillar: Chair & CEO (2004–2010)
	On the board at the Peterson Institute for International Economics; member of the Aspen Economic Strategy Group

CEO impact

Dug the US industrial company out of stagnation with a clear strategic vision based on geographical and end market segments focus, performance objectives, product/service offerings, operational excellence, and rising employee involvement and satisfaction. Nearly doubled market cap and optimized the cost structure so the highly cyclical company could sustain profitability through the financial crisis.

Fast facts

Received the National Foreign Trade Council's World Trade Award, 2007

●　　●　　●

Sundar Pichai

Alphabet
Revenue: $162B, Market cap: $923B
Employees: 119k in 50 countries
Career highlights
Alphabet: CEO (2019–present); CEO, Google (2015–present)
Advisor, CapitalG

CEO impact

Led the technology company's rapid growth beyond its core product offering while winning accolades for his empathetic, collaborative, and optimistic leadership style. Quadrupled stock price of parent company Alphabet since taking over as CEO of Google.

Fast facts

Appeared in the *TIME* 100 list of the world's most influential people, 2020

Received Carnegie Corporation's "Great Immigrants: The Pride of America" Award, 2016

Received US-India Business Council's Global Leadership Award, 2019

Named in Comparably's Best CEOs for Diversity, 2020

●   ●   ●

Henrik Poulsen

Ørsted
Revenue: $11B, Market cap: $44B
Employees: 7k in 6 countries
Career highlights
Ørsted: CEO (2012–2020)
TDC Group: CEO (2008–2012)
Deputy chair of Carlsberg and ISS; on the boards of Novo Nordisk, Ørsted, and Bertelsmann; member of the Presidium, WWF Denmark

CEO impact

Divested the former state-owned Danish energy company of much of its legacy fossil-fuel businesses to focus exclusively on offshore wind and soon became the world's biggest developer. Tripled market cap and EBITDA, instilling an execution culture that enabled a rapid strategic transformation and turnaround of the company's financial performance.

Fast facts

Ørsted ranked first on Corporate Knights' Global 100 list of the world's most sustainable companies, 2020

●   ●   ●

Patrick Pouyanné

Total
Revenue: $176B, Market cap: $143B
Employees: 108k in 80 countries
Career highlights
Total: CEO (2014–present), Chair (2015–present)
On the board of Capgemini

CEO impact

Broadened the French oil major's investments to diversify its energy mix into renewables, while updating the organizational design to stress people, social responsibility, strategy, and innovation. Delivered 8 percentage points of excess shareholder return relative to the sector.

Fast facts

Named Energy Intelligence's Petroleum Executive of the Year, 2017

Appointed a French Knight of the Legion of Honor

Ken Powell

General Mills
Revenue: $18B, Market cap: $32B
Employees: 35k in 26 countries
Career highlights
General Mills: Chair & CEO (2007–2017); Cereal Partners Worldwide, CEO (1999–2004)
University of Minnesota, Chair of Regents; on the boards of Medtronic and CWT

CEO impact

Responded to changing customer preferences to move the US consumer-foods giant toward healthier products, while also embedding a deep understanding of local cultural context. Almost doubled market cap and delivered more than 5 percentage points of excess shareholder return relative to the sector.

Fast facts

Received the Keystone Policy Center's Founders award, 2016

Received the Committee for Economic Development's Corporate Citizenship Award, 2013

Topped Glassdoor's America's Most Beloved CEO list, 2010

Kasper Rørsted

Adidas

Revenue: $27B, Market cap: $64B

Employees: 53k in 9 countries

Career highlights

Adidas: CEO (2016–present)

Henkel: CEO (2008–2016)

On the boards of Nestlé and Siemens

CEO impact

Brought a razor-sharp focus on performance and strategy execution to the German consumer-goods company Henkel, improving operating margins by more than 600 basis points and tripling market cap. Leading a digital transformation at Adidas, improving both top- and bottom-line performance while almost doubling shareholder return since taking over.

Fast facts

Appeared in *HBR*'s Top 100 CEOs, 2018

Ranked in the top five in *Fortune*'s Businessperson of the Year list, 2018

Played handball for Denmark's national youth team

● ● ●

Gil Shwed

Check Point Software

Revenue: $2B, Market cap: $17B

Employees: 5k doing business in over 150 countries

Career highlights

Check Point Software: Founder & CEO (1993–present)

Chair of the Board of Trustees of the Youth University of Tel Aviv University, and chair of the Yeholot Association

CEO impact

Grew this Israeli tech start-up into a global cybersecurity company by shifting the business model to an integrated hardware and software solution, and recognizing that easy-to-use products scale better.

Fast facts

Awarded the inaugural Israel Prize in Technology, 2018

Named Ernst & Young's Israeli Entrepreneur of the Year, 2010

Named Globes's Person of the Year, 2014

Named in the World Economic Forum's Global Leaders for Tomorrow Program, 2003

● ● ●

Roberto Setúbal

Itaú Unibanco
Revenue: $29B, Market cap: $84B
Employees: 95k in 18 countries
Career highlights
Itaú Unibanco: Co-chair (2017–present), CEO (1994–2017)
Federal Reserve Bank of New York, International Advisory Committee (2002–present)

CEO impact

Transformed the Brazilian bank into a top-ten global financial institution, masterminding a series of acquisitions to expand both geographically and into investment banking. Grew revenue twenty-fivefold and market cap more than thirtyfold.

Fast facts

Named Euromoney's Banker of the Year, 2011

Appeared twice in *HBR*'s Top 100 CEOs (once in top 5)

●   ●   ●

Feike Sijbesma

DSM
Revenue: $10B, Market cap: $25B
Employees: 23k in 50 countries
Career highlights
DSM: Honorary chair (2020–present), Chair Managing Board & CEO (2007–2020)
Co-chair, Global Center on Adaptation (with Ban Ki-moon)
On boards of Philips and Unilever
Named a World Bank Group Global Climate Leader (2017) and carbon price champion (2019)

CEO impact

Headed a purpose-led transformation of the Dutch company out of bulk chemicals into nutrition, health, and material science through an emphasis on innovation and sustainability and more than twenty acquisitions and divestments. More than tripled market cap and delivered over 450 percent total shareholder return.

Fast facts

Appeared in *HBR*'s Top 100 CEOs, 2019

Named on *Fortune*'s 50 World's Greatest Leaders list, 2018

Named UN Association of New York's Humanitarian of the Year, 2010

Honorary doctorates from universities of Maastricht (2012) and Groningen (2020)

Royal award as Grand Officer in order of Orange Nassau for his contribution to sustainability and society (2021)

DSM named on *Fortune*'s Change the World list for three consecutive years (ranked second in 2017)

•   •   •

Brad D. Smith

Intuit

Revenue: $7B, Market cap: $68B

Employees: 9k in 6 countries

Career highlights

Intuit: Chair (2016–present), CEO (2008–2019)

Nordstrom: Chair (2018–present)

On the board of SurveyMonkey; founded the Wing 2 Wing Foundation to advance education and entrepreneurship in overlooked areas of the country

CEO impact

Changed the American software company's model from desktop to cloud and focused on delighting customers through his mission to "power prosperity around the world." Doubled revenue and grew market cap almost fivefold.

Fast facts

Appeared twice in *HBR*'s Top 100 CEOs

Ranked twice in *Fortune*'s Businessperson of the Year list (once in top 10)

Member of the President's Advisory Council on Financial Capability for Young Americans, 2014–2015

•   •   •

Lars Rebien Sørensen

Novo Nordisk

Revenue: $18B, Market cap: $137B

Employees: 43k in 80 countries

Career highlights

Novo Nordisk: CEO (2000–2016)

Novo Nordisk Foundation and Novo Holdings: Chair (2018–present)

Chair of the advisory board at Axcel, and on the boards of Essity, Jungbunzlauer, and Thermo Fisher Scientific

CEO impact

Sharpened the Danish company's strategic focus by investing heavily in biopharmaceuticals for diabetes treatment, while balancing ethical corporate activity with strong financial performance. Improved operating margins by 20 percent and grew both revenue and market cap fivefold.

Fast facts

Twice ranked top of *HBR*'s Top 100 CEOs (2015 and 2016) and twice in the top 20

Named in *Fortune*'s Businessperson of the Year list, 2016

Appointed a French Knight of the Legion of Honor

Appointed a Knight of the Order of Dannebrog

Novo Nordisk topped Corporate Knights' Global 100 list of the world's most sustainable companies

●   ●   ●

Francesco Starace

Enel

Revenue: $87B, Market cap: $81B

Employees: 68k in 32 countries

Career highlights

Enel: Group CEO and general manager (2014–present); CEO, Enel Green Power (2008–2014)

Vice-chair, Endesa

Chair, UN Sustainable Energy for All

Chair, B20 Italy 2021 "Energy & Resource Efficiency" Task Force (2020)

Co-chair, WEF "Net Zero Carbon Cities—Systemic Efficiency Initiative" (2020)

Co-chair, European Clean Hydrogen Alliance's round table on "Renewable and Low-Carbon Hydrogen Production" (2021)

On the boards of UN Global Compact, Politecnico de Milano

CEO impact

Accelerated the Italian utility's transition to a more sustainable future, while expanding in emerging markets, digitizing the infrastructure and embracing open innovation. More than doubled market cap and increased the rate of new renewable capacity build fourfold, establishing Enel as the world's largest private player in renewables with close to 50 GW capacity.

Fast facts

Awarded orders of merit for business in Brazil, Colombia, Italy, Mexico, Russia

Awarded Global Leadership Award by University of California, Berkeley (2019)

Named Best Utility Manager by *Institutional Investor* (2020)

●   ●   ●

Lip-Bu Tan

Cadence Design Systems

Revenue: $2B, Market cap: $20B

Employees: 8k in 23 countries

Career highlights

Cadence Design Systems: CEO (2009–present)

Walden International: Founder and chair (1987–present)

On the boards of Hewlett Packard Enterprise, Schneider Electric, Softbank, the Electronic System Design Alliance, the Global Semiconductor Association, and Carnegie Mellon University

CEO impact

Turned around this troubled US electronic design company by adopting a singular focus on the customer (mostly semiconductor and chip manufacturers) and expanding into new markets. Improved operating margins by almost 30 percent and grew market cap twentyfold.

Fast facts

Received the Global Semiconductor Association's Dr. Morris Chang Exemplary Leadership Award, 2016

Cadence named six times in *Fortune*'s 100 Best Companies to Work For (2015–2020)

● ● ●

Johan Thijs

KBC

Revenue: $9B, Market cap: $31B

Employees: 42k in 20 countries

Career highlights

KBC: Chair & CEO (2012–present)

On the board of European Banking Federation

CEO impact

Identified serious issues in the Belgian financial services company's risk portfolio, restored trust with all KBC's stakeholders, launched a digital transformation and built a stronger culture. Grew net income fourfold and market cap almost sixfold.

Fast facts

Appeared five times in *HBR*'s Top 100 CEOs (three in top 10)

Named *International Banker*'s Western Europe Banking CEO of the Year, 2016, 2017, 2020

KBC received Euromoney's World's Best Bank Transformation award, 2017

● ● ●

David Thodey

Telstra
Revenue: $18B, Market cap: $30B
Employees: 29k in 21 countries
Career highlights
Telstra Corporation: CEO (2009–2015)
Xero Limited: Chair (2020–present)
Tyro Payments: Chair (2019–present)
Commonwealth Scientific and Industrial Research Association (Australia): Chair (2015–present)
Lead director of Ramsay Healthcare

CEO impact

Led the Australian telecommunications company through a sales-and-service digital transformation that sharpened focus on customers and expanded reach in Asia, resulting in doubling of market cap to $75B and Telstra being named the country's most-respected company in 2014 by *Australian Financial Review*.

Fast facts

Appeared in *HBR*'s Top 100 CEOs, 2015

Appointed as officer in the Order of Australia for distinguished service to business and promotion of ethical leadership

● ● ●

Kan Trakulhoon

Siam Cement Group
Revenue: $15B, Market cap: $16B
Employees: 54k in 14 countries
Career highlights
SCG: President & CEO (2006–2015), Board member (2005–present)
Advanced Info Service: Chair (2020–present)
On the boards of Bangkok Dusit Medical Services, Intouch Holdings, and The Siam Commercial Bank

CEO impact

Dramatically streamlined the Thai conglomerate's portfolio and aligned all the businesses under a unified mission, while bringing a culture of innovation to the commodity producer and building a strong reputation for corporate citizenship. Doubled market cap and delivered 10 percentage points of excess shareholder return relative to the sector.

Fast facts

Named *The Nation*'s Businessman of the Year, 2011

Has a long track record of serving on multiple national advisory boards and committees

● ● ●

Masahiko Uotani

CEO impact

Shiseido
Revenue: $10B, Market cap: $29B
Employees: 45k in 120 countries
Career highlights
Shiseido: President & CEO (2014–present)
President of the Japan Cosmetic Industry Association, and on the board of the Japan Business Federation

Turned this venerable Japanese cosmetics firm into an innovative global beauty powerhouse, by using a hybrid model of leadership that combines a strong Japanese heritage with global marketing capabilities. Improved operating margins by more than 600 basis points and grew market cap more than fourfold.

Fast facts

First external appointment to lead Shiseido in its 142-year history (1872–2014)

First chair of 30% Club Japan, founded to increase female representation on company boards, 2019

● ● ●

Peter Voser

CEO impact

Royal Dutch Shell
Revenue: $345B, Market cap: $231B
Employees: 83k in 70 countries
Career highlights
Shell: CEO (2009–2013)
ABB: Chair (2015–present), interim CEO (2019–2020)
On the boards of IBM, Temasek, and Catalyst; chair of the board of the St. Gallen Symposium; member of the Asia Business Council

Simplified the Anglo/Dutch oil and gas giant's structure, drove accountability, fostered entrepreneurship, and placed new bets on partnerships around the world—all moves that led to Shell's revenue, EBITDA, and market cap growing around 50 percent.

Fast facts

Granted the Most Distinguished Order of Merit of Brunei, 2011

● ● ●

Andrew Wilson

Electronic Arts
Revenue: $6B, Market cap: $31B
Employees: 10k in 16 countries
Career highlights
Electronic Arts: CEO (2013–present)
On the board at Intel; chair, Association of Surfing Professionals North America

CEO impact

Reversed six years of decline by adopting a player-first culture at the US gaming company and improving the quality of titles, which contributed to making EA profitable again and delivering more than 20 percentage points of excess shareholder return relative to the sector.

Fast facts

Ranked twice on *Fortune*'s Businessperson of the Year list (once in top 5)

Named in *Barron's* World's Best CEOs, 2018

Named in *Forbes*'s Innovative Leaders list, 2019

Named twice on *Forbes*'s America's Most Powerful CEOs 40 and Under list (number 3, 2015)

● ● ●

Marjorie Yang

Esquel
Revenue: $1B, Market cap: N/A
Employees: 35k in 5 countries
Career highlights
Esquel: Chair (1995–present), CEO (1995–2008, 2021–present)
On the boards of Budweiser APAC, Serai, and Asia School of Business; chair of the Seoul International Business Advisory Council; Hong Kong, China representative to APEC Business Advisory Council

CEO impact

Globalized the family-owned Hong Kong–based textile manufacturer, moving it upmarket and bucking the trend of relocating production to lower-cost countries in the region. Tripled revenue and made Esquel among the largest woven cotton shirt makers in the world, producing more than 100 million shirts annually.

Fast facts

Awarded the Gold Bauhinia Star by the Hong Kong government

Appeared four times on *Fortune*'s 50 Most Powerful Women list

Listed in *Forbes Asia*'s 48 Heroes of Philanthropy, 2012

Received the Bronze Beaver Award from the MIT Alumni Association, 2011

Notes

1. Top quintile CEO performance sourced from McKinsey's proprietary database containing twenty-five years' worth of data on 7,800 CEOs from 3,500 public companies across seventy countries and twenty-four industries. Calculation based on average annual TRS (Total Return to Shareholders) of large-cap CEOs in the top quintile of performance, with large-cap defined by the companies being in the Forbes Global 1000.
2. See Timothy Quigley, Donald Hambrick, "Has the 'CEO Effect' Increased in Recent Decades? A New Explanation for the Great Rise in America's Attention to Corporate Leaders," *Strategic Management Journal*, May 2014.
3. Based on a study by the Center of Creative Leadership, who conduct original scientific research into the field of leadership development.
4. https://www.forbes.com/sites/susanadams/2014/04/11/ceos-staying-in-their-jobs-longer/?sh=3db21cf567d6; https://www.kornferry.com/about-us/press/age-and-tenure-in-the-c-suite.
5. https://www.strategyand.pwc.com/gx/en/insights/ceo-success.html.
6. See Chris Bradley, Martin Hirt, and Sven Smit, *Strategy Beyond the Hockey Stick: People, Probabilities, and Big Moves to Beat the Odds*, Hoboken, NJ: John Wiley & Sons, 2018.
7. See James Citrin, Claudius Hildebrand, Robert Stark, "The CEO Life Cycle," *Harvard Business Review*, November-December 2019.
8. See transcript of Episode 314 of the Freakonomics radio podcast on "What Does a C.E.O. Actually Do?," where Stephen Dubner interviews Nicholas Bloom, among others, on the role of the CEO.
9. See Henry Mintzberg, *The Nature of Managerial Work*, New York: Harper & Row, 1973.
10. See Steve Tappin's interview with CNN, "Why Being a CEO 'Should Come with a Health Warning'," March 2010.
11. Episode 314 of the Freakonomics radio podcast on "What Does a C.E.O. Actually Do?"
12. Bradley et al., *Strategy Beyond the Hockey Stick*.
13. Jeffrey M. O'Brien, interview with Netflix CEO Reed Hastings, "The Netflix Effect," *Wired*, December 1, 2002. https://www.wired.com/2002/12/netflix-6/
14. Allyson Lieberman, "Many Shoes to Fill; Ceo Latest to Hot-Foot Adidas," *New York Post*, March 3, 2000. https://nypost.com/2000/03/03/many-shoes-to-fill-ceo-latest-to-hot-foot-adidas/

15. https://www.cnbc.com/2018/08/23/intuit-ceo-brad-smith-will-step-down -at-end-of-year.html.

16. Quote from video: https://www.kantola.com/Brad-Smith-PDPD-433-S.aspx.

17. See Daniel Kahneman, Paul Slovic, Amos Tversky, *Judgment Under Uncertainty: Heuristics and Biases*, Cambridge, UK: Cambridge University Press, 1982.

18. Bradley et al., *Strategy Beyond the Hockey Stick*.

19. Piers Anthony, *Castle Roogna*, book 3 in the Xanth series. New York: Ballantine Books, 1987.

20. See Yuval Atsmon, "How Nimble Resource Allocation Can Double Your Company's Value," McKinsey.com, August 2016.

21. See Adam Brandenburger and Barry Nalebuff, "Inside Intel," *Harvard Business Review* magazine, November-December 1996.

22. Academic study by Brian Wansink, Robert Kent, Stephen Hoch, "An anchoring and adjustment model of purchase quantity decisions," *Journal of Marketing Research*, February 1998. Cited by Daniel Kahneman in his book *Thinking, Fast and Slow*, New York: Farrar, Straus and Giroux, 2011.

23. See Stephen Hall, Dan Lovallo, Reinier Musters, "How to Put Your Money Where Your Strategy Is," *McKinsey Quarterly*, March 2012.

24. See Scott Keller, Bill Schaninger, *Beyond Performance 2.0: A Proven Approach to Leading Large-Scale Change*, Hoboken, NJ: John Wiley & Sons, 2019.

25. Ibid.

26. See Charles Duhigg, *The Power of Habit: Why We Do What We Do in Life and Business*, New York: Random House, February 2012.

27. Keller and Schaninger, *Beyond Performance 2.0*.

28. See Rita Gunter McGrath, "How the Growth Outliers Do It," *Harvard Business Review*, January–February 2012.

29. See Scott Keller, Mary Meaney, *Leading Organizations: Ten Timeless Truths*, London: Bloomsbury Publishing, April 2017; based on Phil Rosenzweig, *The Halo Effect: How Managers Let Themselves Be Deceived*, New York: Free Press, 2007; and Dan Bilefsky, Anita Raghavan, "Once Called Europe's GE, ABB and Star CEO Tumbled," *Wall Street Journal*, January 23, 2003.

30. See Tom Peters, "Beyond the Matrix Organization," *McKinsey Quarterly*, September 1979.

31. See Aaron de Smet, Sarah Kleinman, Kirsten Weerda, "The Helix Organization," *McKinsey Quarterly*, October 2019.

32. Keller and Meaney, *Leading Organizations*.

33. Keller and Meaney, *Leading Organizations*.

34. See Ram Charan, Dominic Barton, Dennis Carey, *Talent Wins: The New Playbook for Putting People First*, Boston, MA: Harvard Business Press, March 2018.

35. Keller and Schaninger, *Beyond Performance 2.0*.

36. See Michael Lewis, *The Blind Side: Evolution of a Game*, New York: W. W. Norton and Company, 2006.

37. From Ken Frazier's conversation with Professor Tsedal Neeley of Harvard Business School. https://hbswk.hbs.edu/item/merck-ceo-ken-frazier-speaks -about-a-covid-cure-racism-and-why-leaders-need-to-walk-the-talk.

38. See Fred Adair, Richard Rosen, "CEOs Misperceive Top Teams' Performance," *Harvard Business Review*, September 2007.

39. See Ferris Jabr, "The Social Life of Forests," *New York Times Magazine*, December 2020.

40. See Jan Hubbard, "It's No Dream: Olympic Team Loses," *Los Angeles Times*, June 25, 1992; https://www.latimes.com/archives/la-xpm-1992-06-25-sp-1411-story.html.

41. See Todd Johnson, "'Dream Team' Documentary's 5 Most Intriguing Moments," theGrio, June 13, 2012; https://thegrio.com/2012/06/13/dream-team-documentarys-5-most-intriguing-moments/.

42. See *The Dream Team Scrimmages Against Chris Webber and the 1992 Select Team*, excerpt from *The Dream Team* documentary (released June 13, 2012, directed by Zak Levitt), https://www.youtube.com/watch?v=5xHoYnuMLZQ.

43. Adair and Rosen, "CEOs Misperceive Top Teams' Performance."

44. See Kenwyn Smith, David Berg, *Paradoxes of Group Life*, San Francisco: Jossey-Bass, 1987.

45. See Cyril Northcote Parkinson, *Parkinson's Law, or the Pursuit of Progress*, London: John Murray, 1958.

46. Keller and Meaney, *Leading Organizations*.

47. See Dan Lovallo, Olivier Sibony, "The Case for Behavioral Strategy," *McKinsey Quarterly*, March 2010.

48. Keller and Meaney, *Leading Organizations*.

49. See Danielle Kosecki, "How Do the Tour de France Riders Train," bicycling.com, August 2020; https://www.bicycling.com/tour-de-france/a28355159/how-tour-de-france-riders-train/.

50. See Sun Tzu, *The Art of War*, Harwich, MA: World Publications Group, 2007.

51. From McKinsey Global Board Survey 2019.

52. See The PwC and The Conference Board study, "Board Effectiveness: A Survey of the C-Suite," based on a 2020 survey of 551 executives at public companies across the United States.

53. From the Franklin D. Roosevelt Presidential Library; http://www.fdrlibrary.marist.edu/daybyday/resource/march-1933-4/.

54. "The Group has taken necessary measures in line with its policies and procedures, including disciplinary measures, and in some cases termination/separation of employment of certain staff," said David Ansell, the group chairman designate. "Sexual harassment/assault in the workplace is totally unacceptable. We at Equity Group have chosen to share our experience openly and raise awareness on this issue of public interest," he added. https://nairobinews.nation.co.ke/equity-bank-sacks-manager-accused-of-sexually-harassing-interns/

55. See Franklin Gevurtz, "The Historical and Political Origins of the Corporate Board of Directors," *Hofstra Law Review*: Vol. 33, Iss. 1, Article 3, 2004.

56. See Rakesh Khurana, *Searching for a Corporate Savior: The Irrational Quest for Charismatic CEOs*, Princeton, NJ: Princeton University Press, September 2011.

57. https://en.wikipedia.org/wiki/Gerousia.

58. Based on a June 2011 McKinsey survey of 1,597 corporate directors on governance. See Chinta Bhagat, Martin Hirt, Conor Kehoe, "Tapping the Strategic Potential of Boards," *McKinsey Quarterly*, February 2013.

59. McKinsey Global Board Survey 2019.

60. McKinsey Global Board Survey 2019.

61. PwC and Conference Board study, "Board Effectiveness: A Survey of the C-Suite."

62. See Christian Casal, Christian Caspar, "Building a Forward-looking Board," *McKinsey Quarterly*, February 2014.

63. Story narrated by Jim Carrey to Oprah Winfrey on her show in 1997. https://www.oprah.com/oprahs-lifeclass/what-oprah-learned-from-jim -carrey-video

64. PwC and Conference Board study, "Board Effectiveness: A Survey of the C-Suite."

65. See John Browne, Robin Nuttal, Tommy Stadlen, *Connect: How Companies Succeed by Engaging Radically with Society*, New York: PublicAffairs, March 2016.

66. See Victor Frankl, *Man's Search for Meaning*, Boston, MA: Beacon Press, 2006.

67. See Susie Cranston, Scott Keller, "Increasing the 'Meaning Quotient' of Work," *McKinsey Quarterly*, January 2013.

68. 2017 Cone Communications CSR study; https://www.conecomm.com /research-blog/2017-csr-study.

69. See Achieve Consulting Inc, "Millennial Impact Report," June 2014. https:// www.shrm.org/resourcesandtools/hr-topics/behavioral-competencies/glob al-and-cultural-effectiveness/pages/millennial-impact.aspx.

70. https://www.businessroundtable.org/business-roundtable-redefines-the-pur pose-of-a-corporation-to-promote-an-economy-that-serves-all-americans.

71. Based on a study by Ernst & Young along with *Harvard Business Review*; https://assets.ey.com/content/dam/ey-sites/ey-com/en_gl/topics/purpose/pur pose-pdfs/ey-the-entrepreneurs-purpose.pdf.

72. Based on a McKinsey Organizational Purpose Survey of 1,214 managers and frontline employees at US companies, October 2019.

73. See 2019 Edelman Trust Barometer Special Report, "In Brands We Trust?" https://www.edelman.com/sites/g/files/aatuss191/files/2019-06/2019_edel man_trust_barometer_special_report_in_brands_we_trust.pdf.

74. https://battleinvestmentgroup.com/speech-by-dave-packard-to-hp-manag ers/.

75. https://www.jpmorganchase.com/impact/path-forward.

76. See Jonathan Emmett, Gunner Schrah, Matt Schrimper, Alexandra Wood, "COVID-19 and the Employee Experience: How Leaders Can Seize the Moment," McKinsey.com, June 2020.

77. See Peter Drucker, "The American CEO," *Wall Street Journal*, December 30, 2004.

78. Drucker, "The American CEO."

79. See Sanjay Kalavar, Mihir Mysore, "Are You Prepared for a Corporate Crisis?," McKinsey.com, April 2017.

80. Remarks of Senator John F. Kennedy, Convocation of the United Negro College Fund, Indianapolis, Indiana, April 12, 1959.

81. See Ronald A. Heifetz, Marty Linsky, *Leadership on the Line: Staying Alive Through the Dangers of Leading*, Boston, MA: Harvard Business Press, 2002.

82. See Neal H. Kissel and Patrick Foley, "The 3 Challenges Every New CEO Faces," *Harvard Business Review*, January 23, 2019.

83. See Jim Loehr, Tony Schwartz, "The Making of a Corporate Athlete," *Harvard Business Review* magazine, January 2001.

84. Inspirational story attributed to Mahatma Gandhi. See "Breaking the Sugar Habit"; https://www.habitsforwellbeing.com/breaking-the-sugar-habit-an -inspirational-story-attributed-to-gandhi/.

85. See Paul Hersey, *The Situational Leader*, Cary, NC: Center for Leadership Studies, 1984; See Kenneth Blanchard, Spencer Johnson, *The One Minute Manager*, New York: HarperCollins, 1982.

86. See Annie McKee, Richard Boyatzis, Frances Johnston, *Becoming a Resonant Leader: Develop Your Emotional Intelligence, Renew Your Relationships, Sustain Your Effectiveness,* Boston, MA: Harvard Business Press, 2008.

87. https://leadershipdevotional.org/humility-7/.

88. See Hermann Hesse, *Journey to the East*, New Delhi: Book Faith India, 2002.

89. See https://www.greenleaf.org/what-is-servant-leadership/.

90. NPR, "Decathlon Winner Ashton Eaton Repeats as the 'World's Greatest Athlete,'" CPR News [Colorado Public Radio], August 19, 2016. https:// www.cpr.org/2016/08/19/decathlon-winner-ashton-eaton-repeats-as-the -worlds-greatest-athlete/.

91. See Bill George, "The CEO's Guide to Retirement," *Harvard Business Review* magazine, November-December 2019.

92. See Friedrich Nietzsche, *The Genealogy of Morals*, North Chelmsford, MA: Courier Corp., 2012.

93. See Violina P. Rindova and William H. Starbuck, "Ancient Chinese Theories of Control," *Journal of Management Inquiry* 6 (1997), pp. 144–159. http:// pages.stern.nyu.edu/~wstarbuc/ChinCtrl.html.

Index

About the Authors

Carolyn Dewar

Carolyn is a Senior Partner in the San Francisco office of McKinsey & Company, having joined the firm in 2000. Carolyn co-leads McKinsey's CEO Excellence service line, advising many Fortune 100 CEOs to maximize their effectiveness in the role, and lead their organizations through pivotal moments (hyper-growth, merger, strategic shift, crisis). She has invested deeply to understand and elevate the "role of the CEO" as a critical role unto itself—one that requires intergenerational guidance, and new thoughts for the future. She plays a faculty role for a number of the firm's client master classes for sitting CEOs and those preparing for the role. Additionally, she has published more than thirty articles in the *Harvard Business Review*, The Conference Board, and the *McKinsey Quarterly* including "The CEO's Role in Leading Transformation," "The Mindsets and Practices of Excellent CEOs," and "The CEO Moment: Leadership for a New Era." Carolyn is also a keynote speaker and panelist at conferences across industries and geographies.

Carolyn was born and raised in Canada, before moving to the UK to study economics and international relations at the University of St. Andrews in Scotland. Both disciplines underscored the importance of marrying an analytical view with a deep understanding of behavioral dynamics and the ripple impact of individual decisions and actions. After her graduate work in the UK, she returned to her native Canada before moving to Northern California.

Outside of work, Carolyn enjoys the California sunshine, cooking from the bounty of the farmers' market, and reliving her love of art with her young children, Gray and Evening, and her husband, Thomas Czegledy.

Scott Keller

Scott is a Senior Partner in McKinsey's Southern California office, having joined the firm in 1995. He co-leads (with Carolyn) the firm's global CEO Excellence service line. A mechanical engineer by training, he spent most of his early consulting years working on business strategy and operational topics, until his life was turned upside down by his second child, who was born with profound special needs. After taking time off to tend to his family, Scott returned to McKinsey with the clarity to bring the best of psychology, social science, and the field of human potential into the workplace.

Ten years later, Scott coauthored the Inc.com bestseller *Beyond Performance: How Great Organizations Build Ultimate Competitive Advantage* (Wiley, 2011). He has since written five more books on leadership and organization effectiveness and has published over fifty articles for the *Harvard Business Review, Forbes, Chief Executive Magazine,* The Conference Board, *Inc.* magazine, and the *McKinsey Quarterly.* He is also a featured speaker at CEO roundtables and is guest lecturer at multiple US and European business schools.

Outside of McKinsey, Scott is a cofounder of Digital Divide Data, a multi-award-winning social enterprise. Further afield, Scott is a featured musician in *Rock Camp: The Movie* (2021), has played guitar on movie and TV soundtracks, and is also credited as a songwriter and music and documentary producer. He's also one of a few hundred people in history known to have traveled to every country in the world. His favorite place, however, is Seal Beach, California, where he lives with his wife, Fiona, and his three boys, Lachlan, Jackson, and Camden.

Vikram Malhotra

Vikram (Vik) Malhotra is a Senior Partner at McKinsey & Company, where he has worked for the past thirty-five years. Vik has had several leadership roles within McKinsey, including serving on the Board of Directors from 2004 to 2017, serving as Managing Partner of the Americas and on McKinsey's Operating Committee from 2009 to 2015, chairing McKinsey's Senior Partner Committee from 2015–2020, and currently chairing McKinsey's Professional Standards Committee.

Vik joined the firm in 1986 and has spent his career in the New York office. During his time at McKinsey, his consulting experience has covered a broad range of assignments on performance transformation, corporate strategy, business unit strategy, growth strategies, organizational effectiveness, and operational improvement. Much of Vik's current focus is on counseling CEOs and boards on a range of issues.

Vik is also active with major nonprofits outside McKinsey. He currently serves as the Chairman of the Board at the Wharton School of the University of Pennsylvania. He's also a Trustee of The New York City Partnership, a Trustee Emeritus of the Asia Society, and a former Trustee of The Conference Board.

Before joining McKinsey, Vik graduated from the Wharton School at the University of Pennsylvania. Prior to receiving his MBA he worked at the accounting firm of Ernst & Whinney in London, England. Vik received his undergraduate degree in economics from the London School of Economics in 1980.